CONTENTS

LIST OF PLATES

THEORIZING MODERNIS

At a time when postmodernism seems to have achieved
position in cultural and critical theory the contributors to
provide a much-needed corrective to the misleading images o
which have dominated recent debate.

Richard Sheppard's account of European modernism fo
profound ideological crisis which beset Western culture b
and 1930 and examines the ways in which artists and inte
sponded to it; Bernard McGuirk analyses the ambivalent
Apollinaire and Alberti to the machine age; David Wragg inv
aesthetic and epistemological underpinnings of verbal and
cism in the work of Wyndham Lewis, and Mike Johnson
potential for a (post)modernist political aesthetic in the Merz
Schwitters. And finally, Steve Giles's Afterword provides a
overview of the relationship between modernism and the
postmodernism and modernity.

This volume makes an important contribution to our und
modernism, and through the use of contemporary critical
new light on current controversies surrounding postmodern
essential reading for all those interested in Critical The
Studies and Comparative Literature.

Steve Giles is a lecturer in German and Critical Theory at
of Nottingham. He is the author of *The Problem of Acti
European Drama* (1981).

NOTES ON CONTRIBUTORS

Steve Giles is a lecturer in German and Critical Theory at the University of Nottingham. He is the author of *The Problem of Action in Modern European Drama* (1981).

Mike Johnson has recently completed his PhD in Critical Theory at the University of Nottingham. He is currently a freelance writer and part-time adult education lecturer.

Bernard McGuirk is Reader in Romance Literatures at the University of Nottingham.

Richard Sheppard is Fellow and Tutor in German at Magdalen College, Oxford, and Lecturer in German at Christ Church, Oxford. He was previously Professor of European Literature at the University of East Anglia. He has published extensively on topics relating to European modernism.

David Wragg completed his MA in Critical Theory at the University of Nottingham, where he continued with doctoral studies on Wyndham Lewis and Critical Theory. He is a tutor with the Open University and has contributed to *Over Here* and the *Journal of American Studies*.

PREFACE

At a time when postmodernism, together with its ideological counterparts post-structuralism, post-Marxism and post-feminism, seems to have achieved a hegemonic position in the cultural sphere comparable to that of Thatcherism in the socio-economic realm, reopening the debate on modernism might well appear to represent the anachronistic residue of a bygone age. But in the wake of the irresistible demise of Thatcherism's arch protagonist, a volume theorizing modernism is, perhaps, untimely in Nietzsche's positive sense.

The essays that follow engage with modernism in the light of contemporary critical theories, and earlier versions of some of them were presented as discussion papers at the Modernism Seminars convened by Dave Wragg under the auspices of Nottingham University's Postgraduate School of Critical Theory. The principle aim of this volume is to provoke a rethinking not only of modernism, but also of the vibrant clichés of postmodern theorizing. Richard Sheppard's meticulous and encyclopaedic account of European modernism has as its primary focus that profound ideological crisis which beset Western culture in all its manifestations, particularly between 1890 and 1930, as humanist and Enlightenment conceptions of reality, human nature, language and history were shattered. This widespread sense of crisis amongst European artists, intellectuals and scientists generated a multiplicity of responses, including one might add contemporary postmodernism and post-structuralism. The three essays which follow, by Bernard McGuirk, David Wragg and Mike Johnson, elaborate through detailed case studies on the themes and conceptual parameters articulated by Sheppard. McGuirk analyses the ambivalent reactions of modernist poetry in France and Spain to the machine age, Wragg engages in a complex meditation on the aesthetic and epistemological presuppositions of verbal and visual Vorticism in the work of Wyndham Lewis, while Johnson investigates the potential for a (post)-modernist political aesthetic embedded in the Merz texts of Kurt Schwitters. The Afterword to the volume dissects key theoretical problems informing the debate on modernism, looking especially at the relationships between modernism and the avant-garde, modernism and postmodernism, and modernism and modernity.

It was originally intended that this volume would appear with Pinter Press as part of an ongoing project presenting Nottingham Studies in Critical Theory. This explains the format of *Theorizing Modernism*, consisting as it does of two extensive essays by established scholars – one external and one internal to the Nottingham University Postgraduate School of Critical Theory – and two by postgraduate members of the School. In Spring 1991, Pinter Press withdrew from Humanities publishing, and this volume was transferred to Routledge with Pinter's Humanities list. I am very grateful to Routledge for publishing *Theorizing Modernism* in its original format.

Steve Giles
Nottingham

ACKNOWLEDGEMENTS

The editor and publisher are grateful to the following for their kind permission to reproduce copyright material: Tate Gallery Publications, the Victoria and Albert Museum, Black Sparrow Press, and the Sprengel Museum, Hanover.

German modernism clearly saw, it is time both to stop 'reducing modernism to this or that set of criteria' and to pose 'the question of history and politics in the [modernist] text . . . with renewed vigor'.[20]

Given the limitations of this first approach, more than a few critics have felt the need to develop a second, more broadly-based strategy – quite often as a spin-off from the first. Having identified one or more allegedly key features of modernism or the modernist avant-garde, critics then attempt to bring these into sharper focus by setting them in a one-dimensional historical, literary-historical or sociological context. Thus, modernism has been viewed as a continuation of[21] or a contrast with[22] Romanticism; as a reaction, in its extreme avant-garde forms, against Aestheticism;[23] as an inversion of the conventions of Realism;[24] as a contrast with Expressionism, Futurism and Surrealism;[25] as a precursor of postmodernism;[26] as a product of the megalopolitan experience[27] and/or the Great War;[28] and as a result of the 'serious arts' being forced to cede their 'utilitarian function' to the 'mass media of communication and entertainment'.[29] All of these positions are more or less tenable, but none is exclusively so. Precisely because, as Alan Wilde observed, the modernists were 'heirs to a tradition they revolted against' (p. 40), they simultaneously used *and* reacted against aesthetic conventions which marked several earlier and contemporary artistic movements. Moreover, fused with such purely aesthetic considerations, the experience of modernity (of which the mass city is but one, major aspect)[30] is equally important to most, if not all, important modernist texts: either visibly or as the equally significant 'repressed Other' in such works as Rilke's *Neue Gedichte* (*c*.1903–8) (translated as *New Poems* (1964)), most of Kandinsky's pre-1914 visual work,[31] or E. M. Forster's *A Passage to India* (1922–4). Furthermore, as Spears so clearly saw (p. 42), the Great War did not of itself generate modernism, but rather foregrounded that awareness of the darker side of reality and human nature which had already been present in the work of several major non-modernist writers of the nineteenth century. And while modernism and postmodernism overlap to such an extent that a large number of *surface* features are common to both phenomena,[32] there are, as Wilde's and Hassan's books show, basic ontological differences between the two modes. Bathrick and Huyssen are right to reject simple categorical contrasts, but their own work, speaking as it does of 'the modernist aesthetic of transcendence and epiphany',[33] points to a nostalgia or desire for epiphany, transcendence and closure which has no place within the flat surfaces and eternal present of postmodernism. As with the movements which preceded modernism, its relationship with its successor is far from simple. What Fredric Jameson said of any cultural or historical

3

period is especially true of modernism, given that modernism is more a transitional phenomenon than a period or a movement. What is designated by the label does not ' "express" some unified inner truth – a worldview or a period style or a set of structural categories which marks the whole length and breadth of the "period" in question'.[34] Modernism not only evolved from, reacted against and anticipated a multiplicity of other artistic phenomena, it also developed out of a complex of socio-historical experiences, of which the shocks caused by the modern megalopolis and the Great War were simply the most violent.

We shall, I suggest, get further with the problem by developing a third strategy which is more or less manifest in works on modernism or the modernist avant-gardes by Schwartz, LeRoy and Beitz, Bürger, Jameson, Renate Werner,[35] Jeffrey Herf,[36] and Huyssen and Bathrick, and if we then combine their insights with the central thesis of Horkheimer's and Adorno's *Dialektik der Aufklärung* (1947) (translated as *Dialectic of Enlightenment* (1972)).[37] Basing his argument on a concept borrowed from the American scientist Thomas S. Kuhn,[38] Schwartz argues that the modernist epoch involved a 'global shift' (p. 5) across a range of disciplines, and that to understand this shift, we need to develop a 'matrix approach' which 'makes it possible . . . to compare individuals who have no direct ties to one another but exhibit similar patterns of thought' (p. 9). Like the much looser matrix which is used in *Les Avant-gardes littéraires au XXe siècle*, the matrix established by Schwartz to investigate the poetry of Pound and Eliot derives primarily from the natural sciences, mathematics and philosophy. But the work of the other writers named above implies that the paradigm shift which those disciplines, like the arts, underwent during the modernist period derived from a much more fundamental seismic upheaval. In 1974, Bürger, following Adorno, connected that upheaval (which generated both Aestheticism and the avant-garde reaction against it) with imperialism (p. 44). And in 1973, LeRoy and Beitz were even more precise about that generative source when they described it as 'the transition to the epoch of imperialism' (p. 1158), which they then analysed as follows:

> Turning then to some changes brought about by the transition to imperialism, we can say first that the ideals of the French Revolution, which had held up reasonably well during two thirds of the nineteenth century (in England and the United States, at any rate), become markedly less tenable. The same thing happens to the notion associated with Adam Smith that the existing economic system has the capacity to correct its own ills and bring about an

4

equitable distribution of the wealth. Profound doubts now arise as to whether man has the capacity to dominate the historical process. With a suddenness that would be surprising if one knew nothing about the causes, the idea of progress collapses. When we seek an explanation for these changes, it is relevant to note how in the epoch of monopoly the decision-making process becomes invisible, the real decisions coming to be made more and more by those in command of the monopolies; ordinary people, even those in some-what privileged positions, come to feel – and justifiably – that they lack the kind of leverage that the humanist tradition had always made one feel entitled to command. A further cause lies in the intensifying irrationalities in the existing order, the vast increase in productive capacity along with economic stagnation, technological progress, and the neglect of human needs, breath-taking scientific advances that seemed to promise a solution to the age-old problem of human want, but with no mechanism for connecting these advances with the demand which in theory they ought to be able to meet . . . . Still another cause of the new doubts about the existing order is a new kind of alienation from work. This results in part from gigantism in industrial development and corresponding efficiency in techniques for managing the work force.

(pp. 1159–60)

For all its perceptiveness, monocausalism never lurks far behind the surface of this avowedly Marxist account of the origins of modernism, and in 1981, Jameson offered a corrective to that tendency when he warned against viewing modernism as 'a mere reflection of the reification of late nineteenth-century social life' (p. 42). More importantly still, Jameson, like Bürger seven years before, saw modernism in dialectical terms: its works are not just reflexes, transcriptions or symptoms of a profound cultural upheaval, but, *simultaneously*, responses through which the authors of those works try to pictorialize their understanding and so make sense of that upheaval. Bürger had asserted that the literary work was not just an 'Abbild, d.h. . . . Verdoppelung der gesellschaftlichen Realität' ('image, that is to say . . . replication of social reality'), but the 'Resultat einer Tätigkeit, die auf eine als unzulänglich erfahrene Wirklichkeit *antwortet*' ('product of an activity which *responds* to a reality that is experienced as inadequate')(p. 12). And Jameson implied a similarly dialectical conception of modernism when he wrote:

we are first obliged to establish a continuity between these two regional zones or sections – the practice of language in the literary

5

work, and the experience of *anomie*, standardization, rationalizing desacralization in the *Umwelt* or world of daily life – such that the latter can be grasped as that determinate situation, dilemma, contradiction, or subtext, to which the former comes as a symbolic resolution or solution.

(p. 42)

Indeed, towards the end of the same work, Jameson broadened out that dialectical conception by indicating that it was necessary to understand modernism not as a single, unified response, but as a range of responses to a perceived crisis (pp. 225 and 236–7). In doing this, he implied that it was possible to account coherently for the diverse phenomena which the concept involves, but without falling prey to the reductionism and oversimplification which the first two strategies described above involve.[39] Because, Jameson suggested, modernism was the product of an age in a process of radical change, it was not simply, but multiply Janus-faced (and in the case of Dada, anus-faced into the bargain), with the result that any account of it has to look not just in two, but in several directions at once. And it is this dual awareness that modernism is both an active response to a seismic upheaval and a heterogeneous phenomenon which constitutes one of the greatest strengths of the major essays in Huyssen's and Bathrick's recent book.[40]

Werner and Herf enable us to go further still. Herf noted that many (conservative) German modernists were born between 1885 and 1895 into a country which was modernizing rapidly (i.e. rationalizing its institutions and industrializing), and in which the humanist, liberal democratic tradition was relatively weak (pp. 10 and 48). And Werner pointed out that in common with most other major artists and intellectuals in nineteenth-century Germany, most German modernists had come from one class (the 'Bildungsbürgertum' – 'educated middle class') and attended one educational institution (the 'Gymnasium' – 'classical grammar school'). This latter was dominated by 'ein klassizistischer Normenkanon, die doktrinäre Verfestigung der klassisch-idealistischen Ästhetik, die Vorstellung, dem Kunstwerk als einem in sich harmonisch gegliederten Organismus komme die symbolische Repräsentanz einer göttlich geordneten Welt zu' ('a quasi-classical set of norms, the canonical institutionalization of a classical-idealist aesthetic, the notion that a work of art could stand symbolically for a divinely ordered world to the extent that it itself was a harmoniously structured organism') (p. 215).[41]

Similar things could be said, *mutatis mutandis*, of modernists from other European cultures. Consequently, it can be argued that at one level, the concept of modernism designates a heterogeneous range of responses to a global process of modernization by a generation which had internalized a set of assumptions in conflict with the values inherent in that process, and which, as a result, experienced modernization as a cultural cataclysm. It should, however, be stressed that the nature and intensity of the conflict varies from culture to culture. In Germany, for example, the classical ideal described by Werner was particularly remote from reality; the process of modernization was exceptionally rapid; and the liberal democratic, humanist ideal had a comparatively weak hold in the public domain. Consequently, many German modernists experienced the conflict particularly intensely. In England, however, the Arnoldian ideal was more robustly ethical than its German counterpart; the process of modernization, having begun much earlier, had been less rapid than in Germany; as Dagmar Barnouw has argued,[42] the liberal democratic, humanist ideal continued to play a comparatively important role in the public domain throughout the modernist period; and the Great War did not produce the same social upheaval as it did on the Continent. Consequently, it was easier for intellectuals in Britain to find more common ground with their societies [43] so that what was in essence the same conflict was, on the whole,[44] experienced less apocalyptically. As a result, it generated much smaller, less radical and less threatening avant-gardes (i.e., the Georgians, Imagists and Vorticists) than was the case on the Continent.[45] So, for all the criticisms which can be levelled at Bürger's theory of the avant-garde,[46] he was fundamentally correct in describing its work as the 'Ausdruck der Angst vor einer übermächtig gewordenen Technik und einer gesellschaftlichen Organisation, die die Handlungsmöglichkeiten des Einzelnen extrem einschränkt' ('expression of a profound anxiety in the face of a technological system which had become excessively powerful and a social system which imposes extreme limitations on the individual's freedom of action') (p. 97).

It is no accident that Georg Heym's first use of the neologism 'Weltstadt' ('world city' – i.e. 'city which has become the whole world') should have occurred in a poem, 'Berlin VIII', which was written in December 1910 – that precise juncture when, according to Virginia Woolf, 'human nature' and 'all human relations' changed. [47] By late 1910, a significant number of major modernist artists and intellectuals were foregrounding a powerful sense that a global process was affecting *all* areas of human life. But modernism was more than just a reflex, it also involved an active attempt to understand and pictorialize the complexities of that process. More importantly still, modernism, in its extreme forms, involved the prophetic urge to investigate the long-term implications of those complexities – both for the individual and society in general. Consequently, Horkheimer and Adorno, writing from America in the 1940s, enable us to add a final dimension to our understanding of the context which generated modernism via their analysis of the dialectical turn which, they contend, the central project of the Enlightenment had taken by the mid-twentieth century. In their view, those very constructs of human reason whose original purpose was to free mankind from its thralldom to Nature and feudalism, had turned into an autonomous system which was running madly out of control, depriving its creators of any real autonomy, and enslaving them more effectively than ever Nature or feudalism had done:

> Die Herrschaft des Menschen über sich selbst, die sein Selbst begründet, ist virtuell allemal die Vernichtung des Subjekts, in dessen Dienst sie geschieht, denn die beherrschte, unterdrückte und durch Selbsterhaltung aufgelöste Substanz ist gar nichts anderes als das Lebendige, als dessen Funktion die Leistungen der Selbsterhaltung einzig sich bestimmen, eigentlich gerade das, was erhalten werden soll.
>
> (p. 70)

> Man's self-mastery, in which his sense of selfhood is grounded, almost always involves the destruction of that very subject in whose name the process of self-mastery is undertaken. For the substance which is thereby mastered, suppressed and dissolved is that self-same vital force from which all that is achieved in the name of self-preservation uniquely derives – i.e. precisely that element which is supposed to be preserved.
>
> (p. 55)

Viewed in this context, modernism ceases to be merely the artistic manifestation of a conflict between conservative, humanist sensibilities and a modernizing, non-humanist world, and becomes the manifestation of a more or less shocked realization that modernization required more than the development of a new, appropriate sensibility. Rather, a significant number of modernists saw that for all its ideology of scientific rationality, the process of modernization was, like the Golem of Paul Wegener's expressionist film *Der Golem* (1920), the monstrous product of an originally emancipatory impulse which was now running amok. Many of the modernists had, during their youth, been imbued by their liberal humanist background with the Enlightenment belief that it was possible for Man increasingly to understand, rise above, dominate and utilize the external world by means of his *logos* – understood either as a purely secular faculty or as one which was grounded in the divine *logos*. But, paradoxically, that very generation which had grown up amid the triumphant achievements of increasingly confident nineteenth-century science, technology and economics, now felt that these systems were becoming dysfunctional and potentially totalitarian. Moreover, by virtue of the law by which the repressed always returns in a destructive form, they also felt they were in danger of turning into their opposite: the entropic chaos which the sociologist Emile Durkheim had, in *Le Suicide* (1897) (translated as *Suicide* (1952)) and *De la Division du travail social* (1902) (translated as *Division of Labour in Society* (1933)), called *anomie*. And it was this feeling of normlessness (which, according to Durkheim, was induced by modernity's destruction of traditional communities) that generated the 'panic terror' (see note 15 above) which informs so many modernist works.

Marcel Duchamp's *La Mariée mise à nu par ses célibataires, même (The Bride Stripped Bare by her Bachelors, Even*; also known as the *Large Glass* (1915–23)); the dystopic vision of Yevgeny Zamyatin's My (1920) (translated as We (1924)); Breton's claim in the first Surrealist Manifesto (1924) that we are increasingly being forced to live in a rationally constructed cage from which, 'sous couleur de civilisation, sous prétexte de progrès' ('using civilization and progress as pretexts'), everything is banished which does not conform to convention;[48] and such paintings from the 1930s by Max Ernst as *La Ville entière (The City as a Whole)* (1935–6 and 1936) and *La Ville petrifiée (The Petrified City)* (1935) catch the first movement of the dialectic described by Horkheimer and Adorno, as does Balázs's and Bartók's image of Duke Bluebeard's Castle. In their opera the triumph of (male) rationality is shown to bring immense wealth and power, but at a terrible cost. Against Duke Bluebeard's intention and despite his desire to be redeemed from his own creation by Judith, his castle holds him more securely captive than ever Nature could do. It induces in him a sense of powerlessness; turns the female and the elemental into dead things locked behind the seventh door of his castle and so divorces him from those powers which might save him from himself.

But Franz Kafka's 'In der Strafkolonie' (1914) (translated as 'In the Penal Colony' (1914)); Henri Barbusse's *Le Feu* (1915–16) (translated as *Under Fire* (1917)); Georg Kaiser's *Gas* trilogy (1916–19) (translated by various hands 1924 and 1971); the concluding pages of Italo Svevo's *La coscienza di Zeno* (1919–22) (translated as *Confessions of Zeno* (1930)); the war paintings of Otto Dix from the 1920s and 1930s (one of which, *Flandern (Flanders)* (1936), was inspired by the concluding pages of *Le Feu*); Alfred Döblin's *Berge Meere und Giganten (Mountains Seas and Giants* (1921–3)), especially Books One and Two; and the slaughter-house chapters from Book Four of Döblin's *Berlin Alexanderplatz* (1927–9) (translated 1931) transcribe both movements of Horkheimer's and Adorno's dialectic. In all six cases, a rationally constructed system – a machine for executing convicts; the military-industrial complex; mechanized warfare; the technological megalopolis; and a food production process – has turned or is in danger of turning into its opposite. In all six cases, an elemental, irrational system is running out of control, treating people as though they were animals or reducing them to dead primal matter, and threatening to destroy both its creators and itself as it does so.

Indeed, because of the very tenacity with which Western Man clung to the fiction of the rationality of the process which was enslaving him, many modernists felt that he was all the more perilously exposed to those anti-rational powers which the Enlightenment had thought it possible, in some final sense, to subdue, harness and control: psychopathological urges and demonic Nature. Kandinsky, whose seven *Compositionen (Compositions)* (1909–13) are marked by a violent sense of impending Apocalypse,[49] put that sense into words when, in *Über das Geistige in der Kunst* (1900–10) (translated as *The Art of Spiritual Harmony* (1914)), he wrote as follows on the state of contemporary civilization: 'Der alte vergessene Friedhof bebt. Alte vergessene Gräber öffnen sich, und vergessene Geister heben sich aus ihnen' ('The old forgotten graveyard is quaking. Old forgotten graves are opening and forgotten spirits/ghosts are rising up from them').[50] And Hugo Ball, one of the founders of Dada in Zurich in February 1916, echoed the diagnosis when lecturing on Kandinsky in Zurich on 7 April 1917: 'Die Titanen standen auf und zerbrachen die Himmelsburgen' ('the Titans rose up and smashed the celestial castles into pieces').[51] Thus, it is precisely because Mann's Gustav von Aschenbach clings so stubbornly to the illusion that his attraction for Tadzio derives from high, Apollonian motives that he falls prey so destructively to Dionysiac obsession. And it is precisely because the utopian Dream Kingdom of Perle in Alfred Kubin's *Die andere Seite* (1908) (translated as *The Other Side* (1967)) has been created so artificially that its final collapse into anarchy is so violent and so total. The same sense also explains why madness and the city are so closely connected in so many modernist texts. As Spears put it, that institution which had originally been constructed as 'a society of individuals who subscribe to an ideal of rational order' (p. 70) was felt to be turning dialectically into the 'Weltstadt', the insane megalopolis which, in all major pre-war

Expressionist poetry and painting, is associated with darkness, demonic ingression, elemental inundation and the dystopic machine. It is not simply, as Bathrick suggests,[52] that 'quotidian modernity' is felt to *cause* madness. Rather, for all its claims to rationality, the modern city itself is perceived to have 'den charakter des offenen Wahnsinns' ('to be characterized by public insanity'). [53] One work which graphically demonstrates this connection *in extenso* is Rilke's novel *Die Aufzeichnungen des Malte Laurids Brigge* (1910) (translated as *The Notebook of Malte Laurids Brigge* (1930)). In this text, the central character is so profoundly affected by the dislocated insanity of modern Paris that, as Huyssen has shown (see note 33), the shock uncovers the fragmentary nature and latent paranoia of his own personality: insane city and unhinged self are mirror images of one another. By the same token, Michael Fischer in Döblin's *Die Ermordung einer Butterblume* (*The Murder of a Buttercup*) (*c*.1905), a small-scale entrepreneur; the madman in Heym's story *Der Irre* (*The Head-case*) (1911), a psychopath who is associated with an industrial landscape; and Anton Gross in Franz Jung's *Der Fall Gross* (*The Case of Anton Gross*) (*c*. 1920), a draftsman, are metonymic. While convinced of their sanity, all are motivated by pathological drives which they cannot control, and these lead them to do violence to the natural, the innocent and the female, and, ultimately, to destroy themselves.

Because we can, with hindsight, understand modernist texts in a total context in a way which many of their creators could not, Althusser's concept of a 'problématique' is of relevance. In *Pour Marx* (1965) (translated as *For Marx* (1977)),[54] Althusser argues that any 'problématique' as that is perceived subjectively will be more or less mismatched with the objective state of things (pp. 67–9), and so will tend to de-form, obscure or repress factors which are not compatible with the epistemological position of the perceiver. If we apply this idea to modernism, it becomes easy to see why the phenomenon is so diverse. First, because of the subjective elements involved in the dialectic encounter from which any given text is generated, two texts which derive from the same objective 'problématique' may appear to be unconnected at the surface level.[55] Second, texts will vary greatly in the manner in which they transcribe and foreground the objective 'problématique' from which they have been generated. Where some will display an 'explicit consciousness of their own ideologies',[56] others will distort, simplify or repress those ideologies and the objective 'problématique' which underpins them – 'manage' them, 'forget' them, drive them underground.[57] Thus, some modernist texts, like Hugo von Hofmannsthal's 'Vorfrühling' ('Early Spring') (1892), the early work of Gustav Klimt, or the poems of

Georg Trakl (1910–14) allow the objective 'problématique' of modernism to manifest itself only as more or less dark intimations of an impending threat. Others, like Musil's *Die Verwirrungen des Zöglings Törless* (1902–3) (translated as *Young Törless* (1955)) naturalize that 'problématique' into something more manageable (an adolescent crisis in this particular case). Others, like Egon Schiele's paintings *Selbstbildnis mit Lampionfrüchten* (*Self-portrait with Chinese Lanterns*) (1912), *Mutter und Tochter* (*Mother and Daughter*) (1913) and *Liesbesakt* (*Act of Love*) (1915), show terrified human figures in contorted and defensive postures but provide no background which indicates what is causing their terror. Others, like Andrey Bely's *Petrburg* (1911–13) (translated as *Petersburg* (1959; revised and improved in 1978)), Balász's and Bartók's *A Kékszakállá herceg vára* (*Duke Bluebeard's Castle*) (1911), Thomas Mann's *Der Tod in Venedig* (1911) (translated as *Death in Venice* (1928)), or Franz Kafka's *Der Proceß* (1914) (translated as *The Trial* (1929)), foreground a very powerful sense of the objective 'problématique', but do so in terms which are mythological, quasi-mythological or surreal rather than overtly modern. And others, like Ludwig Meidner's *Apokalyptische Landschaften (Apocalyptic Landscapes)* (1913–14), or the major poetry of the German Expressionists, foreground the objective 'problématique' using images which are derived from the modern, i.e. urban/technological world.

Furthermore, modernist texts vary greatly in the degree of complexity with which they present the 'problématique' which they are confronting and trying to resolve. Some, like the poetry of the German Expressionist August Stramm,[58] evince a sense that the 'problématique' is so tangled, so multi-dimensional, that it vitiates the very medium – in Stramm's case language – which is being employed. While others, like the poetry of the German Activists (1914–20), such late novels by Lawrence as *The Plumed Serpent* (1923–5), or Heidegger's *Einführung in die Metaphysik* (1935; second (revised) edition 1953) (translated as *An Introduction to Metaphysics* (1959)), involve a subjective 'problématique' which is relatively simple, notwithstanding the portentous weight of their rhetoric. Finally, modernist works vary extensively in the nature and complexity of their response to the perceived 'problématique'. On the one hand, it is perfectly possible for important modernist works – like many of Rilke's *Neue Gedichte* or Kandinsky's post-1910 visual work – to involve a highly complex response to a perceived 'problématique' which is so repressed, concealed or 'veiled'[59] that we seem to be dealing with Art for Art's sake in its purest form. While on the other hand, an excessively simple perception of the 'problématique' can, and indeed tends to provoke a correspondingly simplistic response and so generate works which, although modernist, are utopian, and even totalitarian in one form or another.[60]

These variables have been the (often unrecognized) source of critical debate along at least two axes: which works belong in the modernist canon and how important is any given modernist work or author? Although such debates are important, I wish, in this essay, to sidestep them for the sake of two more descriptive aims. First, I wish to chart the major aspects of the modernist 'problématique' within the context established above. And second, I want to chart some of the major ways in which a range of modernists responded to and attempted to resolve that 'problématique' as they perceived it. The point of drawing such a map is not to make it unnecessary to explore individual texts. Rather, the point is to bring those texts into some kind of relationship with one another and so give readers some kind of idea of the issues they may expect to find there when they throw away the map and engage with the texts themselves.

MODERNISM AS DIAGNOSIS

At the heart of the 'problématique' perceived by a large number of major modernist artists and intellectuals lay the sense, more or less explicitly formulated and explained in any given case, that contemporary European culture was experiencing the subversion of the most fundamental assumptions and conceptual models on which the liberal humanist epoch had been based. Although the remotest origins of that epoch could be traced back to the thought of Aristotle, it was felt to have begun in earnest during the Renaissance, to have reached its apogee during the Enlightenment, and now to be nearing its end.[61] Hugo Ball, drawing heavily on Nietzsche (whose ideas were the source for many a modernist diagnosis of the cultural situation), put it thus in his lecture on Kandinsky: 'Eine Zeit bricht zusammen. Eine tausendjährige Kultur bricht zusammen. Es gibt keine Pfeiler und Stützen, keine Fundamente mehr, die nicht zersprengt worden wären. . . . Eine Umwertung aller Werte fand statt' ('An epoch is collapsing. A culture which has lasted for a millenium is collapsing. There are no pillars and supports, no foundations any longer which have not been blown to smithereens. . . . A transvaluation of all values came about') (pp. 688–9). And the German theologian, Paul Tillich, recorded how, crawling across the battlefield at Verdun at almost exactly the same time amid the bursting shells and the piles of corpses, he came to the conclusion 'daß der Idealismus zerbrochen war' ('that Idealism was shattered').[62]

More precisely, Ball's global 'transvaluation of all values' involved three major aspects: (1) a change in the concept of what constituted reality;

13

(2) a change in the concept of what constituted human nature; and (3) a change in the sense of the relationship between Man and reality.

The changing sense of reality

By the last decades of the nineteenth century, mainstream European science had come to three basic conclusions about the nature of physical reality. First, that it was material, composed of irreducible particles of matter (i.e. atoms). Second, that it was in a state of harmony with itself, endowed with a certain staticness inasmuch as the amount of energy in the universe stayed constant. And third, that it worked according to the mechanical principle of causality, i.e. regularly and predictably through the interaction of the irreducible atoms. These assumptions derived from Newton's mechanical model of the universe and were based on the static, unchanging, three-dimensional space of Euclidian geometry. However, James Clerk Maxwell's discovery of a phenomenon which could not be accounted for in Newtonian terms, the electrical field of force (*On Physical Lines of Force* (1861–2)), put a question mark over these assumptions. The Newtonian model of irreducibly solid bodies moving predictably through empty space according to the laws of causality and the rules of mathematics might still be valid for the 'zone of middle dimensions' (i.e. the realm of everyday experience). However, advances made in the areas of sub-atomic and astro-physics during the high modernist period by Albert Einstein, Louis de Broglie, Erwin Schrödinger and Paul Dirac (which almost certainly owed something to the more global cultural upheavals which were taking place) showed that, beyond the apparently stable and harmonious world of classical physics, there lay a 'meta-world' which was not describable in Newtonian terms. This 'meta-world' was radically different from the physical reality investigated by classical physics, being composed of decentred, multi-dimensionally fluctuating energies rather than centred, regularly orbiting material particles. Moreover, far from being linear or continuous with itself, that 'meta-world' was observed to involve leaps, jerks, gaps, irregularities and discontinuities. Finally, within this 'meta-world', the principle of causality seemed not to apply, and classical space and time changed from independent and absolutely valid grids of reference into concepts which were relative to the velocity of the object observed and the location of the observer.[63]

The opening up of this 'meta-world' caused similar disruptions during the same period to the stable relationships of Euclidian geometry. Where, for over two thousand years, it had been assumed that Euclid's *Elements* gave an accurate and final picture of stable physical space, Henri Poincaré's *La Science et l'hypothèse* (1903) (translated as *Science and Hypothesis* (1905)) argued that Euclidean geometry was simply conventional and relative: 'neither a transcript of the forms of external space', nor 'a necessary a priori form through which the mind orders spatial experience, as it was for Kant', but simply 'a useful convention for organizing spatial relations'. As with Newtonian physics, Euclidean geometry continued to work well 'at the scale of ordinary experience', but, Poincaré saw, there existed 'meta-worlds' beyond that zone where 'non-Euclidian geometries' were 'more convenient'.[64] Concerning this changed sense of reality, Heisenberg wrote: 'modern physics is in some way extremely near to the doctrines of Heraclitus. If we replace the word "fire" [for Heraclitus the basic element] by the word "energy", we can almost repeat his statements [about the dynamic nature of reality] word for word from our modern point of view.'[65]

One does not need to look very far within the fields of philosophical and literary modernism to find counterparts of and parallels to this changed sense of reality. Indeed, F. T. Marinetti's reference to 'Brownian movements' – the random, discontinuous motion of sub-atomic particles – in his Manifesto of 11 May 1913 dealing with 'parole in libertà' ('words in freedom'),[66] Ball's reference in his lecture on Kandinsky to the strange, dynamic effect which the new 'Elektronenlehre' ('electron theory') had had on all (static) planes, lines and forms (p. 690) and the lecture given by the 'Oberdada', Johannes Baader, on 25 September 1920 in Berlin linking Dada with the Theory of Relativity[67] at a time when Einstein was under attack for his views, are simply three concrete examples of members of the avant-garde using scientific ideas to express or reinforce their own sense that reality is fluctuating, ephemeral and mysterious. Moreover, the centrality for Nietzsche's philosophy of such vitalist concepts as Dionysos, the Will to Power and the Will to Life (together with their widespread reception by large numbers of the European avant-garde); the importance of the thought of Schopenhauer and Bergson during the pre-war decade; the attraction of so many continental intellectuals to Eastern philosophy, especially Taoism, during the modernist period; the conversion of the scientist Alfred North Whitehead to philosophical vitalism as instanced by his Gifford Lectures of 1927 (published two years later as *Process and Reality*); the terms of Karl Jaspers's analysis of the modern situation in the Introduction to his *Die geistige Situation der Zeit* (1931) (translated as *Man in the Modern Age* (1933)); Rimbaud's transmutation of solid objects into decentred lines of energy in, for example, 'Les Ponts' (*c.* 1872) (translated as 'Bridges' (1953)); the 'dinamismo universale' ('universal dynamism') hymned in the manifestos of Italian Futurism; the centrality of the dynamic concept of 'Verkehr' ('traffic') in Kafka's *Der Verschollene* (1912) (translated as *America* (1938));[68] the move away from a noun-based syntax and towards one based on intransitive and reflexive verbs that is so evident in such major German expressionist poems as Ernst Stadler's 'Fahrt über die Kölner Rheinbrücke bei Nacht' ('Journey over the Rhine Bridge at Cologne by Night') (1913); the dynamic nature of Kandinsky's concept of 'Das Geistige' ('The Spiritual') in his seminal work on abstraction *Über das Geistige in der Kunst*; the amazing description of the Parisian Restaurant Lejeune in the first edition of Wyndham Lewis's novel *Tarr* (1914–15);[69] the Dadaist sense that reality is in a state of anarchic, multi-dimensional flux;[70] the celebration of perpetual transformation which is central to Rilke's *Sonette an Orpheus* (1922) (translated as *Sonnets to Orpheus* (1936)) – especially II/12 and II/15; the fluctuating, a-causal presentation of the city which marks Robert Musil's *Der Mann ohne Eigenschaften* (c. 1924–42) (translated as *The Man without Qualities* (1953–60)), James Joyce's *Ulysses* (c. 1915–21), Hermann Broch's *Die Schlafwandler* (1929–32) (translated as *The Sleepwalkers* (1932)) and Döblin's *Berlin Alexanderplatz* – all these are examples of a general, albeit differentiated sense that reality is energetic, fluctuating and chaotic rather than material, unchanging and regularly patterned. As Ball summarized it in his lecture on Kandinsky: 'Die Welt zeigte sich als ein blindes Über- und Gegeneinander entfesselter Kräfte. . . . Das Feste zerrann. Stein, Holz, Metall zerrannen' ('The world revealed itself to be a blind, unfettered flux of forces which overlay and collided with one another. . . . What was solid dissolved. Stone, wood, metal dissolved') (pp. 689 and 690).

Furthermore, a large number of major modernist texts deal centrally with the irruption of a 'meta-world' into the 'middle zone of experience'; with the overturning of an apparently secure, common-sense, bourgeois world by powers which are sub- or inhuman, cosmic, or, at the very least, non-commonsensical. Such disruptive powers are personified by Jarry's Ubu, Wedekind's Lulu, Anastasia in *Tarr* and Hermine in Hermann Hesse's *Der Steppenwolf* (1922–27) (translated 1929). They are also manifested both in the elemental, demonic forces which irrupt into the literary and visual works of German Expressionism, and in the nightmare images which suffuse and subvert the world of everyday objects in surrealist art. In such major modernist texts as Joseph Conrad's *Heart of Darkness* (1898–9), Thomas Mann's *Der Tod in Venedig* and *Der Zauberberg* (1913–24) (translated as *The Magic Mountain* (1928)), Kafka's *Der Proceß*, D. H. Lawrence's *Women in Love* (1913–20),

16

Forster's *A Passage to India* and Jean-Paul Sartre's *La Nausée* (1931–3) (translated as *The Diary of Antoine Roquentin* (1949)), various central characters suddenly discover that the 'real' – i.e. conventional – world of objects and relationships in which they had thought to be securely at home is actually permeated by and subject to elemental powers over which they have no final control, but with which they have to come to terms or be destroyed. The sense that conventional reality is surrounded and permeated by a dynamic 'meta-world' is also embodied in the surreal city which interpenetrates with the 'real' St Petersburg in Bely's novel; in the disconcertingly mysterious country of Perle in Kubin's *Die andere Seite*; in the (to K.'s mind) chaotic world of the Castle and village in Kafka's *Das Schloß* (1922) (translated as *The Castle* (1930)); in the multi-layered, ungrammatical, fluctuating discontinuities of the Dublin of Joyce's *Finnegan's Wake* (1922–38) which, as Spears observed, 'breaks with liberal humanism and with rationality as previously understood in order to reveal a different and more complex view of reality' (p. 98); and in the topsy-turvy worlds of Mr Nott's house in Samuel Beckett's *Watt* (1943–4) and Gonzales's *estancia* in Witold Gombrowicz's *Trans-Atlantyk* (*Trans-Atlantic*) (1953).

Like the modernist scientist, all these modernist writers have a developed sense that reality is not reality as perceived and structured by the Western bourgeois consciousness. Moreover, they all sense that within and behind reality as it is conventionally understood, there lies a realm full of dynamic energies whose patterns are alien to liberal humanist or classical notions of order, and, to the extent that such patterns exist at all, elusive and mysterious. Rilke gave voice to the sense of shock at that discovery when, in the first of the *Duineser Elegien* (1912/22) (translated as the *Duino Elegies* (1939)), he wrote: 'und die findigen Tiere merken es schon, / daß wir nicht sehr verläßlich zu Haus sind / in der gedeuteten Welt.' ('and the resourceful animals already notice / that we are not very reliably at home / in the interpreted world'). And thereafter, in the other nine *Elegies*, he investigated what it meant for Man to exist in an 'angelic' universe – i.e. one which was governed by awesome, supra-human, barely expressible energies over which 'dispossessed' mankind had no control.

In order to communicate the strangeness of the 'meta-worlds', modernist painters increasingly gave up the fixed point of perspective inherited from the Renaissance. Similarly, modernist writers of prose fiction increasingly moved away from the linear sequentiality, omniscient and reliable narrators, fixed narrative relationships and consistency of narrative mode by means of which their nineteenth-century predecessors had accounted 'realistically' for their relatively secure sense of reality.[71]

17

Instead, modernist novelists experiment with techniques which accentuate the discontinuity between the conventional understanding of reality and the sense of reality which informs their works. These techniques include distortions of linear causal/temporal order (as in Mann's *Der Zauberberg*, Proust's *A la Recherche du temps perdu* (1908–22) (translated as *Remembrance of Things Past* (1922–31)) and Joyce's *Ulysses*). They include narrators whose perspective is limited, peculiar or unreliable (like that of Kafka's short story 'Ein Hungerkünstler' (1922) (translated as 'The Hunger Artist' (1938)), Marlow in Conrad's *Heart of Darkness*, Dowell in Ford Madox Ford's *The Good Soldier* (1913–14), Jason Compson in William Faulkner's *The Sound and the Fury* (1928) and Serenus Zeitblom in Mann's *Dr Faustus* (1942–7) (translated 1949)); multi-perspectivism (as in Virginia Woolf's *The Waves* (1928–31), Broch's 'polyphonic novels' like *Die Schlafwandler*, Joyce's *Finnegan's Wake* and Musil's *Der Mann ohne Eigenschaften*); and elastic or elusive relationships between author, narrator and protagonist (as in Mann's *Der Tod in Venedig*, Kafka's two major novels and André Gide's *Les Faux-Monnayeurs* (1919–25) (translated as *The Counterfeiters* (1928))). And they include montage techniques (as in *Berlin Alexanderplatz*) which derive from a-perspectival (i.e. post-Renaissance) visual modes,[72] together with a range of pastiche, parodic and other rhetorical devices. These foreground the writer's consciousness of a 'problématique' by drawing the reader's attention as forcibly to the relative status of the literary signifier as they do to the unconventional sense of reality which they signify. In all cases, we are dealing with what the Russian Formalist theoretician, Viktor Shklovsky, writing in St Petersburg during the Great War, called 'ostraneniye' ('defamiliarization'),[73] and what Brecht was later to call 'Verfremdung' ('alienation'). Modernist artists attempt to break the hold over their audience's minds of conventionalized, nineteenth-century modes of perception; compel their audience to confront an alternative 'meta-world' whose nature transcends the conventional reality principle; and so challenge their audience to rethink their epistemological and, ultimately, their ontological categories.[74] Or, to put it another way, the modernist sense that reality is threatening to run out of control generates texts which, through both content and form, aim to shock their audience into facing that insight with all its attendant consequences.

The changing sense of human nature

Like his Enlightenment predecessor, the nineteenth-century liberal humanist assumed that Man was moral by nature and endowed with a power of rationality which enabled him both to unlock the secrets of Nature and to exercise control over himself. As such, he could, by means of education, be brought to a state of autonomy. Having dispensed with God, the enlightened nineteenth-century free thinker filled that gap with Man, who, he assumed, was the measure of all things, at home in and entitled to do what he pleased with the world of which he was the securely centred mid-point.

As early as 1886, Ernst Mach had gained a certain notoriety for asserting, in *Beiträge zur Analyse der Empfindungen* (translated as *Contributions to the Analysis of Sensations* (1897)): 'das Ich ist unrettbar' ('the ego cannot be saved'). And he developed this position in *Erkenntnis und Irrtum* (1905) (translated as *Knowledge and Error* (1976)) when he characterized the concept of the ego as a fictional label without substance denoting clusters of sensations. But it was above all Nietzsche's philosophy, which made its major initial impact during the high modernist period, that constituted the most damaging polemic against nineteenth-century liberal assumptions. For example, Nietzsche's jottings from the 1880s, later synthesised by his sister into *Der Wille zur Macht* (translated as *The Will to Power* (1909–10)) for the Large Octavo Edition of his works (1900–26), contain several penetrating remarks to the effect that the existence of the shifter 'Ich' ('I') should not mislead us into thinking that there exists a unified substance or organic cell which corresponds to it.[75] And in the works published during his lifetime, Nietzsche's polemic against nineteenth-century conceptions of the self is encapsulated in his attacks on such notable liberals as the theologian David Friedrich Strauß and George Eliot (who had translated Strauß's best-known work, *Das Leben Jesu* (1835–6) as *The Life of Jesus* (1846)). She, Nietzsche claimed, was one of those 'moral fanatics' who, having got rid of the Christian God, believed all the more tenaciously in the need to hang onto Christian morality.[76] For Nietzsche, human nature was fundamentally Dionysiac, governed by the amoral god of unreason and drunkenness, who 'evokes the sense of dark underground forces mysteriously stirring, from Freud's Unconscious to Marx's masses, from Lawrence's Dark Gods to the sleeping giant of *Finnegan's Wake* and Yeats's gods and Sidhe ...'.[77]

As this quotation suggests, similar ideas are to be found in the work of Sigmund Freud, Carl Gustav Jung and Alfred Adler, all of whom were more or less avowedly indebted to Nietzsche.[78] Western behavioural science had been gradually moving towards a 'dynamic psychiatry' since the late eighteenth century.[79] Nevertheless, it was only during the high modernist period, from the turn of the century onwards,[80] that the view gained wide currency in intellectual circles, largely as a result of the psychoanalytical school around Freud, that human behaviour was impelled by unconscious powers. These were said to be irrational and amoral; controllable only in a limited way by conscious reason and moral imperatives; knowable, like the sub-atomic world, only indirectly, via dreams and neuroses; and deeply offensive to and so ignored by conventional wisdom. At a remarkably early date, Freud showed that he was to some extent aware of the analogy between the paradigm shift from the Conscious to the Unconscious which was taking place in the field of the behavioural sciences and the direction in which the physical sciences were moving when he wrote, in *Die Traumdeutung* (1900) (translated as *The Interpretation of Dreams* (1913)):

> Das Unbewußte ist das eigentlich reale Psychische, *uns nach seiner inneren Natur so unbekannt wie das Reale der Außenwelt, und uns durch die Daten des Bewußtseins eben so unvollständig gegeben wie die Angaben unserer Sinnesorgane.*

> The unconscious is the true psychical reality; *in its inner nature it is as much unknown to us as the reality of the external world, and it is as incompletely presented by the data of consciousness as is the external world by the communications of our sense organs.*[81]

The corrosive impact of Freud's teachings on nineteenth-century assumptions about the inherent rationality and morality of human nature would be hard to overestimate. Far from being the autonomous or transcendental ego of the post-Kantian idealist tradition, Man was seen to be at the mercy of basic unconscious drives whose nature could be known only imperfectly. Far from being rational, Man was seen to be innately irrational. Far from being inherently moral, Man was seen to be fundamentally animal. The human ego, claimed Freud, was a bundle of discrete structures without substantial unity. Correspondingly, the structures of human culture had been built over and at the cost of the repressed Unconscious, which Freud described in 'Das Unbewußte' ('The Unconscious') (1913) as analogous to 'einer psychischen Urbevölkerung' (X, p. 294) ('an aboriginal population of the mind' (XIV, p. 195)) – a highly revealing image given the connections made earlier between modernism and the age of imperialism. Far from being a god in his little world, Western man, Freud argued, was at the mercy of more primitive divinities whom, in his hubris, he thought he had abolished or chose to ignore. And the result of this decision was, Freud concluded, the Great War in particular and a profound unease in general. In 'Zeitgemäßes über Krieg und Tod' ('Thoughts for the Time on War and Death') (1915), he claimed, personifying Death,[82] that one of the major psychological reasons for the sense-

rer can investigate either the 'JE' which has become problematic or nature of the mysterious 'autre'.

Accordingly, therefore, the very titles of a large number of major modernist texts denote a move beyond the 'zone of middle dimensions' – the well-defined and apparently secure world of nineteenth-century bourgeois reality in which human beings, apparently governed by free will, seem to be in moral control of their actions – and into that *ungeborgen* ('exposed', 'unprotected') realm which Mann's Hans Castorp entered when he went to the Berghof Sanatorium and Rilke evoked in his poem 'Aus-gesetzt auf den Bergen des Herzens . . .' ('Exposed upon the Mountains of the Heart . . .') (1914). Where the titles of many major nineteenth-century novels consist in the names of people or humanly created places (e.g. *Madame Bovary, Daniel Deronda, Effi Briest, La Chartreuse de Parme, Mansfield Park, Die Chronik der Sperlingsgasse*), the titles of many major modernist novels have a more metaphorical resonance (*Heart of Darkness, To the Lighthouse, Der Proceß, Die andere Seite, My*), signalling their author's awareness that there is more to reality and human nature than can be humanly determined, appropriated, named and explained. As Mark Anderson put it, modernist texts are frequently 'traveling narratives' which work to destabilize the identity of the protagonist as well as the structures of genealogy and property with which this identity is bound up (p. 153). Correspondingly, Conrad's Kurtz, Döblin's Michael Fischer, Mann's von Aschenbach, Kafka's Josef K., Wyndham Lewis's Tarr, Lawrence's Gerald Crich, Elias Canetti's Professor Peter Kien (in *Die Blendung* (1930–1) (translated as *Auto da Fé* (1965)), Sartre's Roquentin and Camus's Meursault are all characters who have acquired what initially looks like a secure and stable identity by neglecting, repressing, or doing violence to the shifting, spontaneous, natural, unconscious sides of their beings. All are characters who have become over-cerebral, over-confident and/or over-conventionalized; who labour under the illusion that they are centaurs in their dragon worlds. And all are, in consequence, brought low and in some cases transformed by a series of encounters with mythological beings or elemental powers – i.e. with objective correlatives of unconscious drives which are, in the strict sense, more primitive and more powerful than what Lawrence, in his letter to Edward Garnett of 5 June 1914, called the 'old stable *ego* – of the character'.[86]

However, precisely because 'the old stable *ego*' is felt to be under so great a threat from what Ball called 'eine Anarchie der befreiten Dämonen und Naturmächte' ('an anarchy of liberated demons and natural powers' (p. 689)), many modernists, as several critics have pointed out, make the preservation of consciousness their chief concern. In a pioneering essay of

less and, apparently, unstoppable slaughter of the Great War, was 'die Störung des bisher von uns festgehaltenen Verhältnisses zum Tode' (X, p. 341) ('the disturbance that has taken place in the attitude which we have hitherto adopted towards death' (XIV, p. 289)). But precisely because we have ignored Death, Freud continued, Death has returned all the more violently to force his reality onto us via the War: 'Der Tod läßt sich jetzt nicht mehr verleugnen; man muß an ihn glauben' (X, p. 344) ('Death will no longer be denied; we are forced to believe in it [him]' (XIV, p. 291)). Thus, Freud concluded, because Western man realized deep down that the repressed divinities and the psychic powers which they represent will not disappear just because he wants them to, he felt profoundly ill at ease. And although he might try to disguise the resultant psychic suffering from himself through such sublimations as religion, culture and the pursuit of knowledge, such displacement activities were ultimately powerless. Thus, in *Das Unbehagen in der Kultur* (*Civilization and its Discontents*) (1929–30), Freud came to the following, wry conclusion:

> Nun hat [der Mensch] sich der Erreichung dieses Ideals sehr angenähert, ist beinahe selbst ein Gott geworden... . Im Interesse unserer Untersuchung wollen wir aber auch nicht daran vergessen, daß der heutige Mensch sich in seiner Gottähnlichkeit nicht glücklich fühlt.
>
> (XIV, pp. 450–1)
>
> To-day [Man] has come very close to the attainment of this ideal, he has almost become a god himself... . But in the interests of our investigations, we will not forget that present-day man does not feel happy in his Godlike character.
>
> (XXI, pp. 91–2)

Ironically, given Freud's attitude to religion, modernist theology runs parallel to psychoanalysis over the question of human nature. Where nineteenth-century liberal Christianity had tended on the one hand to divinize man, stressing his ethical potential and the godlike nature of his character; and on the other hand to humanize God, ignoring those facets of Christian teaching which did not fit this rapprochement, modernist theology, as instanced above all by the work of Rudolf Otto and Karl Barth, drew attention to the 'numinous', the non-rational, the awe-inspiring and the meta-ethical aspects of religious experience.[83] In *Das Heilige* (1917) (translated as *The Idea of the Holy* (1923)), Otto described 'das Unterste und Tiefste in jeder starken frommen Gefühlsregung' ('the deepest and most fundamental element in all strong and sincerely felt religious emotion') in irrationalist, Dionysiac terms, claiming that it can lead people 'zu Rausch, Verzückung und Ekstase' ('to intoxicated frenzy, to transport, and to ecstasy').[84] And in the (completely rewritten) second edition of his commentary on St Paul's *Epistle to the Romans* (1921), a text in which the influence of Kierkegaard, Dostoevsky and Nietzsche is particularly marked, Barth also described the divine-human encounter in irrationalist, almost expressionist terms. Far from informing mankind of its divinity or telling men how they might become divine,[85] God is said to irrupt cataclysmically into the human world in order to convict man of his smallness and impotence, to bring him to a more appropriate awareness of his place in the scheme of things, and thereby, paradoxically, to make him anew. Both the psychoanalytical school who followed Freud and the dialectical theologians who followed Barth were, for all their differences, in agreement over one essential point: human beings were governed by and at the mercy of irrational, primitive powers. These might be psychological or metaphysical, but to ignore or defy them was to court disaster.

Once again, modernist art and literature provide extensive parallels. The beast- or mask-like heads on the female bodies in Picasso's *Les Demoiselles d'Avignon* (*The Maids of Avignon*) (1907) graphically speak of the modernist sense that the *logos* (conventionally located in the head) and ego-identity (conventionally located in the face) are illusions covering a more primitive, more bestial, non-humanist reality. Similar sentiments are encapsulated in the opening lines of Gottfried Benn's poem 'Der Arzt II' ('The Doctor II') (*c*.1912): 'Die Krone der Schöpfung, das Schwein, der Mensch: – / geht doch mit anderen Tieren um' ('The crown of Creation, the swine, mankind: – / has commerce with the other beasts indeed') or the lines from Ezra Pound's eighty-first *Pisan Canto* (written in a prison camp near Pisa in 1945): 'The ant's a centaur in his dragon world. / Pull down thy vanity, it is not man / Made courage or made order or made grace.' In their different ways, both Benn and Pound are saying that Man can no longer be regarded as the moral centre of a rationally ordered world, as a being who is ontologically distinct from and in some sense above it. Like the 'ant' in his 'dragon world', Man may labour under the self-centred illusion that he is semi-superior to the rest of Creation – a 'centaur' who is half animal and half something else. But in fact, he is just another of the animals and as such, subject to non-rational drives which are beyond his control. Ball was even more explicit on the effects of modernity in his lecture on Kandinsky:

> Der Mensch verlor sein himmlisches Gesicht, wurde Materie, Zufall, Konglomerat, Tier, Wahnsinnsprodukt abrupt und unzulänglich zuckender Gedanken. Der Mensch verlor seine

> Sonderstellung, die ihm die Vernunft gew
> Partikel der Natur, vorurteilslos gesehen ein
> storchenähnlich, mit disproportionierten G
> Gesicht abstehenden Zacken, der sich Nase
> Zipfeln, die man gewohnt war 'Ohren' zu nenne
> göttlichen Illusion entkleidet, wurde gewöhnlic
> ter als ein Stein es ist, von denselben Gesetz
> beherrscht, er verschwand in der Natur, man hatte
> ihn nicht zu genau zu besehen, wenn man nicht vol
> Abscheu den letzten Rest von Achtung vor diesem
> des gestorbenen Schöpfers verlieren wollte.

Man lost his heavenly visage, became matter, chan
erate, animal, the crazy product of though
spasmodically and inadequately. Man lost that specia
reason had accorded him. He became a particle of Na
without prejudice a being akin to a frog or a stork, wi
of proportion to one another, a protruberance sticking
face called a nose, points sticking up from his head
generally been known as 'ears'. Man, divested of the illu
divinity, became ordinary, no more interesting than a s
structed and governed by the same laws, he disappeared in
and there was every reason not to look at him too closely i
not want to be filled with horror and disgust and lose the l
respect for this wretched image of the dead Creator.

(Translated by the

This passage reads like an anticipation of Beckett's *Watt* in
that the human(ist) subject has been radically 'decentred'. And t
(which, as Schwartz rightly perceived, derived in part from 'the
turn-of-the-century assumption that ordinary consciousness is str
by forces of which it is unaware' (p. 213)), had two major, complen
effects on modernist literature. Although Beebe saw these effec
contradiction (p. 1074), they are more accurately regarded as two si
the same spinning (i.e. decentred) coin. Where some modernist w
investigate the extent to which human beings are subject to motivatio
lower (i.e. animal) or higher (i.e. metaphysical) irrational powers, ot
are centrally concerned with the problem of consciousness. Or to pu
epigrammatically, Rimbaud's famous dictum in his letters to Georg
Izambard and Paul Demeny of 13 and 15 May 1871– 'JE est un autre'
is an other') – opens up two complementary routes. The moderni

1903 entitled 'Die Großstadt und das Geistesleben' (translated as 'The Metropolis and Mental Life' (1936)), the sociologist Georg Simmel had singled out an attitude of blasé intellectuality as the most appropriate stance for the modern city-dweller who wished to preserve the integrity of his person in the face of the continuous shocks of great city life.[87] Many modernist texts offer parallels to that insight. The 'cool rationalism and ironic scepticism' of so many major modernists;[88] the centrality, for such modernist works as Italo Svevo's *La coscienza di Zeno* or Benn's poem 'Synthese' ('Synthesis') (1917), of the 'individual consciousness, which tries to make itself immune from external influences in order to observe the world from an independent position';[89] the Cubists' and Imagists' concern with controlled, analytical impersonality;[90] Prufrock's tortured self-irony;[91] the ego-inflation which marks so many Expressionist poems and the heroes of the so-called *Ich-Dramen*; and the excoriating analysis of the self which leaps out from so many Expressionist (self-)portraits (like Ludwig Meidner's *Ich und die Stadt* (I and the City (1913)) and all aspects of 'the burden of subjectivity'[92] in a situation where the symbiotic relationship between stable self and ordered world has been fractured.[93] In such a destabilized situation, the individual consciousness, painfully aware of the relativity of its perspective and always on the point of being overwhelmed by the sub- and supra-human powers evoked by Benn's imagery of 'Höhlen, Himmeln, Dreck und Vieh' ('Caves, heavens, filth and beast') ('Synthese'), is left either desperately asking *what* it is or emphatically insisting *that* it is. Consequently, when a point of epiphanic meaning unexpectedly presents itself, it has to be seized and pinned down as precisely as possible. Hence Pound's simultaneous connection of Imagism with 'the "search for oneself" ', definition of an Imagist poem as the recording of 'the precise [epiphanic] instant when a thing outward and objective transforms itself, or darts into a thing inward and subjective'; and explication of his ideal form of modern art in terms of the equation which, in Cartesian geometry, generates the circle.[94] In a highly confusing, irrational universe, where the the self is at best out of control and at worst non-existent, Pound is advocating opening oneself to, and by means of an aesthetic of impersonality, attempting to hold on to those rare instants at which the rift between decentred self and disordered outer world is, or seems to be overcome in a single, transcendent instant.

The changing understanding of the relationship between Man and reality

Given the above situation, it follows that the modernist understanding of the relationship between Man and reality is radically different from that of mainstream nineteenth-century thinkers and writers. By and large, nineteenth-century thinkers and writers posited, or at least sought to posit, a consonance, correspondence or substantial unity between the logical structure of the material world, the structure of the human *logos*, and, if they were believers, between those two dimensions and the divine *Logos* – between what Fokkema and Ibsch called 'the world of appearances and a higher world of absolute Beauty and Truth' (p. 41). In contrast, the modernists were afflicted by a greater or lesser sense of dislocation between the material, the human and the metaphysical. This shift was graphically prefigured by the contrast between two poems by Baudelaire. In 'Correspondances' ('Correlatives' / 'Correspondences') (*c*. 1845– after 1851), Man is at home in the temple of Nature, surrounded by forests of (friendly) symbols which speak to his mind and senses. But in 'Le Coucher du soleil romantique' ('The Setting of the Romantic Sun') (1862), that sense of harmony has become a memory. God is withdrawing; irresistible night is coming on; and the poet finds himself on the edge of a grimpen, haunted by the smell of the grave. Such a sense of dispossession, of not being at home, is central to the modernist experience. It generates the desolate imagery of Eliot's *The Waste Land* (1921–2) and the cry at the end of Rilke's Second Duino Elegy: 'Fänden auch wir ein reines, verhaltenes, schmales / Menschliches, einen unseren Streifen Fruchtlands / zwischen Strom und Gestein' ('If only we too could find an unsullied, half-hidden, narrow / strip of humanness, a plot of fertile land which was our own / between the torrent and the rocky place'). This sense of radical alienation manifests itself particularly clearly in the modernist treatment of four questions: the status of reason; the status of language; the nature of history and the status of Western culture.

Over and over again within modernist literature, one finds attacks on the supremacy of human reason on behalf of other faculties of human nature. Apollonian reason is attacked by disciples of Nietzsche in the name of Dionysiac vitality; by the Futurists in the name of energy; by the Expressionists in the name of ecstasy; by the Dadaists (for whom, Ball relates, Bergson was particularly important during the founding period in Zurich)[95] in the name of spontaneity, intuition and the imagination; and by the Surrealists in the name of dream and the unconscious. The fluctuations of reality and the complexities of human nature, invisible to the eye of empirical reason guided by conventional common sense, can, it is variously claimed, be approached, visualized and grasped only by those faculties in human nature which come from below or beyond rational faculties.[96] One might well expect such claims from avant-garde artists out to shock. All the more surprising is it then to find mathematicians (like

Poincaré) insisting on the centrality of intuition, and physicists (like Heisenberg and Planck) spelling out the limitations of reason. The scientist working within the Cartesian-Newtonian paradigm had assumed a structural homology between 'the "syntactic" order of semiotic systems (particularly language)', 'the logical ordering of "reason"', and 'the structural organization of a world given as exterior to both these orders'[97] such that the laws of the latter could be translated exhaustively into abstract formulations by means of the former. In contrast, the scientist working in the field of sub-atomic physics dispensed with these assumptions and, following Mach, insisted that reason described not Nature in itself, but only Nature as exposed to our method of questioning. Consequently, the apparently rational picture which the scientist constructs of Nature is said inevitably to involve an element of anthropomorphic subjectivity which it is impossible, in any final sense, to remove,[98] especially at the sub-atomic level where the very act of observing has an effect on what is observed.

Similarly then, language for the modernist proves to be equally limited. When Nietzsche noted: 'Ich fürchte, wir werden Gott nicht los, weil wir noch an die Grammatik glauben . . .' ('I fear we are not getting rid of God because we still believe in grammar . . .'),[99] he was saying epigrammatically what Ferdinand de Saussure was to argue scientifically in his posthumously published *Cours de Linguistique générale* (1907–11) (translated as *Course in General Linguistics* (1960)) – namely, that although language feels as though it has some absolute and immutable (i.e. divinely legitimized) status to those who live 'inside' it, it is actually a relative and continuously evolving system of arbitrary signs. As such, it has no *a priori* connection with reality: there is no one-to-one correspondence between immutable material objects and a noun-based syntax which names and orders those objects. For modernist 'Sprachkritiker' ('critics of language') such as Nietzsche, Mach, Fritz Mauthner, Bergson, Ernest Fenollosa and the Dadaists, no substance exists to substantiate substantives (i.e. to cement together the world of language and the world of material objects). Indeed, although, at one level, Wittgenstein's *Tractatus Logico-Philosophicus* (1914–18) (translated 1922) sets out and refines upon the assumptions of nineteenth-century positivism and its relation to reality, at another – as the image of the disposable ladder in Proposition 6.54 suggests – it deconstructs and offers an alternative, modernist set of assumptions about the same topic. In Propositions 2.027, 3.1431, 3.203, 4.0311 and 4.12, for example, Wittgenstein states that the universe is composed of material objects, that nouns name those things, and that the worlds of language and material reality are held together by one common factor: 'logical form'. But because, as the aporias of Propositions 4.12 and 4.121 clearly indicate, Wittgenstein saw that the very concept of 'logical form' could not be depicted by language, that concept, subverted the very system which it was supposed to underpin. Consequently, Wittgenstein also set up a parallel series of propositions within the *Tractatus* which clearly point forward to the linguistic conventionalism of the *Philosophische Untersuchungen* (1935–48) (translated as *Philosophical Investigations* (1953)). Nowhere is the self-deconstructive nature of the *Tractatus* more evident than in Proposition 4.01. Its first part ('Der Satz ist ein Bild der Wirklichkeit' ('The proposition is a picture of reality')) involves nineteenth-century positivist assumptions about language and reality. But its second part ('Der Satz ist ein Modell der Wirklichkeit, so wie wir sie uns denken' ('The proposition is a model of reality to the extent that and according to the manner in which we conceive of it')) involves a relativism which is entirely compatible with the thinking behind de Saussure's analysis of the linguistic sign into the (arbitrary) signifier and the (conventionally agreed) signified.

Modernist science, dealing with even more elusive matters, runs parallel with philosophy and linguistics over the question of language. When Heisenberg and Bohr first met, in the early summer of 1920, Bohr replied as follows to a question of Heisenberg's about the nature of the language he was using to describe atomic and sub-atomic relationships: 'We must be clear that, when it comes to atoms, language can be used only as in poetry. The poet, too, is not nearly so concerned with describing facts as with creating images and establishing mental connections.'[100] And a subsequent chapter in the same book, 'Discussions about Language (1933)' (pp. 123–40) (which, interestingly enough, takes place outside the 'zone of middle dimensions', in the rarified air of the Bavarian Alps), makes it clear that the inexactitude of language, even mathematical language, was one of the central problems for the most advanced scientists of the time. Here, Bohr is quoted as saying: 'One could, of course, say that the mathematical formulae with which we theoretical physicists describe nature ought to have this degree of logical purity and strictness. But then the whole problem reappears in different guise just as soon as we try to apply these formulae to nature' (p. 135). And in *Physics and Philosophy*, Heisenberg reiterated the problem by saying that the language in which we talk about atomic events is 'not a precise language', but 'a language that produces pictures in our mind', and furthermore, that those pictures 'have only a vague connection with reality ... represent only a tendency towards reality' (p. 156). So, in order to get at the 'strange kind of reality' which lies beyond the world of immediate sense-data, Heisenberg formulated his principle of complementarity, according to which the scientist needs to play with logically incompatible, but complementary pictures (p. 50).

Similar, and in several cases even more devastating doubts about the adequacy of language exist by accident or design throughout modernist literature. The impossibility of putting a precise number on the elemental Malabar Caves in *A Passage to India*; the silences of Rimbaud, Valéry, Rilke and Hofmannsthal's Lord Chandos and the failure of Mallarmé's *grand oeuvre*; the abstract and nonsense poetry of the Russian Futurists (*zaoum*), the Dadaists and the Surrealists; the telegrammatic style of the Italian Futurists and several major Expressionist poets and dramatists; the use of non-verbal, sound and ideogrammatic elements to help out a medium (i.e. language) which is felt to be in a bad way; and the ironic attitude towards language in general and overweening linguistic confidence in particular which is so important in the work of Mann, Joyce, Svevo and Beckett – all are indices of the modernist awareness of the arbitrariness, inexactitude and unreliability of language. And to the extent that we are talking about conscious literary devices, these exist in modernist works to break the hold of conventional syntax and received meanings over the readers' imaginations and open them to strange, alternative, sub- and supra-human 'meta-worlds'.

A third fundamental difference between modernists and their nineteenth-century predecessors involves their conceptions of history and time. For the pre-modernist thinker, whether an Idealist like Hegel, a Materialist like Marx, an Evolutionist like Herbert Spencer, or a Christian theologian like Adolf von Harnack, time was a progressive process moving ever upwards in a dialectical or linear manner as Man brought ever more of the natural world under his rational, moral, economic or cultural control. The modernist experiences of flux, decentring and apocalypse explode these ideas. In the realm of the natural sciences, sub-atomic physics made such nonsense of the Kantian notion of time as a universally valid, *a priori* category of the transcendental consciousness that Heisenberg came to the conclusion that one might have to reckon with sub-atomic processes in which certain events seem to take place 'en sens inverse de l'ordre causal' ('in a way which runs counter to causal order').[101] And in 'Das Unbewußte,' Freud wrote that the processes of the Unconscious are timeless in the sense that they are not ordered temporally, not altered by the passage of time, and have no relation at all with time as that is normally understood (X, p. 286; XIV, p. 187). Similarly, for the modernist writer, time ceases to be a regular and common-sense process in which a precise but fixed gap, the present, separates the past from the future. Instead, it becomes either elastic (as in

Der Zauberberg), with the present moment expanding and contracting according to the situation of the observer, or incipiently apocalyptic (as in so many early Expressionist poems), or a kind of simultaneity in which past, present and future merge into one. Similarly, history ceases to be a progressive movement upwards and becomes something akin to an irregular series of surges in no particular direction. Each surge may have its shape, but a gap will separate it from the next, differently shaped and differently extended surge – which may well move in a different direction or, alternatively, prove to be a recurrence of the same. In his appropriately named *Apocalypse* (1929), D. H. Lawrence welcomed the overturning of the nineteenth-century conceptions, describing 'our idea of time as a continuity in an eternal, straight line' as something which 'has crippled our consciousness cruelly'.[102] And before he went to Berlin in 1912 and began to revert to a classicism, T. E. Hulme had been an enthusiastic Bergsonian, not least because he felt that Bergson's more fluid sense of time had liberated him from a linear, mechanical and ultimately deterministic view of the universe.[103] But more often than not, when confronted with the same phenomenon, modernists echoed the desperate cry of Nietzsche's madman in *Die fröhliche Wissenschaft* (1882) (translated as *The Joyful Wisdom* (1910)):

> Was taten wir, als wir diese Erde von ihrer Sonne [i.e. the fixed point of reference] losketteten? Wohin bewegt sie sich nun? Wohin bewegen wir uns? Fort von allen Sonnen? Stürzen wir nicht fortwährend? Und rückwärts, seitwärts, vorwärts, nach allen Seiten? Gibt es noch ein Oben und ein Unten? Irren wir nicht wie durch ein unendliches Nichts?[104]

> What did we do when we unchained this earth from its sun? Whither is it moving now? Whither are we moving now? Away from all suns? Are we not continually falling headlong? And backwards, sideways, forwards, in every direction? Is there still an above and a below? Are we not straying as though through an endless Nothingness?

For a generation reared on the idea of history as progress, the modernist experience easily gave rise to radical *Kulturpessimismus*. And as we shall see, many major modernists, trying to make sense of history in the teeth of their experience of the chaotic megalopolis and/or the Great War, saw, like Oswald Spengler in his two-volume *Der Untergang des Abendlands* (*c.*1914–17) (translated as *The Decline of the West* (1926)), the modern age as a trough, in a state of dire fallenness and in urgent need of messianic redemption.

Finally, from such an elastic, decentred, multi-dimensional view of time and history, it was only a short step to a profound doubt in that assumed supremacy of Western civilization which had sustained so much nineteenth-century thinking and political action. In *Abstraktion und Einfühlung* (1906) (translated as *Abstraction and Empathy* (1953)), the German aesthetician Wilhelm Worringer had distinguished between 'empathetic' and 'abstract' art, arguing that whereas the former was produced in cultures marked by a sense of being at home in the world, the latter was produced in cultures suffering from a sense of being at the mercy of hostile elemental or mythological powers. From this, Worringer concluded that one should not evaluate 'abstract' art (like that of the Middle Ages, the Orient and so-called 'primitive' cultures) in terms of 'empathetic' categories specific to Western, post-Renaissance humanism. He also argued that one should certainly not regard non-realistic, 'abstract' art as inferior to representational, 'empathetic' art. The implications of Worringer's highly influential thesis are clear. Apparently 'primitive' cultures, though technologically less advanced than the modern West, may in fact be better equipped to deal with the totality of a universe in which Man is not at home, of which he is not the centrepiece, and in the face of which he inevitably experiences a profound sense of *Angst*. The same feeling informs much modernist writing and painting. Tolstoy's withdrawal to the life and Kandinsky's celebration of the art of the Russian peasantry; Rimbaud's cry from the first part of *Une saison en enfer* (c.1871–3) (translated as *A Season in Hell* (1939)) 'Je retournais à l'Orient et à la sagesse première et éternelle' ('I returned to the Orient and to primal and timeless wisdom'); Gauguin's move to Tahiti; Delacroix's attraction to the life of the desert Arabs; Karl Kraus's essay attacking European ethnocentrism 'Die chinesische Mauer' ('The Great Wall of China') (1909); the attraction, for so many modernist intellectuals, of pseudo-primitive, tribalistic communities like that at Worpswede near Bremen or that on the Monte Veritá near Ascona in the years before and after the Great War; Bartók's fascination with the peasant culture of Hungary and Romania during the first decade of the century when he recorded and transcribed approximately 10,000 folk-songs; the Expressionist attraction to non-Western and 'primitive' art which is encapsulated in the *Almanach der blaue Reiter* (1912) (translated as *The blaue Reiter Almanac* (1974)), Carl Einstein's *Negerplastik* (*African Sculpture*) (1915) and so many paintings, woodcuts and sculptures by members of the *Brücke* (*Bridge*) group; the neo-primitivism of the Vorticists Henri Gaudier-Brzeska and P. Wyndham Lewis; the Dadaists' attraction to the art of children and experimentation with pseudo-primitive poetry and rituals; Hesse's and Döblin's fascination with the Orient; Federico García Lorca's celebration of Spanish gypsy culture in *Romancero Gitano* (*c*.1923–4) (translated as *Gypsy Ballads* (1938–53)); Martin Buber's attraction to the Chassidic communities of Eastern Europe and the non-European setting of such major modernist novels as Gide's *L'Immoraliste* (1899–1901) (translated as *The Immoralist* (1930)), *Heart of Darkness*, *Die andere Seite*, *Kangaroo* (1922), *A Passage to India* and *The Plumed Serpent* all involve one common sentiment. Such pre-modern and non-Western cultures have not abstracted the *logos* from the rest of the personality and coexist with rather than seek to dominate external Nature. Thus, rightly or wrongly, they are felt to enjoy a freedom and balance which the modernizing West is perceived to have lost or to be losing because of the dialectical turn which the central project of the Enlightenment is felt to be taking.[105]

The work which perhaps best summarizes the modernists' changed sense of reality, human nature and the relationship between them is Hofmannsthal's eleven-page masterpiece *Ein Brief* (1901–2) (translated as *The Letter of Lord Chandos* (1952)). Here, the fictional author, Philipp Lord Chandos, writes in 1603 to Francis Bacon, the man responsible for formulating the theory of the inductive procedure which came to underpin the classical Western scientific attitude,[106] explaining why it is impossible for him to write any more. From this letter it emerges that Chandos has undergone a psychological crisis which replicates *in nuce* the paradigm shift analysed above. Before his crisis, Chandos had felt himself to be a rational, integrated self at home in his society and the mid-point of a concentric world. This was in a state of harmony with itself, ontologically secure, historically grounded and exhaustively knowable by human reason. However, as a result of a series of increasingly disturbing experiences, culminating in the famous 'rats in the cellar' episode, Chandos loses his sense of security and identity and is forced to see that he is actually adrift in a decentred universe in a state of chaotic, multi-dimensional flux. This non-anthropocentric universe is shot through with mysterious powers that are simultaneously 'göttlicher, tierischer' ('more divine, more bestial');[107] has no fixed points or continuous patterns; is characterized by unpredictably alternating moments of total illumination and periods of devastating emptiness; and is not decipherable by human reason and language. In other words, Chandos is undergoing the Death of God experience proclaimed by Nietzsche's madman and experiencing the full force of the lines from Yeats's poem 'The Second Coming' (1916): 'Things fall apart; the centre cannot hold; / Mere anarchy is loosed upon the world.' Like the real Rimbaud thirty years before, the fictitious Adrian

Leverkühn forty years later, and so many modernists who experienced the night side of the city and/or the horrors of trench warfare at first hand, Chandos is spending an enforced season in Hell. And during this season he has to find some way to adjust his former, humanist-logocentric assumptions to an inner and an outer reality which have not only ceased to conform to them, but appear to be running out control.

MODERNISM AS RESPONSE

By the early 1930s, it was a commonplace among artists and intellectuals, especially on the Continent, that European civilization was at a cross-roads. C. G. Jung's *Seelenprobleme der Gegenwart* (*Spiritual Problems of the Present Day*) (1931), especially the chapter entitled 'Das Seelenproblem des modernen Menschen'; [108] Karl Jaspers's *Die geistige Situation der Zeit*; Edmund Husserl's lecture of 7 and 10 May 1935 'Die Krisis des europäischen Menschtums und die Philosophie' (translated as 'Philosophy and the Crisis of Modern Man' (1965)); [109] and, of course, Heidegger's *Einführung in die Metaphysik* all evince a more or less pronounced awareness that Western humanist and/or idealist culture was in a state of crisis. The scientist Max Planck put it thus:

> We are living in a very singular moment of history. It is a moment of crisis, in the literal sense of that word. ... Many people say that these symptoms mark the beginnings of a great renaissance, but there are others who see in them the tidings of a downfall to which our civilization is fatally destined.[110]

But the art of modernism had anticipated and gone beyond such a straightforwardly optimistic/pessimistic reaction to the perceived crisis, and at the risk of excessive categorization, it is possible to identify at least nine fairly well distinguished types of response to that crisis which recur throughout modernist art.

First, and most negatively, there is the nihilist response. Faced with a situation which Durkheim had, in *Le Suicide* and *De la Division du travail social*, described as one of *anomie*, more than a few modernist artists and intellectuals succumbed to the feeling that an apocalyptic end was approaching beyond which there was only the 'endless darkness . . .' with which *A Kékszakállá herceg vára* concludes, or that human relationships were irredeemably locked into that sado-masochistic double bind which marks Kafka's early writings and Georg Kaiser's *Von morgens bis mitternachts* (1912) (translated as *From Morn to Midnight* (1920)). Consequently, a significant number either went insane (Nietzsche, van Gogh,

Jakob van Hoddis, Antonin Artaud); or took their own lives (Virginia Woolf, Jacques Vaché, Jacques Rigaut, René Crevel, Georg Trakl, Ernst Toller, Kurt Tucholsky, Vladimir Mayakovsky, Sergey Yesenin); or died prematurely in a state of near total despair (Rimbaud, Alfred Lichtenstein, August Stramm).[111]

Second, several modernists – and this response is particularly typical of the early Expressionists[112] – sought to relieve their sense of crisis by means of the experience of ecstatic release, sometimes aided by drugs, alcohol or violent experience. Following Rimbaud's stated aim in his letters of 13 and 15 May 1871 of arriving at the Unknown by deranging all his senses, several early Expressionists, not to mention the *alter egos* who form the mid-point of their so-called *Ich-Dramen*, would have assented to the view which Georg Heym recorded in his diary on 6 July 1910 and 15 December 1911: that one instant of intoxicated enthusiasm, even though it may lead to death, is preferable to the suffocating banality and oppression of everyday modern life.[113] And Ludwig Rubiner's highly influential essay of mid-1912, 'Der Dichter greift in die Politik' ('The Poet intervenes in Politics'),[114] with its call for dynamism, intensity, ecstasy and the will to catastrophe (col. 715), was almost certainly one of the immediate stimuli for such hymns to ecstasy as Benn's 'Untergrundbahn' ('Underground Train/Railway') (1913), Stadler's 'Der Aufbruch' ('The Beginning'/'The Break-Out') (*c.* 1912) and 'Fahrt über die Kölner Rheinbrücke bei Nacht' and Ernst Wilhelm Lotz's 'Aufbruch der Jugend' ('Youth Bursts Out') (*c.* 1913–14). In these and similar works, no attempt is made to analyse or understand. The threatened ego seeks to overcome its sense of isolation and constriction by tapping the irrational powers of the psyche and inducing what Freud called the 'oceanic feeling', regardless of where that might lead. And in several cases, it led, via the war hysteria of 1914, to the trenches and an early death (Lotz, Stadler, Hans Leybold, Franz Marc and August Macke) or to rapid disillusion with ecstatic irrationalism (Ludwig Rubiner, Oskar Kokoschka, Wilhelm Klemm, Hugo Ball and Rudolf Leonhard). As Freud was to argue in *Jenseits des Lustprinzips* (XIII) (translated as *Beyond the Pleasure Principle* (XVIII)) which he published in 1920 in the wake of the Great War: if you open up the Unconscious, you are as likely to release the destructive power of the Death Instinct (*Thanatos*) as the creative power of the Life Instinct (*Eros*).

Third, a significant number of Modernists turned to mysticism as a way of resolving their sense of crisis. This might take the form of a latter-day Platonism (like that of Kandinsky's *Über das Geistige in der Kunst*); a panentheism (like that informing the theory and practice of Hans Arp and Paul Klee); an esoteric hermeticism (like that of Yeats);[115] or a more or less westernized Eastern mysticism (like that embodied in the blue-eyed people who preside over and survive the concluding apocalypse of *Die andere Seite*; or that implied by the concluding (Sanskrit) words of Eliot's *The Waste Land*; or that involved in Hesse's *Siddhartha* (1919–22) (translated 1954) and *Narziß und Goldmund* (1927–9) (translated as *Death and the Lover* (1932)). But the mysticism might also take more secular forms like Chandos's final openness to inexplicable epiphanic moments; Breton's alchemically inspired quest for 'le merveilleux' ('the marvellous') in *Nadja* (1927–8) (translated 1960);[116] the importance of music in Symbolist and Symbolist-derived aesthetic theory; the use of music imagery throughout *A Passage to India* and in the concluding pages of *La Nausée*, *Dr Faustus* and Kafka's 'Die Verwandlung' (1912) (translated as 'The Metamorphosis' (1937)); or what has been variously termed the 'individualist mysticism' and 'the aesthetic of transcendence and epiphany'[117] of such works as *Die Aufzeichnungen des Malte Laurids Brigge*, *My*, *Das Schloß*, *Der Steppenwolf* and *Berlin Alexanderplatz*. In all cases, we are dealing with an attempt, albeit one which expresses itself in very different ways and with varying degrees of confidence, to arrive at a sense which is deeply repugnant to those critics who have accepted the (anti-)ontology of postmodernism. Beyond or within what looks like entropic chaos or unresolvable conflict, there exists a firm spiritual substratum. This substratum may be either psychological or metaphysical, but it permits what Jung termed 'integration' and the emergence of what the Existentialists were to call a sense of Being out of Nothingness: it is a melody, as Roquentin puts it in the final pages of *La Nausée*, which persists even after the record has been broken.

Fourth, and closely related to the mystical response, is the aestheticist one. As Bürger has shown, the attempt to establish art as something autonomous, a-historical and removed from the realm of rationalization and commercialization goes back to the end of the eighteenth century (pp. 57–8). But towards the end of the nineteenth century the sense intensified that the world had not only been desacralized, but was also being increasingly afflicted by the radical sense of uncertainty generated by the dialectical turn taken by the central project of the Enlightenment. Consequently, such practitioners of Art for Art's sake and aestheticism as the Symbolists, the Decadents, the George Circle and the Imagists felt the ever more urgent need to proclaim the sacral nature of art and thereby hold on to an allegedly a-temporal enclave of meaning, stability and transcendence. It is this desire which informs Mallarmé's essay 'Averses ou Critique' ('Rainshowers or Criticism') (1886–95; better known as 'Crise de vers' 'Crisis in Poetry' (1897)); Rilke's book on Rodin (1903–7) (translated

1946) and Hofmannsthal's essay 'Der Dichter und diese Zeit' ('The Poet and this Age' (1906)). In an age when, as Hofmannsthal puts it, the representative things lack spirit and the spiritual things do not stand out in relief; which has no Eleusinian Mysteries or Seven Sacraments with which people can lift themselves above everyday life, it is the artist's task to redeem the world by recapturing that lost sense of mystery.[118]

From here, it is only a short step to the fifth response, the decision to turn one's back on the modern age. After the Great War, for instance, Rilke, Yeats and Ball expressed that decision in a 'flight out of time' – the emigration to a 'still point' or the fixed centre of a 'gyre' which was geographically as far removed as possible from the confusions of the modern age.[119] In Rilke's case, this meant the little château at Muzot; in Yeats's case, the tower in Galway; and in Ball's case, Montagnola in the Tessin (where he became Hesse's secretary and biographer) and the certainties of ultra-orthodox Catholicism. Eliot and Pound (whose early thinking about art and poetry, especially in respect of the need for impersonality,[120] owed much to Symbolism) expressed a very similar decision in a somewhat different way. After the Great War, both moved backwards in time to associate themselves with a pre-modern conscious-ness and system of beliefs which, they felt, were free from the uncertainties, instability and sense of meaninglessness which marked the modern age. In *The Waste Land*, Eliot came to the conclusion that the modern world was an arid desert full of broken images and that all he could do about it was to put his own lands in order. And he rationalized that conclusion in his essay 'The Metaphysical Poets' (1921) by means of the extremely influential notion of the 'dissociation of sensibility' according to which English culture had undergone a historical fall from grace during the seventeenth century from which it had never recovered. On the basis of that conclusion, Eliot committed himself publicly, in his preface to *For Lancelot Andrewes* (1928), a book dedicated to an English divine who had died in the pre-lapsarian year of 1626, to classicism in literature, royalism in politics and Anglo-Catholicism in religion[121] – i.e. to those attitudes which Eliot believed to have been most finely developed in the last part of the sixteenth century, before the historical fall. And it was the quintessential spirit informing those attitudes which Eliot sought to celebrate in *Little Gidding* (1941–2), the last of the *Four Quartets*, which takes as its starting point a religious community near Huntingdon founded one year before Andrewes's death by Nicholas Ferrar, but looted and dissolved by the Roundheads in 1646. Pound voiced a similar disgust with contemporary European civilization in *Hugh Selwyn Mauberly* (1919–20), describing it as 'an old bitch gone in the teeth, / . . . a botched civilization'. He then left England, and after a stay in Paris, finally settled in 1924 in Mussolini's Italy (which he saw as a modern version of the corporate medieval state and hence free from the mechanization, systematization and 'the black death of the capitalist system')[122] in order to write his own, latter-day version of the *Divine Comedy*: the *Cantos*. These were, as Schwartz put it, 'designed to challenge the corrupted values of Western civilization and to inspire reverence for the highest values – the "eternal state of mind" – which will lay the groundwork for a new and more humane society' (p. 148).[123] Likewise, Hofmannsthal and George went down their own, not dissimilar paths leading from Aestheticism to various forms of high conservatism.[124]

Where Pound and Eliot turned their backs on the complexities and confusions of the present in the name of an ideal, hieratic past, other modernists, especially during the immediate post-war years, turned their back on the same complexities and confusions in the name of an ideal, socialist future.[125] Thus, the more or less short-lived left-wing utopianism of, for instance, Ernst Toller, Johannes R. Becher, Rudolf Leonhard, Kurt Hiller, Ludwig Rubiner, Lyonel Feininger, Bruno Taut and the members of the *Arbeitsrat für Kunst* in Germany,[126] or of Kandinsky, Mayakovsky, Alexander Blok, El Lissitzky, Vladimir Tatlin and Alexander Rodschenko in Russia, was the obverse of the right-wing nostalgia of Eliot, Pound, Hofmannsthal and George. Both groups of modernists were marked by a deep yearning for a total, centred world in which the New Man under socialism or redeemed humanity under God could rediscover a secure identity and transcendent sense of purpose.[127] It is wrong to say, as some critics have, that all modernist utopianism issued in a totalitarian commitment. However, Pound's extreme right-wing illusions did lead him to become the propagandist for a fascist state; and Becher's extreme left-wing illusions did lead him to become the first Minister of Culture of a Stalinist state, the GDR, and the composer of its national anthem. In both cases, a flawed sense of 'problématique' ultimately generated a frighteningly simple, totalitarian response.

The sixth response can be broadly described as a 'primitivism'. Non-European or pre-modern cultures are used not just as sources of aesthetic inspiration, but as a cultural model for emulation. Hence the importance of the Hindu philosopher Professor Godbole in *A Passage to India* and the black community of Harlem in Section II of Lorca's *Poeta in Nueva York* (1929–30) (translated as *Poet in New York* (1940)). Godbole's intuitive, non-rational cast of mind makes him the character who is best adapted to the mysteries, ambiguities and open-ended fluidity which Forster designated with the non-topographical shifter 'India'. And in

Lorca's poem, it is the elemental, mythological, 'great and desperate' King of Harlem (whose beard is said to stretch down to the sea) who offers the inhabitants of New York, especially its black community, their only hope of redemption from the anguished frustration and cancered blood which derive from their enslavement by the banality and materialism of industrial civilization.[128]

The seventh response, aptly characterized by Pär Bergman as 'modernolatry',[129] is characteristic of Italian Futurism, early Vorticism and that group of writers, of whom Ernst Jünger is the best known, described by Herf as 'reactionary modernists'. Where the first six responses described above all, in various ways, involve a withdrawal from or transcendence of the contemporary world, the three latter groups celebrated their unreserved commitment to it. The Futurists and the reactionary modernists did so because of the speed, energy, size and sheer modernity of industrial society, and, conversely, its ability to destroy what had been inherited from the past. The Vorticists did so because of the tension they perceived between the massively static, abstract machine forms of modernity and the violence which was stored up within them. But where the Futurists' hymn to the machine, the city and material energy led several of the major members of the movement towards 'embarrassingly reactionary' attitudes[130] – the inhuman celebration of mechanized warfare, Man's ability to master his environment by machine brutality and, ultimately, Mussolini's fascism – most of the Vorticists moved away from their early attitudes and towards less abstract and more humane modes of art. Indeed, Jacob Epstein (who belongs stylistically to the Vorticist group even though he refused to exhibit with them in June 1915) went so far as to destroy what is arguably the major example of Vorticist sculpture, his massive *Rock Drill* (1913–15), probably because he felt that it celebrated the machine violence which had issued in the Great War.[131] Unlike Epstein, but like several major Futurists, Jünger failed to learn more humane attitudes from his war experience. And in books like *In Stahlgewittern* (1920; second (revised) edition 1924) (translated as *The Storm of Steel* (1929)) and *Der Arbeiter* (*The Worker*) (1932), he actually seems to approve of the process by which human beings lose their autonomy and become aspects of a supra-human military or industrial machine. But like the early Vorticists, it was the staticness and stability of huge machines which attracted him; and this, together with his ingrained aristocratism, generated in the late 1930s the totalitarian (albeit anti-Nazi) 'static hierarchy of value' and 'haven of paradisaical permanence' which forms the resolution of his novel *Auf den Marmorklippen* (1939) (translated as *On the Marble Cliffs* (1947)).[132]

The change of heart on the part of most of the Vorticists forms an obvious bridge to the eighth response. Utopian and messianic socialism was doomed to disillusion as the real nature of the German and Russian revolutions became apparent; and Futurist affirmation of the modern was unacceptable to many modernists because of its blindness to or indifference towards the reality and implications of machine violence. So, in order to avoid these pitfalls, those modernists who suffered from a sense of cultural crisis but who wished to stay with the contemporary world had to develop more modest, more ambiguous and more ironic attitudes to the complexities of modernity. It was this desire to negotiate a middle way which generated Constructivism and *Neue Sachlichkeit* (New Objectivity), with their assertion of the need for a modern classicism, their commitment to modern materials and their desire to rescue Western civilization from the barbarism to which it had succumbed over the previous decade. But above all, whether they understood it in these terms or not, the proponents of both movements were trying to reverse the dialectical turn which the central project of the Enlightenment had taken and bring it back onto its central and proper course. Hence their attempts to bring technology back to manageable human dimensions through the design and construction of aesthetically pleasing cities where imperialist capitalism was not permitted to turn into a chaotic, autonomous system, but was, instead, subject to reasonable and humane control. One might describe this general attitude as a pared-down humanism: Man was reinstated at the centre of things but not necessarily regarded as the measure of all things. And human reason, while retaining its centrality, was not over-estimated vis-à-vis the powers of unreason inside and outside human nature. Such was the spirit informing Bruno Taut's move away from utopianism and acceptance of the post of City Architect in Magdeburg;[133] Sartre's Existentialism; Jung's central doctrine of 'integration'; Ernst Bloch's *Spuren* (*Traces*) (1930);[134] Döblin's revision of his apocalyptic *Berge Meere und Giganten* into *Giganten* (*Giants*) (1932) (in which human autonomy and technological ability were celebrated);[135] and, perhaps of all literary works, Thomas Mann's *Joseph* tetralogy (1926–42) (translated as *Joseph and his Brothers* (1934–45)). Here, as Ritchie Robertson has perceptively observed, Mann, instead of 'surrendering blindly to the primitive or trying to deny its power', sought to 'explore and understand it with the aid of his modern consciousness' and so developed an ironic stance as 'a means of keeping the primitive at bay while acknowledging its authority and appeal'.[136]

And finally, one can identify a strand in modernism which points forward very clearly to McHale's definition of the postmodernist condition as an acceptance of 'an anarchic landscape of worlds in the plural' (p. 37) in which artists renounce the nostalgia or desire for epiphany, transcendence and closure. From the modernist point of view, this double attitude of acceptance and renunciation can be experienced either as a loss (as in Virginia Woolf's last, posthumously published *Between the Acts* (1938–41), and, less tragically, in *Ulysses* and *Watt*). Or it can be experienced as a liberation (as in *Finnegan's Wake* and *Der Mann ohne Eigenschaften*). Or it can be experienced as both at the same time. The best example of this latter, ambiguous response is undoubtedly provided by Dada with its anarchist roots, plurality of poetic registers (including deliberate banality), wide-ranging use of various kinds of collage components, recognition that the cinema rather than the printed word is the art form of modernity, aggressive challenging of classical humanist assumptions, metaleptic mistrust of hierarchies, disrespect for allegedly impermeable boundaries (like that between 'Art' and 'life'), hostility to final solutions and closures, parodic use of machinery, experimentation with heteroglossia via the simultaneous poem, carnival imagery, willingness to accept its own disposability/death, anti-illustrations and repeated insistence that Dada involves the ability to say 'yes' and 'no' at the same time.[137] It can be argued that Dada left too many of the tragic aspects of life out of account, and in his later years, Arp came to see this.[138] Nevertheless, Dada involves the 'suspensive irony', the 'more comprehensive "both-and"', the 'willingness to live with uncertainty, to tolerate and, in some cases, to welcome a world seen as random and multiple, even, at times absurd' and the ability to accept 'the gaps and discontinuities' which Wilde identified as central features of postmodernism (pp. 44 and 48–9). Dada also evinces virtually all the characteristics which, in McHale's view, typify postmodernism – so that it comes as something of a surprise to discover that neither of these critics accords Dada so much as a mention![139]

It is an artistic landscape like that constructed by Dada in which Ulrich, Musil's 'Möglichkeitsmensch' (literally 'possibilitarian') lives and moves: 'without the fiction of the self as entelechy unfolding and growing according to some inner law'; untroubled by 'the futile and frequently self-destructive searches for selfhood as wholeness, which neglect the potential rewards of openness toward the other'; and without the need for certainty.[140] Indeed, Ulrich's refusal to look for any final solution outside his situation, his ability to hold an ironic balance between the conflicting, overlapping and fluctuating possibilities which inform his situation, and his preparedness to live without any final certainty in an elastic situation where reason is of limited help all make him an example of that 'non-Euclidian humanity' which can live in a 'Lobatchevskyan' universe. Eliot glimpsed precisely this possibility when he published his essay on Ben Jonson in the *TLS* on 13 November 1919, but having achieved his own sense of centred, 'Euclidean' certainty, he repressed that awareness when he published his *Selected Essays* in 1932.[141] Ulrich's attitudes also put him in the same category as those quintessentially modernist heroes Chaplin and Keaton – little men who, when everything is ranged against them, manage to keep their balance in an insane modern universe.

Because the modernists could see, with varying degrees of clarity, complexity and acceptance, the implications of an accelerating process which, in our own era, has turned the world into an electronic stage,[142] or, as Wilde put it, a global shopping mall (p. 166), they constituted in the literal sense an avant-garde scouting out an unknown territory. But because that process had not yet turned into a total and accepted way of life legitimized by what Horkheimer and Adorno were to call the 'culture industry' (pp. 139–89), it was still possible for the modernists to respond to it in ways which are closed to the postmodernists. Hence the frequent and hotly debated charge that postmodernism is not an oppositional phenomenon. The modernists were still able, either literally or imaginatively, to seek out alternative or geographical enclaves which had not yet been colonized by the media or the leisure industry.[143] They could call to mind a past which was in danger, but not irrevocably so, of being lost and had not been reified by the nostalgia or heritage industries. They could hope in a hieratical or socialist utopia which had not been discredited by Nazi or Stalinist atrocities. They could withdraw into arcane areas of the mind which had not been invaded by the religious or the fantasy industries. And they could use a variety of innovative artistic techniques and psychological ploys which enabled them to retain a greater or lesser sense of selfhood and autonomy, but which had not yet been assimilated by the advertising, fashion and lifestyle industries.[144] Although modernism anticipated what McHale has called 'the pluralistic and anarchistic ontological landscape of advanced industrial cultures' (p. 38), most modernists disliked what they espied from their advanced position. As Barnouw (p. 248) and Wilde suggest, this was partly because of a nostalgia for a (probably imaginary) ideal stability, but partly, too, because of three more serious reasons. First, many modernists suspected that what McHale describes as 'pluralism' might actually be nothing more than a multi-coloured surface concealing a commodified uniformity. Second, the more socially aware realized that that 'anarchistic' landscape was not a flat one, but involved large, possibly growing areas of systematically created physical and psychological misery. And third, the more

41

psychoanalytically aware feared that the abolition of metaphors of depth – one of the central features of the postmodernist imagination[145] – inevitably involved a blindness to or the repression of those dark, Dionysiac powers which return from the forgotten depths all the more potently and destructively for being ignored.

Given the unmistakeable consequences which are now issuing from the dialectical turn taken by the central project of the Enlightenment – escalating environmental problems, the growing gap between the haves and the have-nots, the boredom, violence and alienation which haunt our advanced societies, the difficulties involved in making relationships within a system which is inherently hostile to *Gemeinschaften* – the anxiety of modernism may well be a more appropriate response to that turn than postmodernism's ludic acceptance. Ever since Kierkegaard, the Existentialists, with the exception of the later Sartre, have been telling us that our capacity to experience *Angst* betokens a very deep realization that the prevailing system which constructs what Lawrence called the 'old stable *ego*' (see note 86) is at odds with the profoundest stratum of the personality.[146] And the central project of German aesthetics since Kant, admirably analysed by Andrew Bowie in terms of the 'concern with those aspects of subjectivity which are incompatible with wholesale rationalisation',[147] points to the same awareness. We may not be able to return in good faith to the security of religious orthodoxy, cling on to the centred categories and confident correspondences of classical humanism, or find refuge in any of the enclaves still available to many of the modernists. But in the face of the massive problems faced by Western or westernizing humanity, all of which can, ultimately, be understood in terms of Horkheimer's and Adorno's analysis, it has become a matter of urgency to undertake a transvaluation of values. And that means defying the massively oracular authority of the patriarchs of the 1980s like Lacan and Derrida;[148] finding a power with which to fill the gap at the heart of postmodernist aesthetics and psychology; undoing the post-Enlightenment equations of Geist-as-spirit with Geist-as-ego and self with ego; relegitimizing metaphors of depth; and rediscovering that decentred fluidum at the heart of the human personality which many ancient cultures referred to by means of metaphors of breath. The problematics of modernism are still with us, albeit in a more drastic form. Thus, by studying the variety of ways in which modernist writers, thinkers and artists responded to them and understanding the implications and end results of those responses, we are given the means of avoiding the modernists' mistakes and making decisions about the nature of reality, our relationship with reality and our relationship with ourselves which can, in some measure at least, help us to look for a way out of the *impasse* into which our civilization seems currently to be heading.

NOTES

1 Wherever possible, I have provided the date of composition of the texts cited. In some few cases, I have not been able to discover that date and have provided the date of publication instead. The date which follows the title of the English translation denotes the year in which that translation was first published. Where a straight translation follows the title in the original language but precedes the date of composition of the original, I have not been able to locate an English translation. Where no translation of the title in the original language is provided, the title of the English translation is identical with that of the original.

2 Jan Mukařovský, 'Dialectic Contradictions in Modern Art' (1935), in *Structure, Sign, and Function*, edited by John Burbank and Peter Steiner, New Haven and London, 1978, pp. 129–51, p. 129.

3 Monroe K. Spears, *Dionysus and the City: Modernism in Twentieth-Century Poetry*, New York, 1970, p. 3.

4 Malcolm Bradbury and James McFarlane, 'The Name and Nature of Modernism', in Malcolm Bradbury and James McFarlane (eds), *Modernism 1890–1930*, Harmondsworth, 1976, pp. 22–3.

5 Douwe Fokkema and Elrud Ibsch, *Modernist Conjectures: A Mainstream in European Literature 1910–1940* (1984), London, 1987, pp. 22, 318.

6 See Spears, op. cit., pp. 9–10 and 13; also Maurice Beebe, 'What Modernism Was', *Journal of Modern Literature*, vol. 3, no. 5, 1973, pp. 1065–80, p. 1066.

7 Beebe, op. cit., pp. 1080–4; Bradbury and McFarlane, op. cit., pp. 641–64; Jean Weisgerber (ed.), *Les Avant-gardes littéraires au XXe siècle*, 2 vols, Budapest, 1984, II, pp. 1155–87.

8 Beebe, op. cit., p. 1071.

9 Harry Levin, 'What Was Modernism?' (1960), in *Refractions: Essays in Comparative Literature*, New York, 1966, pp. 271–95, p. 292; cf. Beebe, op. cit., p. 1066 and Fokkema and Ibsch, op. cit., p. 31.

10 Spears, op. cit., p. 14, citing the introduction to Irving Howe's anthology *Literary Modernism*, Greenwich, Conn., 1967.

11 Spears, op. cit., p. 20; cf. also Alan Wilde, *Horizons of Assent: Modernism, Postmodernism, and the Ironic Imagination*, Baltimore and London, 1981, p. 16.

12 Spears, op. cit., p. 35; cf. also Lionel Trilling, 'On the Teaching of Modern Literature', in *Beyond Culture: Essays on Literature and Learning*, London, 1966, p. 19 and John Burt Foster Jr, *Heirs to Dionysos: A Nietzschean Current in Literary Modernism*, Princeton, 1981.

13 Beebe, op. cit., p. 1073.

14 Tom Gibbons, 'Modernism and Reactionary Politics', *Journal of Modern Literature*, vol. 3, no. 5, 1973, pp. 1140–57, p. 1150.

15 William J. Brazill Jr, 'Art and "The Panic Terror" ', in Gerald Chapple and Hans H. Schulte (eds), *The Turn of the Century: German Literature and Art 1890–1915*, Bonn, 1981, pp. 529–39, pp. 531–3.

16 Wilde, op. cit., pp. 3, 6, 9–10, 16 and 41.
17 Fokkema and Ibsch, op. cit., p. 60.
18 Sanford Schwartz, *The Matrix of Modernism: Pound, Eliot, and Early Twentieth-Century Thought*, Princeton, 1985, pp. 71–4, following Frank Kermode, *Romantic Image*, London, 1957 and Robert Langbaum, *The Poetry of Experience*, London, 1957.
19 Gaylord LeRoy and Ursula Beitz, 'The Marxist Approach to Modernism', *Journal of Modern Literature*, vol. 3, no. 5, 1973, pp. 1158–74, p. 1158.
20 David Bathrick and Andreas Huyssen, 'Modernism and the Experience of Modernity', in Andreas Huyssen and David Bathrick, *Modernity and the Text: Revisions of German Modernism*, New York, 1989, pp. 1–16, esp. pp. 4–5.
21 Mukařovský, op. cit., pp. 132–3; cf. Spears, op. cit., pp. 16–19, discussing the views of Edmund Wilson, Northrop Frye and Frank Kermode; also Schwartz, op. cit., pp. 71–4, and Robert Langbaum, *The Modern Spirit*, London, 1970.
22 Mukařovský, op. cit., p. 132; Schwartz, op. cit., pp. 104 and 172–3. Several of the essays in Karl Ludwig Schneider, *Zerbrochene Formen*, Hamburg, 1967 show how German Expressionist poets used and inverted Romantic imagery.
23 Peter Bürger, *Theorie der Avantgarde*, Frankfurt am Main, 1974, *passim*.
24 Fokkema and Ibsch, op. cit., p. 37; Schwartz, op. cit., p. 174.
25 Fokkema and Ibsch, op. cit., pp. 3 and 46.
26 Wilde, op. cit., *passim*, but especially pp. 22, 27, 44, 108, 131–2 and 185; Fokkema and Ibsch, op. cit., p. 89; Schwartz, op. cit., p. 213; Ihab Hassan, 'POSTmodernISM: A Paracritical Bibliography', in *The Postmodern Turn*, Columbus, 1987, pp. 25–45; Brian McHale, *Postmodernist Fiction*, New York and London, 1987, pp. 6–11.
27 Levin, op. cit., p. 291; Spears, op. cit., p. 74; Edward Timms and David Kelly (eds), *Unreal City: Urban Experience in Modern European Literature and Art*, Manchester, 1985.
28 Spears, op. cit., p. 60; Fokkema and Ibsch, op. cit., p. 25.
29 Bradbury and McFarlane, op. cit., p. 27; Fokkema and Ibsch, op. cit., p. 25.
30 Cf. Klaus R. Scherpe, 'The City as Narrator: The Modern Text in Alfred Döblin's *Berlin Alexanderplatz*', in Huyssen and Bathrick, op. cit., pp. 162–79, especially p. 169. Scherpe's essay (p. 177, n. 10 and n. 15) contains useful bibliographical information on secondary literature dealing with the image of the modern(ist) city. For an earlier bibliography on the same topic, see John Z. Guzlowski and Yvonne Shikany Eddy, 'Studies of the Modern Novel and the City: A Selected Checklist', *Modern Fiction Studies*, vol. 24, 1978–9, pp. 147–53.
31 See Richard Sheppard, 'Kandinsky's *oeuvre* 1900–14: The *Avant-garde* as Rear-guard', *Word and Image*, vol. 6, no. 1, 1990, pp. 41–67.
32 For a check-list of similarities and differences, see Hassan, op. cit., pp. 40–4.
33 Andreas Huyssen, 'Paris/Childhood: The Fragmented Body in Rilke's *Notebooks of Malte Laurids Brigge*', in Huyssen and Bathrick, op. cit., pp. 113–41, p. 137.
34 Fredric Jameson, *The Political Unconscious: Narrative as a Socially Symbolic Act*, Ithaca, 1981, p. 27.
35 Renate Werner, 'Das Wilhelminische Zeitalter als literarhistorische Epoche',

in Jutta Kolkenbrock-Netz, Gerhard Plumpe and Hans Joachim Schrimpf (eds), *Wege der Literaturwissenschaft*, Bonn, 1985, pp. 211–31.

36 Jeffrey Herf, *Reactionary Modernism: Technology, Culture, and Politics in Weimar and the Third Reich*, Cambridge, 1985.

37 Max Horkheimer and Theodor W. Adorno, *Dialektik der Aufklärung: Philosophische Fragmente* (1947), Leipzig, 1989. My translation is based on but not identical with *Dialectic of Enlightenment* (1972), translated by John Cumming, London, 1973.

38 Thomas S. Kuhn, *The Structure of Scientific Revolutions*, Chicago, 1970.

39 Such a dialectical understanding is rare among critics before the mid-late 1980s, but it is more or less explicitly present in Mukřovský, op. cit., pp. 140–5; Spears, op. cit., p. 62; Stoddard Martin, *Wagner to the Waste Land*, London and Basingstoke, 1982, pp. 208 and 240; Fokkema and Ibsch, op. cit., p. 240; Schwartz, op. cit., p. 214 and Werner, op. cit., p. 223. However, as a glance at the pagination rapidly indicates, most of these writers tend to arrive at a dialectical stance relatively late on in their works, in tacit admission that a one-dimensional approach cannot make coherent sense of the heterogeneous phenomena which they have confronted in the preceding pages.

40 Huyssen and Bathrick, op. cit., pp. 3, 7–8, 38, 50, 65–7, 86, 90–3, 106, 142–3, 156, 169–71.

41 Ibid., p. 215. For information on the sociological origins of a significant section of German modernists – the so-called Expressionists – see Paul Raabe, *Die Autoren und Bücher des literarischen Expressionismus*, Stuttgart, 1985, pp. 575–9 and 600–1; also Werner Kohlschmidt, 'Zu den soziologischen Voraussetzungen des literarischen Expressionismus in Deutschland' (1970), in Hans Gerd Rötzer (ed.), *Begriffsbestimmung des literarischen Expressionismus*, Darmstadt, 1976, pp. 427–46.

42 Dagmar Barnouw, *Weimar Intellectuals and the Threat of Modernity*, Bloomington, Indiana, 1988, pp. 27–30.

43 Cf. Richard Sheppard, 'Expressionism and Vorticism: An Analytical Comparison', in Janet Garton (ed.), *Facets of European Modernism*, Norwich, 1985, pp. 149–74.

44 D. H. Lawrence is, of course, the great native English exception to this statement. Many of the other leading British modernists were not English.

45 It is easy to forget that in their day, both the Georgians and the Imagists were considered avant-garde. See Christian Karlson Stead, *The New Poetic*, London, 1964.

46 See W. M. Lüdke (ed.), *'Theorie der Avantgarde': Antworten auf Peter Bürgers Bestimmung von Kunst und bürgerlicher Gesellschaft*, Frankfurt am Main, 1976.

47 Virginia Woolf, 'Mr Bennett and Mrs Brown' (1924), in *Collected Essays*, 4 vols. London, 1966–9, I, p. 321.

48 André Breton, *Les Manifestes du surréalisme*, Paris, 1955, p. 12.

49 For a discussion of the *topos* of apocalypse, see Gunter E. Grimm, Werner Faulstich and Peter Kuon (eds), *Apokalypse: Weltuntergangsvisionen in der Literatur des 20. Jahrhunderts*, Frankfurt am Main, 1986.

50 Wassily Kandinsky, *Über das Geistige in der Kunst* (1912), 9th edn, Berne, 1970.

51 Andeheinz Mößer (ed.), 'Hugo Balls Vortrag über Wassily Kandinsky in der

Galerie Dada in Zürich am 7.4.1917', *Deutsche Vierteljahresschrift für Literaturwissenschaft und Geistesgeschichte,* vol. 51, 1977, pp. 676–704, p. 689. Translated in Hugo Ball, *Flight out of Time,* edited by John Elderfield, New York, 1974.

52 David Bathrick, 'Speaking the Other's Silence: Franz Jung's *Der Fall Gross*', in Huyssen and Bathrick, op. cit., pp. 19–35, p. 28.

53 Horkheimer and Adorno, op. cit., p. 70.

54 Louis Althusser, *For Marx* (1965), London, 1977.

55 Cf. Beebe, op. cit., p. 1074.

56 Cf. Judith Ryan, 'Each One as She May: Melanctha, Tonka, Nadja', in Huyssen and Bathrick, op. cit., pp. 95–109, esp. p. 96.

57 For examples of critics disentangling the subjective 'problématique' which is embedded in various important modernist works from a deformed, obscured or repressed objective 'problématique', see Michael Long, 'The Politics of English Modernism: Eliot, Pound, Joyce', in Edward Timms and Peter Collier (eds), *Visions and Blueprints: Avant-garde Culture and Radical Politics in Early Twentieth-Century Europe,* Manchester, 1988, pp. 98–112, especially pp. 103–5; Barnouw, op. cit., pp. 12–13 and 20–1; Theodor W. Adorno, 'George und Hofmannsthal: Zum Briefwechsel: 1891–1906', in *Prismen,* Frankfurt am Main, 1955, pp. 232–82, pp. 280–1; Jameson, op. cit., p. 266 and Fredric Jameson, 'Modernism and its Repressed: Robbe-Grillet as Anti-Colonialist', *Diacritics,* vol. 6, no. 2, 1976, pp. 13–14.

58 Cf. Richard Sheppard, 'The Poetry of August Stramm: A Suitable Case for Deconstruction', in Richard Sheppard (ed.), *New Ways in Germanistik,* Oxford, 1990, pp. 211–42.

59 For the importance of the concept of 'veiling' for Kandinsky, see Rose-Carol Washton Long, *Kandinsky: The Development of an Abstract Style,* New York and Oxford, 1980, pp. 72–3 and Sheppard, 'Kandinsky's *oeuvre* 1900–14', p. 61.

60 Cf. Peter Uwe Hohendahl, 'The Loss of Reality: Gottfried Benn's Early Prose', in Huyssen and Bathrick, op. cit., pp. 81–94, esp. pp. 90–1.

61 Cf. Spears, op. cit., p. 42; Brazill, op. cit., p. 533 and Wilde, op. cit., p. 40.

62 Quoted in Heinz Zahrnt, *Die Sache mit Gott: Die protestantische Theologie im 20. Jahrhundert,* Munich, 1966, p. 384.

63 For introductions to the scientific revolution which took place in the modernist period, see John P. Briggs and F. David Peat, *Looking Glass Universe* (1984), London, 1985, p. 34; Fritjof Capra, *The Tao of Physics* (1975), London, 1976 and *The Turning Point* (1982), London, 1983.

64 Schwartz, op. cit., pp. 15–16.

65 Werner Heisenberg, *Physics and Philosophy,* London, 1959, p. 61.

66 F. T. Marinetti, 'Destruction of Syntax – Imagination without Strings – Words-in-Freedom 1913', in Umbro Apollonio (ed.), *Futurist Manifestos,* New York, 1973, pp. 95–106, esp. p. 96.

67 Anon., 'Dadaistische Aufklärung', *Vorwärts* (Berlin), vol. 37, no. 473, 27 September 1920, p. 2.

68 See Mark Anderson, 'Kafka and New York: Notes on a Traveling Narrative', in Huyssen and Bathrick, op. cit., pp. 142–61, esp. pp. 142–3 and 156–7.

69 See Richard Sheppard, 'Wyndham Lewis's *Tarr*: An (Anti-)Vorticist Novel?' *Journal of English and Germanic Philology,* vol. 88, 1989, pp. 510–30, esp. p. 515.

70 Cf. Richard Sheppard, 'What is Dada?', *Orbis Litterarum*, vol. 34, 1979, pp. 175–207. For a comparison of futurist and Dada concepts of dynamism, see Richard Sheppard, 'Dada und Futurismus', in Wolfgang Paulsen and Helmut G. Hermann (eds), *Sinn aus Unsinn: Dada International*, Berne and Munich, 1982, pp. 29–70.

71 Cf. Spears, op. cit., pp. 23–8; Fokkema and Ibsch, op. cit., pp. 39 and 66.

72 Cf. Bürger, op. cit., pp. 97–8.

73 The origins of this concept are to be found in Shklovsky's 'Art as Technique' (1917), in Lee T. Lemon and Marion J. Reis (eds), *Russian Formalist Criticism*, Lincoln, Nebraska, 1965, pp. 3–24.

74 McHale, op. cit., argues that where the 'dominant' of modernist fiction is epistemological, that of postmodernist fiction is ontological. But as he himself admits, this distinction is one of emphasis:

> it specifies the order in which different aspects are to be attended to, so that, although it would be perfectly possible to interrogate a postmodernist text about its epistemological implications, it is more urgent to interrogate it about its ontological implications.
>
> (pp. 9–10)

75 Friedrich Nietzsche, *Werke*, edited by Karl Schlechta, 5 vols, Frankfurt am Main, 1972, IV, pp. 48, 72, 92, 129, 204, 369, 434, 442, 455, 487, 490, 501 and 507.

76 Friedrich Nietzsche, 'Streifzüge eines Unzeitgemässen', para. 5, in *Götzen-Dämmerung* (1888), *Werke*, III, p. 993.

77 Spears, op. cit., p. 40.

78 Although Freud denied any early knowledge of Nietzsche, recent research has shown this to be untrue (see Anthony Storr, *Freud*, Oxford, 1989, p. 120). The basis of Adlerian 'Individual Psychology', the urge to power, is clearly very close to Nietzsche's concept of the Will to Power. And a glance at the index to Jung's *Collected Works* quickly shows how important the writings of Nietzsche, especially *Zarathustra*, were to him. To quote Henri Ellenberger: 'More even so than Bachofen, Nietzsche may be considered the common source of Freud, Adler, and Jung' (*The Discovery of the Unconscious*, London, 1970, p. 276).

79 Ellenberger, op. cit.

80 Cf. Schwartz, op. cit., p. 213.

81 Sigmund Freud, *Die Traumdeutung*, in *Gesammelte Werke*, edited by Anna Freud and Marie Bonaparte, 18 vols, London and Frankfurt am Main, 1940–68, II/III, pp. 617–8. All subsequent German references to Freud within the text relate to the relevant volume of this edition. Sigmund Freud, *The Interpretation of Dreams*, in *The Standard Edition of the Complete Psychological Works of Sigmund Freud*, edited by James Strachey and Anna Freud, 24 vols, London, 1953–74, V, p. 613. All subsequent English references to Freud within the text relate to the relevant volume of this edition.

82 The English translation obscures Freud's personification by rendering the accusative masculine pronoun 'ihn' ('him' or 'it') by the unambiguous 'it'.

83 For an introduction to the theological paradigm shift which took place during the modernist period, see Zahrnt, 'Die grosse Wende', in op. cit., pp. 13–65.

84 Rudolf Otto, *Das Heilige: Über das Irrationale in der Idee des Göttlichen und sein Verhältnis zum Rationalen* (1917), Gotha, 1929, pp. 13–14. Rudolf Otto, *The Idea of the Holy: An Inquiry into the Non-Rational Factor in the Idea of the Divine and its Relation to the Rational* (1923), Harmondsworth, 1959, pp. 26–7.

85 Karl Barth, *Der Römerbrief,* 2nd (revised) edn, Munich, 1922, p. 4. Karl Barth, *The Epistle to the Romans*, Oxford, 1933, p. 28.

86 Harry T. Moore (ed.), *The Collected Letters of D. H. Lawrence,* 2 vols, London, 1970, I, pp. 281–2.

87 Georg Simmel, 'Die Großstadt und das Geistesleben', in *Die Großstadt: Vorträge und Aufsätze zum Städteleben* (Jahrbuch der Gehe-Stiftung zu Dresden, vol. 9, 1903,) pp. 187–206. Georg Simmel, 'The Metropolis and Mental Life', in Edward A. Shils (ed.), *Syllabus and Selected Readings: Second-Year Course in the Study of Contemporary Society*, Chicago, 1936, pp. 221–38.

88 Beebe, op. cit., p. 1066.

89 Fokkema and Ibsch, op. cit., pp. 43 and 217.

90 Schwartz, op. cit., pp. 170–3.

91 Ibid., pp. 194–203.

92 Wilde, op. cit., p. 15.

93 Silvio Vietta and Hans-Georg Kemper, *Expressionismus*, Munich, 1975, pp. 30–213; see also Wilde, op. cit., p. 41.

94 Ezra Pound, 'Vorticism [I]', *The Fortnightly Review*, vol. 96, no. 573 (N. S.) September 1914, pp. 461–71.

95 Hugo Ball, *Die Flucht aus der Zeit* (1927), 2nd (revised) edn, Lucerne, 1946, p. 187. For the English translation, see note 51.

96 Cf. Schwartz, op. cit., pp. 22–30.

97 Timothy J. Reiss, *The Discourse of Modernism,* Ithaca and London, 1982, p. 31.

98 Werner Heisenberg, 'L'Image de la nature selon la physique contemporaine', *Nouvelle Revue Française* vol.7, 1959, pp. 73 and 85.

99 Friedrich Nietzsche, 'Die "Vernunft" in der Philosophie', para. 5, in *Götzen-Dämmerung* (1888), *Werke*, III, p. 960.

100 Werner Heisenberg, *Physics and Beyond: Encounters and Conversations*, London, 1971, p. 41.

101 Heisenberg, 'L'Image de la nature', p. 292.

102 D. H. Lawrence, *Apocalypse*, London, 1932, pp. 97–8.

103 For details, see Sheppard, 'Expressionism and Vorticism', pp. 151–2.

104 Friedrich Nietzsche, 'Der tolle Mensch', in *Die fröhliche Wissenschaft* (1882), Book 3, para. 125, *Werke*, II, pp. 400–2.

105 Francis Ford Coppola's film *Koyannisqatsi* (1983), whose title is a Hopi Indian word meaning 'crazy life', 'life in turmoil', 'life out of balance', 'life disintegrating' and 'a state of life that calls for another way of living', shares exactly the same consciousness.

106 See Briggs and Peat, op. cit., pp. 17–19; Capra, *The Turning Point*, pp. 40–1. For Bacon's importance for the construction of the logocentric model of reality which has been destroyed for Chandos, see Reiss, op. cit., p. 210.

107 Hugo von Hofmannsthal, 'Ein Brief', in *Gesammelte Werke in Einzelausgaben*, edited by Herbert Steiner, Stockholm and Frankfurt am

Main, 1945–59, *Prosa* II, pp. 7–22, esp. p. 16. Hugo von Hofmannsthal, 'The Letter of Lord Chandos', in *Selected Prose*, edited by M. Hottinger and T. and J. Stern, London, 1952, pp. 129–41.

108 Most readily available in English as 'The Spiritual Problem of Modern Man' in Volume X of Jung's *Collected Works*, pp. 74–94.

109 Edmund Husserl, 'Die Krisis des europäischen Menschtums und die Philosophie', in *Husserliana*, edited by Walter Bieme *et al.*, 27 vols, The Hague, Dordrecht, Boston and London, 1950–88, IV, pp. 315–48. Edmund Husserl, 'Philosophy and the Crisis of European Man', in *Phenomenology and the Crisis of Philosophy*, edited by Quentin Lauer, New York, 1965, pp. 149–92.

110 Max Planck, 'Is the External World Real?', in *Where is Science Going?*, edited by James Murphy, London, 1933, p. 65.

111 Cf. A. Alvarez, *The Savage God*, London, 1971.

112 Cf. Gunter Martens, *Vitalismus und Expressionismus*, Stuttgart, Berlin, Cologne and Mainz, 1971.

113 Georg Heym, *Dichtungen und Schriften*, edited by Karl Ludwig Schneider *et al.*, 6 vols, Hamburg, 1960–8, III, pp. 138–9 and 164.

114 Ludwig Rubiner, 'Der Dichter greift in die Politik', *Die Aktion*, vol. 2, no. 21, 22 May 1912, cols 645–52 and vol. 2, no. 23, 5 June 1912, cols 709–15.

115 See George Mills Harper, *Yeats and the Occult*, London and Basingstoke, 1975 and Graham Hough, *The Mystery Religion of W. B. Yeats*, Brighton, 1984.

116 See Michel Carrouges, *André Breton and the Basic Concepts of Surrealism*, University of Alabama, 1974, pp. 10–66.

117 Barnouw, op. cit., p. 248; Huyssen, op. cit., p. 137.

118 Hofmannsthal, op. cit., pp. 264–98, esp. pp. 268–9.

119 The references are to the title of Ball's autobiography (see notes 51 and 95); line 62 of Eliot's *Burnt Norton* from the *Four Quartets* (1935–42); and an image central to Yeats's later poetry which also occurs in the title of an important early book on modernism: Joseph Frank, *The Widening Gyre*, New Brunswick, 1963. It is also of relevance to note that Rilke used the following dictum of Emerson's as an epigraph to his book on Rodin: 'The Hero is he who is immovably centred.'

120 Cf. Schwartz, op. cit., pp. 122–3 and Adorno, 'George und Hofmannsthal', pp. 278–9.

121 T. S. Eliot, *For Lancelot Andrewes*, London, 1928, p. ix.

122 Ezra Pound, *Jefferson and/or Mussolini* (1933), New York, 1935, pp. 63 and 128.

123 See Cairns Craig, *Yeats, Eliot, Pound and the Politics of Poetry*, London and Canberra, 1982, especially pp. 251–89, and Elizabeth Cullingford, *Yeats, Ireland and Fascism*, London and Basingstoke, 1981.

124 Cf. Adorno, 'George und Hofmannsthal', p. 249.

125 Cf. Hohendahl, op. cit., p. 91, where the author speaks of a left and right utopianism.

126 See Joan Weinstein, *The End of Expressionism: Art and the November Revolution in Germany, 1918–19*, Chicago, 1990, pp. 64–5 and 70–5.

127 Cf. Barnouw, op. cit., p. 17.

128 See William Rubin, *'Primitivism' in Twentieth-Century Art*, 2 vols, New York, 1984.

129 Pär Bergman, *'Modernolatria' et 'Simultaneità'*, Uppsala, 1962.

130 John White, *Literary Futurism: Aspects of the First Avant Garde*, Oxford, 1990, p. 72.

131 Richard Cork, *Vorticism and Abstract Art in the First Machine Age*, 2 vols, Berkeley and Los Angeles, 1976, II, pp. 479 and 508–57.

132 See Barnouw, op. cit., pp. 227 and 229.

133 Weinstein, op. cit., p. 229.

134 See Klaus L. Berghahn, 'A View Through the Red Window: Ernst Bloch's *Spuren*', in Huyssen and Bathrick, op. cit., pp. 200–15.

135 For Döblin's own comments on this change of attitude, see Alfred Döblin, 'Epilog' and 'Nachwort zu "Giganten" ', in *Aufsätze zur Literatur*, edited by Walter Muschg, Olten and Freiburg im Breisgau, 1963, pp. 383–99, and 371–4, p. 388.

136 Ritchie Robertson, 'Primitivism and Psychology: Nietzsche, Freud, Thomas Mann', in *Modernism and the European Unconscious*, edited by Peter Collier and Judy Davies, Cambridge, 1990, pp. 79–93, p. 91.

137 For a small range of articles in which some of these points are discussed, see Sheppard, 'What is Dada?' pp. 189–90; Richard Sheppard, 'Dada and Expressionism', *Publications of the English Goethe Society,* vol. 49, 1979, pp. 45–83; Richard Sheppard, 'Dada and Politics', *Journal of European Studies,* vol. 9, 1979, pp. 39–74; Krzysztof Fijalkowski, 'Dada and the Machine', *Journal of European Studies*, vol. 17, 1987, pp. 233–51; Hanne Bergius, 'Dada als "Buffonade und Totenmesse zugleich" ', in *Unter der Maske des Narren*, edited by Stefanie Poley, Stuttgart, 1981, pp. 208–20.

138 Rex Last, 'Arp and the Problem of Evil', in *New Studies in Dada: Essays and Documents*, edited by Richard Sheppard, Hutton, 1981, pp. 60–6.

139 In contrast, Hassan (whom McHale cites) understands the affinity between Dada and postmodernism, going so far to designate it a postmodern phenomenon ('Towards a Concept of Postmodernism', in Hassan, op. cit., pp. 84–96, pp. 91–2).

140 Barnouw, op. cit., pp. 97, 100 and 108.

141 T. S . Eliot, 'Ben Jonson', in *Selected Essays 1917–1932*, London, 1932, pp. 147–60. Between 'world.' and 'They' on p. 156, l. 14 from the bottom, the following sentence has been omitted from the original text: 'It is a world like Lobatchevsky's; the worlds created by artists like Jonson are like systems of non-Euclidean geometry'; and on p. 159, lines 11–12 from the bottom, 'two-dimensional life' originally read 'non-Euclidean humanity'.

142 Cf. Peter Handke's preface to his play *Kaspar* (1967); see also Hassan, op. cit., p. 39.

143 Cf. Horkheimer's and Adorno's remarks on the survival of pre-modern enclaves in Germany (op. cit., pp. 151–2) and Jameson's remarks in *The Political Unconscious*, pp. 92 and 236.

144 Cf. Bürger, op. cit., pp. 80 and 85; Jameson, 'Modernism and its Repressed', pp. 12–13, citing Stanley Cohen and Laurie Taylor, *Escape Attempts* (1976), Harmondsworth, 1978.

145 See Fredric Jameson, 'Postmodernism, or the Cultural Logic of Late Capitalism', *New Left Review*, no. 146, 1984, pp. 60–6.

146 See especially Søren Kierkegaard, *The Sickness unto Death* (1849), Princeton, 1984; cf. in this connection Richard Sheppard, 'Kafka, Kierkegaard and the K.'s: Theology, Psychology and Fiction', *Journal of Literature and Theology*, vol. 5, no. 3, 1991, pp. 277–96.

147 Andrew Bowie, *Aesthetics and Subjectivity from Kant to Nietzsche*, Manchester, 1990, p. 11.

148 Satirized in Juilia Kristeva's novel *Les Samouraïs* (Paris, 1990) and under increasing attack from feminist theoreticians.

2

MACHINATIONS: SHOCK OF THE OLD, FEAR OF THE NEW – APOLLINAIRE AND ALBERTI

Bernard McGuirk

SHOCK OF THE OLD?

To theorize on modernism in this age of the postmodern might seem akin to speculating on the theological arguments for the existence of God in a post-Nietzschean, post-theological era. It may nonetheless be argued that only in retrospect may the project of modernism be identified, all the more clearly, perhaps, for having failed or, at the very least, run out of steam. Fredric Jameson has implied that, in Western culture, modernism accompanied a process of incomplete scientific and industrial modernization which, in its incompletion, still offered the artist not only a sense of endless novelty but also a mission. If not spiritual leadership, this posture undoubtedly retained the appurtenances of elitism associated with the artist no less after Rimbaud's embracing of the role of 'poet-seer' than had been the case for Baudelaire as 'decipherer of the Universe'. In both cases, an ultimate sense of failure in no way diminished the powerful legacy bequeathed to a later generation of poets. A social as well as a spiritual dimension pervades the writings of Mallarmé, Yeats, Pound and Eliot. *Rendre plus purs les mots de la tribu*, however, all too easily became associated with a purity of tribe rather than of words. The risks, politically, are well summed up in the following exchange between Octavio Paz and Leszek Kolakowski:

> *Kolakowski:* Religion, philosophy, art and politics, were somehow part of a unified order voted by the divine wisdom. Now this order, this cosmos, was gradually crumbling and this is precisely what modernity is about.

> *Paz:* And it can be applied, this idea of the breaking of the Old Christian order, not only to communism as a substitute, but also

to Fascism. After all, the great attraction that Fascism had among some poets, English poets or American poets like Ezra Pound, or writers such as Claudel in France. . . . Yes, Céline. All of them were attracted because Nazism and Fascism also tried to substitute Christian order, but now a new order founded in the idea of race, in the idea of state, in the idea of old Rome and many other things. But also it was the idea of order.[1]

L'Ordre et l'Aventure . . . the keynotes of a modernist aesthetics, for Guillaume Apollinaire, entailing risk while at the same time suffused with a pretension to signal and, often, to assume, leadership. In this chapter, I shall presently examine in close detail the interplay and tension of Apollinaire's binary perception, in 'La Jolie rousse', of the early twentieth century's inherited aesthetic imperative. First, however, it is worth pointing out a standard danger in the trajectory of many a poetic discourse, namely, that of 'going transcendental' or, in Octavio Paz's formulation, 'every poem is an attempt to reconcile history and poetry for the benefit of poetry'.[2] To what extent, then, does lyric poetry function historically? Need its so-called autotelic rhythm shift it away from referential traceability? Can the question 'To what does poetry refer?' ever be answered by a more complex response than a mere 'To itself'? For Paz, one possibility certainly exists:

> Now, in modern times this great emptiness of the Western world has been expressed for the best part in the 'Waste Land' of Eliot or some poems by Valéry or Kafka or Céline. . . . Sometimes this religious information is masked through a political affirmation as in Ezra Pound or Neruda, but especially I think all these poets have tried to fill something. I mean desperation, negation, emptiness is one part of the picture. The other is creation.[3]

For Jameson, Paz's proposal would certainly be insufficient but, what is more, might be read as both masking and revealing the deliberate limitations set on art by the anguish-ridden bourgeois subject already despairing of poetry's capacity to affect, rather than merely reflect, reality. My own strategy of departure from Paz's 'emptiness' versus 'creation' formula will be more modest than Jameson's aspiration to define modernism and postmodernity. It will simply examine, in the case studies of Guillaume Apollinaire and Rafael Alberti which follow, modes of claiming and reclaiming. Poetry will be glimpsed, however momentarily, attempting to claim the machine age, just as, previously, as Walter Benjamin and Jürgen Habermas have argued, art and literature set out to reclaim the street.

In Benjamin's famous formulation of the Baudelairean aesthetic trajectory, appropriating the street as antidote to the boredom of bourgeois interiors is conveyed with undisguised euphoria:

> In the words of Guys as quoted by Baudelaire, 'Anyone who is capable of being bored in a crowd is a blockhead'.... The street becomes a dwelling for the flâneur; he is as much at home among the façades of houses as a citizen in his four walls. To him, the shiny enamelled signs of businesses are at least as good a wall ornament as an oil painting is to a bourgeois in his salon. The walls are the desk against which he presses his notebooks; news-stands are his libraries and the terraces of cafés are the balconies from which he looks down on his household after his work is done. That life in all its variety and inexhaustible wealth of variations can thrive only among the grey cobblestones and against the grey background of despotism was the political secret on which the physiologies were based.[4]

Presently it will become apparent just how directly Apollinaire is the inheritor of Baudelaire's 'town' poetic, as the early sequences of 'Zone' virtually perform to Benjamin's stroller's rhythm. Yet two further comparisons arise: first, the stark contrast between Benjamin's emphasis on *flânerie* and the *Spleen de Paris*; second, the parallel political agenda which juxtaposes a public Utopian escapism with a private resignation:

> In Baudelaire's view of modernism, the theory of modern art is the weakest point. His general view brings out the modern themes; his theory of art should probably have concerned itself with classical art, but Baudelaire never attempted anything of the kind. His theory did not cope with the resignation which in his work appears as a loss of nature and naïveté.[5]

A predominant issue to be decided, then, as Apollinaire 'updates' his Baudelairean legacy, will be the extent to which he casts off the classicist's perspectives, of which Benjamin writes, with respect to Baudelaire, 'the allegorist's gaze which falls on the city is rather the gaze of alienated man'.[6] Half a century after Baudelaire, does the shadow of alienation darken the poetics and, indeed, the poetry of Apollinaire, the twentieth century *flâneur*, the adventurer of the machine age?

L'ESPRIT NOUVEAU

The Arts Council of Great Britain chose to open its monumental catalogue of *Dada and Surrealism Reviewed*, the exhibition held at the Hayward

Gallery, London, from 11 January to 27 March 1978, with a section devoted to *Les Soirées de Paris*, the magazine founded by Guillaume Apollinaire in February 1912:

> It contains proto-dada and proto-surrealist works made around 1914 by artists based in Paris – Duchamp, Picabia, de Chirico, Chagall, Picasso. Perhaps the only thing that links them all is that their importance was perceived in the critical writings of Apollinaire, whose poetic work is at different times proto-dada and proto-surrealist, who invented the word 'surrealist' and who is surely this exhibition's patron saint. Many of those critical writings appeared in the magazine he edited, *Les Soirées de Paris*, 1912–14, which can therefore fitly be used as the flag under which, for our purposes, this motley crew of eminences sails.[7]

The choice is wholly consistent with the established (by now, traditional) view of Guillaume Apollinaire as a patron saint of the avant-garde, enthusiastic propagator of *l'esprit nouveau* and indiscriminate popularizer of myriad experimental '-isms'. 'Zone', first published in number 11 of *Les Soirées* ... is catalogued as 'a testament of belief in the modern world – "A la fin tu es las de ce monde ancien"'.[8] The major legacy of Apollinaire's so-called testament, then, even to this day, has been his reputation as upholder of a new, futurist-inspired aesthetic, vaunter of the machine age and believer in a technologically inspired spirituality.

Apollinaire's lecture 'L'Esprit nouveau'[9] has been the source of considerable debate and divergent opinion. Tristan Tzara, forty years later, is enthusiastic:

> La croyance d'Apollinaire en la science et son pouvoir de changer la face du monde est proclamée sur un ton prophétique et optimiste qui tire sa source d'un passé tendre et douloureux. Elle est aussi, de ce fait, un antidote à ces temps révolus.[10]

> The belief of Apollinaire in science and its power to change the face of the world is proclaimed in a prophetic, optimistic tone which draws its source from a tender and unhappy past. It is also, for this very reason, an antidote to these times of upheaval.

André Breton, less generous, is for the purposes of this article, however, more relevant:

> Apollinaire fut un médiocre théoricien. En dehors de la part fondamentale faite dans ce manifeste à la surprise – encore est-ce là une indication bien sommaire – 'l'esprit nouveau', au sens où

nous pouvons l'entendre encore, est aux antipodes de ce qu'il dit: il éclate dans 'Zone' ... et ailleurs, soit partout où la liberté et l'audace d'Apollinaire ont délibérément forcé toutes les écluses pour donner cours à l'inouï.[11]

Apollinaire was a mediocre theoretician. Apart from the fundamental role played in this manifesto by surprise – again rather summarily dealt with – 'l'esprit nouveau', in the sense that we can still understand it, is at the opposite pole of what he says: it breaks out in 'Zone' ... and elsewhere, or wherever the liberty and audacity of Apollinaire have deliberately burst open the flood-gates to unleash the unheard of.

In short, while Apollinaire's theories have been widely scrutinized with a view to proving or disproving his attachment to an aesthetics of the machine age, the evidence of his poetry and, specifically, of 'Zone' has been relatively neglected.[12] By close inspection of 'Zone' itself, and by the juxtaposition of a gloss upon it and a reading of it, Rafael Alberti's 'Carta abierta',[13] this essay will suggest that a portrait of Apollinaire as machine age publicist is an image more relatable to literary history than to textual fact. Alberti's response to and use of Apollinairean echoes suggests that this disparity was already apparent to at least one of the Spanish Generation of 1927, equally misleadingly but so often labelled as surrealist.

'ZONE'

A la fin tu es las de ce monde ancien

Opening with closure. No longer is it relevant, no longer is it possible to begin by looking at an *Ars Poetica*, a poetic prescription. Nor does the opening invite deference, rather a recognition of defiance, self-indulgence, the promise of cultivated inconsistency and a dissatisfaction with established norms of grandiose or conceptually problematical exposition. The downward rhythm, the 'throwaway', colloquial register do not, however, exclude complexity. For the 'tu' recalls that 'JE EST un autre' is now an established dissociation; that the Romantic ego can now but stalk the poem as a reminiscence, a fragment of persona both in time and in aspect. Fragmentation lurks, too, in the antithetical 'ce ... ancien', since the modern, technological world which the poem would initially appear to celebrate will sporadically, damagingly, be reinfused by unjettisoned traditional preoccupations.

Bergère ô tour Eiffel le troupeau des ponts bêle ce matin
Tu en as assez de vivre dans l'antiquité grecque et romaine

The unapologetic immediacy of the opening line gives way, nonetheless, to celebratory distancing, albeit momentarily. Confusion, arising from 'ce … ancien' is extended; the already (by 1912) clichéd symbol of modernity, the Eiffel Tower, is viewed in mock-pastoral perspective, despite the immediate disclaimer. At play, then, in this opening, is the mixture of high/low, ancient/modern which is to inform the poem's development. The deliberately conceived 'shock' image-fusion at once delights in its novelty. 'La surprise est le grand ressort nouveau. C'est par la surprise, par la place important [*sic*] qu'il fait à la surprise, que l'esprit nouveau se distingue.' (Surprise is the great new spring. It is by surprise, by the important place it leaves for surprise, that 'l'esprit nouveau' may be recognized) (Apollinaire, 'L'Esprit nouveau', XIII). But it broaches in its disparate elements *not* the chance association soon to be favoured (a misinterpretation) by the Surrealists but rather the Reverdyan precision of calculated 'justesse'.[14] For it prepares the way for the ensuing paradox:

Ici même les automobiles ont l'air d'être anciennes
La religion seule est restée toute neuve la religion
Est restée simple comme les hangars de Port-Aviation

The keynote of modernity, of inventions and contraptions, is rapid obsolescence, all-too-easy familiarity. Thus, already, a vaunting of the modern world so shot through by nostalgia for spirituality, religion. Though the 'hangars de Port-Aviation' simile remains, at this stage, an unexplained, distant preparation for the later, elaborated comparison of 'Christ'/'aviateurs', it is an apotheosis, too, of the old/new, high/low fusion:

Seul en Europe tu n'es pas antique ô Christianisme
L'Européen le plus moderne c'est toi Pape Pie X
Et toi que les fenêtres observent la honte te retient
D'entrer dans une église et de t'y confesser ce matin

Might obsolescence be avoided by the church, ancient yet adaptable, ship tossed on a trouble-torn sea? Apparent topicality in fact constitutes an ironic aside, a double reference to Pius X, arch-opponent of 'modernity', of the separation of French church and state, yet Eucharistic popularizer inasmuch as introducer of daily Communion for all. The hinge of the irreverence is 'toi'/'toi'; initially Pius, then the self, as the 'flânerie' is interrupted, for the first time, by guilt, the shame of a lost faith. At this early stage, however, a care-free tone is re-established; the need to confess is drowned by the clarion-call of modernity:

> Tu lis les prospectus les catalogues les affiches qui chantent tout haut
> Voilà la poésie ce matin et pour la prose il y a les journaux
> Il y a les livraisons à 25 centimes pleines d'aventures policières
> Portraits des grands hommes et mille titres divers

A new Establishment, a mysticism *à la* Toulouse Lautrec, momentarily diverts introspection and JE becomes AUTRE again in the celebration of a reordered hierarchy of literature where classical genre distinctions are swept aside by the colourful hybrids of the newspaper-stands. Devilishly, the 25 centime titillation of literature by instalment is made to echo Apollinaire's own 'portrait de grand homme', Prince Mony Vibescu, voracious phallocrat of *Les onze mille verges* (1907).

The sequence of self-indulgence brings the opening of the poem, the mixture of enthusiasm for the present and lingering nostalgia for a post-spirituality, to a climax. Confidently, explicitly, JE surfaces for the first time.

> J'ai vu ce matin une jolie rue dont j'ai oublié le nom
> Neuve et propre du soleil elle était le clairon
> Les directeurs les ouvriers et les belles sténo-dactylo-graphes
> Du lundi matin au samedi soir quatre fois par jour y passent
> Le matin par trois fois la sirène y gémit
> Une cloche rageuse y aboie vers midi
> Les inscriptions des enseignes et des murailles
> Les plaques les avis à la façon des perroquets criaillent

The immediacy of 'je', here, contrasts with the mere glimpses of intimate presence in the opening sequence and preludes an attempt at self-persuasion. By sheer vitality, by word-play, by shock image-fusions of rabid clocks or the factory-siren pre-dawn whoring mermaids, by spontaneous delight in the novelty of technical and verbal invention, anywhere – 'I've even forgotten the name of the street' – the *déjà vu* may be transformed:

> J'aime la grâce de cette rue industrielle
> Située à Paris entre la rue Aumont-Thiéville et l'avenue des Ternes

Back to childhood and to innocence, to the tenderness of a mother and a school-chum, named, personalized. The intimacy of clandestine, shared adventure, escape from the 'dorm', forever intermingled with early associations of awed spirituality, the pomp and the ceremony, the pull of the sanctuary-lamp and the headiness of incense. The senses are awakened, enlivened in anticipation of litany:

> C'est le beau lys que tous nous cultivons
> C'est la torche aux cheveux roux que n'éteint pas le vent
> C'est le fils pâle et vermeil de la douloureuse mère
> C'est l'arbre toujours touffu de toutes les prières
> C'est la double potence de l'honneur et de l'éternité
> C'est l'étoile à six branches
> C'est Dieu qui meurt le vendredi et ressuscite le dimanche

The apparent function of the litany, the confirmation, the reaffirmation of faith, is to operate hypnotically, through 'c'est, c'est, c'est, c'est, c'est, c'est', to 'c'est Dieu'. Yet its elements disclose a mingling of the divine with the personal. Little boys have little logic; they fall for the emotional and the incantatory. The superficial faith is frittered away in intimate recollection; to the surface come personal preoccupations, a mother and child abandoned, a hint of Jewish paternity, the cultivated habit of plunging into spirituality to douse and drown the pain. Contemplation of God, incited by the dinning litany, prompts a raising of the eyes, the upward vision of a boy's perception of the stained-glass stigmata, or a faded, smoke-stained, rising Saviour. But a child's concentration falters, his mind is full of other things, including the turn-of-the-century obsession with records, land, sea, air ... distance, height and speed:

> C'est le Christ qui monte au ciel mieux que les aviateurs
> Il détient le record du monde pour la hauteur

The sudden 'trouvaille' of the image-fusion works at several levels, the delineated psychology of the schoolboy with a mind as variedly full as his trouser-pockets; the course of the poem 'Zone', like a switch-back ride, violently confronts elements but glimpsed previously; the filtering of faith through a memory which once fused modernity happily with spirituality and now permits again a thoroughly modern, poetic suspension of disbelief.

The encounter of old with new, formerly a source of unresolved, rapidly concealed tensions, has been brought to harmony linguistically, poetically, through the aesthetic of 'l'esprit nouveau'. There thus follows a remarkable series of image-fusions, the Ascension not only of the risen Christ but, with Him, of an Aesthetic:

> Pupille Christ de l'œil
> Vingtième pupille des siècles comme Jésus monte dans l'air
> Les diables dans les abîmes lèvent la tête pour le regarder

Ils disent qu'il imite Simon Mage en Judée
Ils crient s'il sait voler qu'on l'appelle voleur
Les anges voltigent autour du joli voltigeur
Icare Enoch Elie Apollonius de Thyane
Flottent autour du premier aéroplane
Ils s'écartent parfois pour laisser passer ceux que transporte la
    Sainte-Eucharistie
Ces prêtres qui montent éternellement élevant l'hostie
L'avion se pose enfin sans refermer les ailes
Le ciel s'emplit alors de millions d'hirondelles
A tire-d'aile viennent les corbeaux les faucons les hiboux
D'Afrique arrivent les ibis les flamants les marabouts
L'oiseau Roc célébré par les conteurs et les poètes
Plane tenant dans les serres le crâne d'Adam la première tête
L'aigle fond de l'horizon en poussant un grand cri
Et d'Amérique vient le petit colibri
De Chine sont venus les pihis longs et souples
Qui n'ont qu'une seule aile et qui volent par couples
Puis voici la colombe esprit immaculé
Qu'escortent l'oiseau-lyre et le paon ocellé
Le phénix ce bûcher qui soi-même s'engendre
Un instant voile tout de son ardente cendre
Les sirènes laissant les périlleux détroits
Arrivent en chantant bellement toutes trois
Et tous aigle phénix et pihis de la Chine
Fraternisent avec la volante machine

Four elements are chosen to constitute an aviator-Christ and the marvel of its impact: 'pupille de l'œil', 'Christ', 'vingtième siècle' and 'oiseau'. Taken individually, or even as dismembered parts of the embodied fusion, the elements are easily grasped. Conjoined, they epitomize Pierre Reverdy's famous formulation of 'L'Image':[15]

L'Image est une création pure de l'esprit.
Elle ne peut naître d'une comparaison mais du rapprochement de deux réalités plus ou moins éloignées.
[. . .]
On ne crée pas d'image en comparant (toujours faiblement) deux réalités disproportionnées.
On crée au contraire, une forte image, neuve pour l'esprit, en rapprochant sans comparaison deux réalités distantes
dont *l'esprit seul* a saisi les rapports.

[...]
La pureté de l'esthétique en découle.

The Image is a pure creation of spirit.
It cannot arise from a comparison but from the bringing
together of two more or less distant realities.
[...]
The image is not created by comparing (always weakly)
two disproportionate realities.
On the contrary, a strong image is created, new for the spirit,
by bringing together, without comparison, two distant realities
the relations between which *only the spirit* has grasped.
[...]
From there does the purity of aesthetic flow.

'Esprit', 'esprit nouveau' and, also, 'esprit seul'. At play is the tension between a poem's propensity for uniqueness and a reader's propensity to familiarize or naturalize meaning. In Apollinaire's text, rarely is it possible to conceive of the *déjà vu* elements in a *jamais vu* whole; for at work is the interplay of spirit, mind, wit, invention and imagination. An analytical reading merely focuses on comparisons rather than seizing the inseparable *structural* relations which constitute the 'image forte'. Myriad *cultural* readings are available (flux); but uppermost is 'la pureté de l'esthétique'; as when confronting a Cubist canvas, the *constructive* role of perception is crucial, a process aided by the suppression of punctuation or, elsewhere in Apollinaire's poetry, by experimental typographical syntax.

Such is the shock of the *new* that bewildered groundlings, Paris-streetlings and Hell's inhabitants alike, stare dumbfoundedly. Their attempt to 'read', to 'familiarize', to 'naturalize' the *jamais vu* encounters but a riot of puns, of jokes, cross-cultural, multicultural, universal, mythical, real and surreal. The kaleidoscope, held steady at any moment, throws out half-recognizable elements – anti-Establishment tones, prophets in a list for the *sound* produced but also for the self-elevation of Apollonius/Apollinaire, escapees from the most extravagant of exotic menageries including the traditional cipher of the poet/phoenix and the most novel one-winged pihis, of necessity flying in pairs ('je'/'tu'?) – but, instantly, plunging on in its infinite, pattern-making novelty. The culmination is a mingling communion ('fraternisent') and Hosanna ('chantent bellement'), in response to Arthur Rimbaud's imperative for the 'long, immense et raisonné dérèglement de tous les sens' – of the senses corporal and the senses verbal, of a structured riot of rhymes, rhythms . . . and reason.

The whole of Paris, as besieged as ever by exotic tourists, albeit winged ones ('oiseaux de passage'?), has been forced to a halt in witness of a new Ascension, a miracle of 'l'esprit nouveau'. The poem bears testimony to the spirituality of the new Age ... climactically, momentarily. Reverdy's formulation of the Image, again, is exemplified:

> Il y a la surprise et la joie de se trouver devant une chose neuve.
>
> [...]
>
> La création de l'image est donc un moyen poétique puissant et l'on ne doit pas s'étonner du grand rôle qu'il joue dans une *poésie de création*.
>
> Pour rester pure cette poésie exige tous les moyens concourant à créer une *réalité poétique*.[16]
>
> There is the surprise and the joy of finding oneself before a new thing.
>
> [...]
>
> The creation of the image is therefore a powerful poetic means and there ought to be no astonishment at the great part it plays in a *poetry of creation*.
>
> To remain pure this poetry demands that all means concur to create a *poetic reality*.

Yet 'la pureté de l'esthétique', the distilled lyricism of an impersonal poetic, cannot hold at bay forever a re-emergent, threatening, introspection:

> Maintenant tu marches dans Paris tout seul parmi la foule
> Des troupeaux d'autobus mugissants prés de toi roulent
> L'angoisse de l'amour te serre le gosier
> Comme si tu ne devais jamais plus être aimé
> Si tu vivais dans l'ancien temps tu entrerais dans un monastère
> Vous avez honte quand vous surprenez à dire une prière
> Tu te moques de toi et comme le feu de l'Enfer ton rire pétille
> Les étincelles de ton rire dorent le fond de ta vie
> C'est un tableau pendu dans un sombre musée
> Et quelquefois tu vas le regarder de près

The immediacy of the personal breaks the spell; lost love rises, a lump in the throat of 'le mal aimé'. To walk through Paris, now by day, soon into the night, is a would-be palliative; retreat to a monastery, that old escape, is unavailable to this divided persona, 'je', 'tu', conjoined as 'vous' only in another virtually unrecognizable, disembodied subject, caught by the self at prayer. Guilt mixed with the laughter of self-mockery, like the poem itself, now splutters after the brilliance of the 'feu d'artifice'. Guilt, too, invokes, and immediately suppresses, the shadowy, background presence of 'un tableau pendu dans un sombre musée', later to re-emerge in the overt reference to 'un criminel en état d'arrestation'. Apollinaire, only recently accused of the theft of the Mona Lisa, suddenly *identifies* himself with the picture, stopping to look and to listen closely to his own enigmatic laughter, laughter which conceals 'l'angoisse de l'amour'.Woman. Women. 'Le mal aimé' can never efface the memory:

Aujourd'hui tu marches dans Paris les femmes sont ensanglantées
C'était et je voudrais ne pas m'en souvenir c'était au déclin de la
  beauté

Entourée de flammes ferventes Notre-Dame m'a regardé à
  Chartres
Le sang de votre Sacré-Coeur m'a inondé à Montmartre
Je suis malade d'ouir les paroles bienheureuses
L'amour dont je souffre est une maladie honteuse
Et l'image qui te possède te fait survivre dans l'insomnie et dans
  l'angoisse
C'est toujours près de toi cette image qui passe

The mixture of religion and sexuality echoes the earlier 'les fenêtres observent la honte te retient'. And 'déclin de la beauté' signals the end of the vision just created, the end of love, the degradation of beauty in the fusion and effusion of the blood of the Sacred Heart and of menstruation. 'Les paroles bienheureuses' of an all-forgiving, loving Saviour bequeath but an intensified, unavoidable, sense of shame at a new conjunction – love as venereal disease.[17] No longer occasional self-contemplation through an art-gallery portrait; now, the permanent, unavoidable, sleepless self-confrontation of a persecuted, spied-upon, unconfessable guilt of both JE and TU, never sheddable even in the 'otherness' (AUTRE) of 'cette image'. Forever hounded, today in Paris, but yesterday, yesteryear, elsewhere:

Maintenant tu es au bord de la Méditerranée
Sous les citronniers qui sont en fleur toute l'année
Avec tes amis tu te promènes en barque
L'un est Nissard il y a un Mentonasque et deux Turbiasques
Nous regardons avec effroi les poulpes des profondeurs
Et parmi les algues nagent les poissons images du Sauveur

Tu es dans le jardin d'une auberge aux environs de Prague
Tu te sens tout heureux une rose est sur la table
Et tu observes au lieu d'écrire ton conte en prose
La cétoine qui dort dans le coeur de la rose

Epouvanté tu te vois dessiné dans las agates de Saint-Vit
Tu étais triste à mourir le jour où tu t'y vis
Tu ressembles au Lazare affolé par le jour
Les aiguilles de l'horloge du quartier juif vont à rebours
Et tu recules aussi dans ta vie lentement
En montant au Hradchin et le soir en écoutant
Dans les tavernes chanter des chansons tchèques

Te voici à Marseille au milieu des pastèques

Te voici à Coblence à l'hôtel du Géant

Te voici à Rome assis sous un néflier du Japon

Te voici à Amsterdam avec une jeune fille que tu trouves belle et
    qui est laide
Elle doit se marier avec un étudiant de Leyde
On y loue des chambres en latin Cubicula locanda
Je m'en souviens j'y ai passé trois jours et autant à Gouda

Tu es à Paris chez le juge d'instruction
Comme un criminel on te met en état d'arrestation

On this lightning trip through time and space, attempted evasion offers nothing but correlative after correlative of lost innocence. Evocation of intimate, personal memories fails to extinguish an ever-yellow bitterness on land; at sea a fish-Saviour image tainted with the horrible, tentacular threat of entangled engulfment. Foreign travel, a would-be escape at first dwelt upon, soon mere flash-back, reveals but the worm in the bud and, amid the proliferation of sound-jokes, thinly disguised glimpses of international brothels. Disabused eroticism renders mere fruit/genitalia images in 'pastèque' and the medlar 'rotten ere halfe ripe' (Shakespeare), multiple punned-anuses for hire (Cubicula locanda) and the cheesy non-rhyme of '-anda'/'-ouda' linked, not inconceivably, by smell. The key-note is a mixed tone of obscene humour and desperate searching for spirituality.

In short, flippant word-play and sexual degradation give way to further humiliation, criminality and the Mona Lisa arrest of 1911. Accused of stealing the symbol of beauty. How ironic. Incapable of stealing 'ideal' beauty, I snatched at beauty in brothels; beautiful by night, next morning, ugly. Thus, the earlier need to confess is at last fulfilled as the correlative of the backward-moving Prague clock becomes an undisguised admission that life is lived as a lie.

Tu as fait de douloureux et de joyeux voyages
Avant de t'apercevoir du mensonge et de l'âge
Tu as souffert de l'amour à vingt et à trente ans
J'ai vécu comme un fou et j'ai perdu mon temps
Tu n'oses plus regarder tes mains et à tous moments je voudrais sangloter
Sur toi sur celle que j'aime sur tout ce qui t'a épouvanté

While 'je' may be 'autre' poetically, a commingling of the different selves, in life, has proven relentless as 'je' meets 'tu' in a confrontation of timeless, placeless, pitiless sameness, of two shame-laden hands, unlooked at, yet unavoidably the nausea-bearing tool of a guilt-ridden persona. Ineluctably, self-pity finds a mirroring companionship:

Tu regardes les yeux pleins de larmes ces pauvres émigrants
Ils croient en Dieu ils prient les femmes allaitent des enfants
Ils emplissent de leur odeur le hall de la gare Saint-Lazare
Ils ont foi dans leur étoile comme les rois-mages
Ils espèrent gagner de l'argent dans l'Argentine
Et revenir dans leur pays après avoir fait fortune
Une famille transporte un édredon rouge comme vous transportez votre coeur

Cet édredon et nos rêves sont aussi irréels
Quelques-uns de ces émigrants restent ici et se logent
Rue des Rosiers ou rue des Ecouffes dans des bouges
Je les ai vus souvent le soir ils prennent l'air dans la rue
Et se déplacent rarement comme les pièces aux échecs
Il y a surtout des Juifs leurs femmes portent perruque
Elles restent assises exsangues au fond des boutiques

Tu es debout devant le zinc d'un bar crapuleux
Tu prends un café à deux sous parmi les malheureux

This sequence combines persona's past with migrants' future, the one already revealed as a foolish waste of time, the other naively optimistic, reeking of unpromise. Both find a correlative in 'édredon' – and a plain statement of disillusionment. Taking up Verlaine's correlative ('Walcourt') of the wandering Jew, Apollinaire, however, eschews any association of adventure or exoticism to concentrate on the involuntary

movement of the 'pièces aux échecs' and, echoing 'les femmes . . .
ensanglantées', to focus on the drained exhaustion of 'leurs femmes . . .
exsangues'. Thus does the persona find companionship 'à deux sous parmi
les malheureux'. For this is town poetry, in the Paris tradition of
Baudelaire but with the sordid modernity, and immediacy, of T. S. Eliot's
London or García Lorca's New York. The sordidness is all-pervading, be
it in the Gare St. Lazare or the fine restaurant:

Tu es la nuit dans un grand restaurant

Ces femmes ne son pas méchantes elles ont des soucis cependant
Toutes mêmes la plus laide a fait souffrir son amant

Elle est la fille d'un sergent de ville de Jersey

Ses mains que je n'avais pas vues sont dures et gercées

J'ai une pitié immense pour les coutures de son ventre

J'humilie maintenant à une pauvre fille au rire horrible ma
    bouche

Tu es seul le matin va venir
Les laitiers font tinter leurs bidons dans les rues
La nuit s'éloigne ainsi qu'une belle Métive
C'est Ferdine la fausse ou Léa l'attentive

Et tu bois cet alcool brûlant comme ta vie
Ta vie que tu bois comme une eau-de-vie

Fine restaurant or not, the venality of the female presence overrides a
sympathy with her anaemic desolation. In the immediate present, the
'belle'/'laide' adventure is relived, yet again. An ambivalent, personal
preoccupation rather than any social concern for these women is divulged;
and for one, in particular. Not merely the source for the pun of
'Jersey'/'gercées', a brief encounter arising from 'What's a nice girl like you
doing in a place like this?' provides a further, graphic instance of 'l'amour
dont je souffre est une maladie honteuse'. He knows she's from Jersey, it's
her hard-lucky story. He knows her hands are 'gercées', he feels them over
his body. And the ambivalence reaches a climax in 'j'ai une pitié immense':
compassion for her scars, yet a lingeringly close observation of her belly.

As the rake's progress pursues its classic, early-morning, homeward
path, the separation between Baudelaire's 'l'homme . . . las d'écrire et la
femme d'aimer' ('man … tired of writing and women of loving') is
abolished. For the solitary 'tu', disgorged from the brothel to the sounds

of passing milkmen, watches, disengaged, his own recently shed 'je' of the night disappearing with the dawn, and with the mock-myth women, 'belle Métive, Ferdine la fausse, Léa l'attentive' . . . Irma la douce, or the eternal whores of François Villon: Blanche la Savetière, Guillemette la Tapisserie, Jeanneton la Chaperonnière, Catherine la Boursière – the 'filles de joie' of his 'Ballade de la Belle Heaumière'.

Villon's night-time girls are women with names inseparable from their day-time trades. Baudelaire's poet writes while woman ruts. Apollinaire's persona returns to the zinc bar, 'parmi les malheureux', sharing the early Parisian worker's breakfast of tossed back 'eau de vie'. The sudden sharp burning in the throat concentrates a whole night's, a whole poem's, a whole life's 'honte'. 'Brûlent' . . . life is consumed, life consumes, each swallow a poem of *Alcools*.

Tu marches vers Auteuil tu veux aller chez toi à pied
Dormir parmi tes fétiches d'Océanie et de Guinée
Ils sont des Christ d'une autre forme et d'une autre croyance
Ce sont les Christ inférieurs des obscures espérances

Adieu Adieu

Soleil cou coupé.

Unable to drink down life in alcohol-oblivion, since it burns where emotion rises, where love and shame dwell, in the lump in the throat, the 'tu' is observed, finally, trudging home to Auteuil, beyond the 'cordon sanitaire'. There the black immigrants, the new Wanderers, bringing with them masks and fetishes, to sell, to inspire (the Cubists) ... but also to worship, will share the symbols, the ciphers of a long-sought, though denigrated, spirituality. Obscure, dark hope of all wanderers, of all exiles.

Paradoxically, the coming day throws light only on these 'obscures espérances'. Thus, the closure of 'Adieu' is twofold, culmination of the 'je'/'tu' voice separation of the whole poem, 'autre' in the disembodiment not only of Rimbaud's frantically-sought impersonality of expression, but, more poignantly, in the concomitant sense of 'disinhabitation'. 'Adieu' to the self, 'Adieu' to the reader, but 'Adieu à Dieu', too. And from the final surging awareness of unattained spirituality, an awareness concentrated, still, in the throat, arises the final correlative of the poem, the searing decapitation of the dawn sun, risen alone. Not the head of the risen Christ ... no neck, no body, no Saviour. Burning throat, decapitated sun, unattained spirituality, all are concentrated, finally, in the densest of image-fusions, the starkest of metaphors of castration.

'CARTA ABIERTA'

(Falta el primer pliego.)

. . . The first sheet is always missing. Equally unfailingly, a reading will strive to supply it, under some critical guise, be it the naivest pursuit of influence or the structuralist commonplace of 'literary competence'. This study will seek to establish no hint of influence of 'Zone' on 'Carta abierta'; rather it will take influence for granted, just as it might have paired 'Zone' with Blaise Cendrars's 'Les Pâques' or 'Carta abierta' with a host of other poems.18

'Zone', impurest of impure poetry, not only blends mixed tone with mixed emotions, mixed postures. It also, vitally, ends with aperture. The new day brings nothing but the promise of a renewed cycle of disillusionment emerging from 'obscure hopes'. Modernity of technology, of aesthetic, has failed to satisfy; from 'l'esprit nouveau' there derives no concomitant modern *ethic*. In precisely the same way, the missing first and last sheets of 'Carta abierta' bracket with absence the Albertian version of a modern consciousness. 'Puntos suspensivos' (dots), then, before the plunge into a world of willed, of longed-for suspension of disbelief in innocent innovation:

. . . hay peces que se bañan en la arena
y ciclistas que corren por las olas.
Yo pienso en mí. Colegio sobre el mar.
Infancia ya en balandro o bicicleta.

To some extent, the juxtaposition of 'Carta abierta' with 'Zone' provides, momentarily, for the duration of this essay at least, the reading of a 'primer pliego'. Intertextually, the unapologetic immediacy of 'yo pienso en mí' reminds the reader that Rimbaud's personal adventure in quest of the impersonal, still an issue for a divided personality in 'Zone', is irrelevant to Alberti. Yet this is not an invitation to read the text as a source of information about the poet's life. Rather it is the taking for granted of an integrated poetic personality and, in this case, one integrated in the very 'surprise [qui] est le plus grand ressort nouveau' of Reverdy's formulation. In short, in Alberti's case, the impact of 'l'esprit nouveau' is signalled by the very ease with which the poetic personality absorbs it and is absorbed by it. Consequently, the anti-dualist aspiration of the final words of *Une Saison en enfer*, 'il me sera loisible de *posséder la vérité dans un âme et un corps*' (it will be open to me *to possess truth in one soul and one body*),[19] is achieved, here, in 'Carta abierta', from the outset. The apparently surrealistic images of displacement of the first two lines arise, it is overtly stated, from self-absorption ... but, also, from absorption of the self in external reality.

The temptation to inscribe the autobiographical reminiscences of the 'marinerito' childhood, evoked by Alberti himself thirty years after the publication of 'Carta abierta' in *La arboleda perdida*,[20] is no doubt strong. Alberti's revelations regarding his Andalucian childhood, memories of the joyous sea-obsession of his first celebrated (though his second published) collection *Marinero en tierra* (*Sailor on Land*) (1924)[21] commingled with the day-boy's, the outsider's agonies at the San Luís de Gonzaga Jesuit boarding school, indeed provide one reading of the long, opening sequence. As does, more accessibly even, a childish delight in the cinema, newly arrived in the Andalucian villages, screen set up at dusk against the sea, its cosmopolitan images ever-threatened by the 'dissolving' lantern of the local *guardia*'s shore-patrol. It is easy, too, in this world of moving pictures, to inscribe at the controlling, creative centre of the poem, the machine-age magician–dictator–artist, all-in-one, the unseen projectionist:

Globo libre, el primer balón flotaba
sobre el grito espiral de los vapores.
Roma y Cartago frente a frente iban,
marineras fugaces sus sandalias.

Nadie bebe latín a los diez años.
El Algebra; ¡quién sabe lo que era!
La Física y la Química, ¡Dios mío
si ya el sol se cazaba en hidroplano!

... y el cine al aire libre. Ana Bolena,
no sé por qué, de azul, va por la playa.
Si el mar no la descubre, un policía
la disuelve en la flor de su linterna.

Bandoleros de smoking, a mis ojos
sus pistolas apuntan. Detenidos,
por ciudades de cielos instantáneos,
me los llevan sin alma, vista sólo.

Nueva York está en Cádiz o en el Puerto.
Sevilla está en París, Islandia o Persia.
Un chino no es un chino. Un transeúnte
puede ser blanco al par que verde y negro.

En todas partes, tú, desde tu rosa,

desde tu centro inmóvil, sin billete,
muda la lengua, riges, rey de todo . . .
Y es que el mundo es un álbum de postales.

Multiplicado, pasas en los vientos,
en la fuga del tren y los tranvías.
No en ti muere el relámpago que piensas,
sino a un millón de lunas de tus labios.

Yo nací – ¡respetadme! – con el cine.
Bajó un red de cables y aviones.
Cuando abolidas fueron las carrozas
de los reyes y al auto subió el Papa.

It is not the intention of this analysis to repeat Alberti's or his critics' explanation of the specific refinements of this long, personal evocation of 'marinerito' childhood memory.[22] The point is to emphasize the similarity of technique which unites Alberti and Apollinaire. For the presentation of an initially heralded modernity, versions of technological triumphalism, is always secondary to an effective illusion of *in*habitation, the oneness of world and voice which, for a moment, are to mask all else. Again, an instance of Reverdy's 'pureté de l'esthétique', of 'l'esprit' and of 'l'esprit seul'; again a rendering of 'déjà' as 'jamais vu'. A critic, even Alberti himself, may provide access to one or many of the *cultural* readings available: El Puerto, the Colegio de San Luís Gonzaga, childhood glimpses of foreign sailors ashore, and of the blue colour of telegram forms. At the same time, the same critic is forced to respond to the structural relations which constitute the series of 'images fortes'. And this structure arises, explicitly, in the Alberti poem 'Yo nací – ¡respetadme! – con el cine', from that cinematic world alluded to in 'L'Esprit nouveau' (III, IV), by Apollinaire:

Il eut été étrange qu'à l'époque où le livre populaire par excellence, le cinéma, est un livre d'images, les poètes n'eussent pas essayé de composer des images pour les esprits méditatifs et plus raffinés qui ne se contentent point des imaginations grossières des fabricants de films. Ceux-ci se raffineront un jour et l'on peut prévoir le jour où le phonographe et le cinéma étant devenus les seules formes d'impression en usage les poètes auront une liberté inconnue jusqu'à ce jour.

It would have been strange, in an age where the popular book *par excellence*, the cinema, is a book of images, for poets not to have tried to compose images for the meditative and more refined spirits who do not content themselves with the vulgar imaginations of the film-makers. These will one day become refined and one can foresee the day when, the phonograph and the cinema having become the only 'printed' matter in use, the poets will have a liberty previously unknown.

The presence, the only presence of a 'tú' in the poem, is explicable in terms very different from 'Zone'. In a world, the poem, ruled by the cinema itself, the absorption of the 'yo' by an unseen, imagined, ticketless projectionist 'tú' ('riges rey de todo') constitutes an equivalent to Apollinaire's kaleidoscope sequence of Ascension. Here, however, the images never stand still; the *personal* perspective, once taken over, gives way to the uncontrollable kinesis of cinema. Though never is Rimbaud's 'dérèglement de tous les sens' more 'raisonné'.

The uppermost 'sens', once it has been realized that verbal sense is controllable, is visuality. For the screen-image series, abolishing the strictures of space and time, transforms history into a dissolvable Anne Boleyn, transforms 'mí' into a petrified, Chicago-style victim, brings New York to El Puerto and reduces the globe to the dimension of the family postcard collection. Not once. Innumerably, immortally ('Multiplicado . . . no en tí muere el relámpago'). 'Yo' escapes not into an otherness of a 'tú'; rather into all otherness, the 'EST UN AUTRE' of endless projectionists.

A new, constructed persona, *visualized* by the poem's reader as might be the subject of a cubist canvas, is provided, too, with a fittingly modern astrology, not of 'una estrella' but of 'una red de cables y aviones'. If Apollinaire's persona is still saturated with nostalgia for lost spiritual values in 'Vendémiaire', the last poem of *Alcools*:

> Hommes de l'avenir souvenez vous de moi
> Je vivais à l'époque où finissaient les rois

> Men of the future remember me
> I lived in the age when Kings were coming to an end

the inhabitation of a constructed horoscope in Alberti's case shifts poet, critic and reader away from the 'déjà connu' of an autobiographical self towards the 'jamais lu' of 'Carta abierta' . . . ever open-ended, since always open to rereading, new reading. Aperture is as potential-filled as the mechanical rose of the projector-lens.

From this aperture, from this open-ended potentiality, derives the closing structure of the poem:

Vi los telefonemas que llovían,
plumas de ángel azul, desde los cielos.
Las orquestas seráficas del aire
guardó el auricular en mis oídos.

De lona y níquel, peces de las nubes,
bajan al mar periódicos y cartas.
(Los carteros no creen en las sirenas
ni en el vals de las olas, sí en la muerte.

Y aún hay calvas marchitas a la luna
y llorosos cabellos en los libros.
Un polisón de nieve, blanqueando
las sombras, se suicida en los jardines.

¿Qué será de mi alma que hace tiempo
bate el récord continuo de la ausencia?
¿Qué de mi corazón que ya ni brinca,
picado ante el azar y el accidente?)

Exploradme los ojos y, perdidos,
os herirán las ansias de los náufragos,
la balumba de nortes ya difuntos,
el solo bamboleo de los mares.

Casco de chispa y pólvora, jinetes
sin alma y sin montura entre los trigos;
basílicas de escombros, levantadas
trombas de fuego, sangre, cal, ceniza.

Pero también, un sol en cada brazo,
el alba aviadora, pez de oro,
sobre la frente un número, una letra,
y en el pico una carta azul, sin sello.

Nuncio – la voz eléctrica, y la cola –
del aceleramiento de los astros,
del confín del amor, del estampido
de la rosa mecánica del mundo.

From out of the blue, the 'azure' so beloved of the generation of symbolist writers of the *fin de siècle*, the 'messages' which percolate are no longer aethereally abstract. The machine age brings the post by aeroplane, the choir of angels is to be heard less in the swinging low of a sweet chariot than through the ear-piece of a wireless-set. Although parenthesized, the legacy of decadence (of mermaids, of waltzes, of 'balding' sentimentality and, finally, of yet another pallidly suicidal finisecular archetype, a 'Dame des Camélias' or a French Lieutenant's woman) can never be bracketed out altogether.

When that other inherited institution of Apollinaire's venture, the re-emergence of a personalized 'alma', 'mi alma', occurs, a residue of saving impersonality is on tap to guard against the self-swamping invasion of *dis*inhabitation.[23]

First, however, it is important to note that the nadir of confessional 'desnortamiento',[24] of disorientation, negatively echoes the high point of spiritual ascension in 'Zone':

C'est le Christ qui monte au ciel mieux que les aviateurs
Il détient le record du monde pour la hauteur

Whereas Apollinaire's lines trigger a Hosanna of elevation, Alberti's poem is invaded by an old, suppressed 'yo', a record-holder for absence, non-being. This reintroduction, equivalent to and verbally echoing Mallarmé's 'Un coup de dés jamais n'abolira le hasard', is a realization and, sinisterly, too, a prefiguration. Imminent angels, here ghost-riders of death and destruction, invade the poem but momentarily. They are held at bay by that residue promised above . . . 'Pero también'. The humblest, the most prosaic of reassertions, it serves, nonetheless, to give force to a saving playground image of little-boy-cum-aeroplane and 'el alba aviadora'. At first the dualistic sense of violent alienation is set aside by a trick, the image-fusion of 'un sol en cada brazo', a sense of flight, of mission towards 'l'azur' . . . unofficial ('sin sello') and undelimited. All this, however, is but 'neo-' or, echoing Juan Ramón Jiménez's view, 'sobre-romántico' ('super-/over-romantic'). The crucial depersonalizing, anti-dualist sequence of the penultimate stanza, arising from 'Nuncio – la voz eléctrica y la cola –', again fuses 'yo' with modernity itself. This time, the 'sens raisonné' is not visual but auditory. For the mechanized herald of transcendence announces a thoroughly updated access to 'l'Azur', comet-like, reaching even beyond the confines of love, beyond the separation of the world of nature and the world of technology, through the sonic boom of the final image-fusion 'el estampido de la rosa mecánica del mundo'.

Analysed, the elements of the image-fusion may defy traditional classifications of beauty. As a synthetic, constructed entity, their impact, again, is one of transformation; the 'déjà mais jamais vu'. Yet the poem is not allowed to rest there; in case the reader marvels only at the Apollinaire-like explosion of a mere technical 'nouveauté', the 'esprit', the *moving* spirit of a persona absorbed in the miraculous renovation of external reality, draws attention to itself, to its renewed formal, poeticizing status in 'Sabed de mí, que dije por teléfono / mi madrigal dinámico'. And what is that status? Herald ('a los hombres'), of course; but distanced, indirect ('por teléfono') voice. And the message:

¿Quién eres tú, de acero, rayo y plomo?
– Un relámpago más, la nueva vida.

If 'acero', 'rayo' and 'plomo' constitute the mechanical elements of the *medium*, the telephone, might they not also constitute a new, integrated, fused, 'created' persona? But wait ... have we not seen this before? Where? At the top of some tower? In a Gothic ruin? Constructed of base matter? Plugged in to the lightning conductor? Awaiting the sudden, electrifying, vivifying flash of life . . . 'la nueva vida'? Yes, of course. On the cinema-screen. A vision of Mary Shelley's Frankenstein-monster ... here reiterated in Alberti's monster-creation, the poetic persona of 'Carta abierta', the poet-author of the dynamic madrigal which is but one version of 'l'esprit nouveau'.

The Albertian ego (JE), born in the *place* of El Puerto, cedes before *im*personality (EST UN AUTRE) in 'Yo nací – ¡respetadme! – con el cine', cedes before the revelation of a totally new, constructed, dynamic persona.

What life awaits this new creation, what 'nueva vida'? But that's another story, a cliff-hanger. . . . Come back next week!

(*Falta el último pliego.*)

FEAR OF THE NEW?

In 'The Mechanical Paradise', the first programme and the first chapter of *The Shock of the New*, the 1980 BBC series and book,[25] Robert Hughes opens yet another discussion of art in the machine age by selectively misquoting from 'Zone':

At last you are tired of this old world.
O shepherd Eiffel Tower, the flock of bridges bleats this morning
You are through with living in Greek and Roman antiquity
Here, even the automobiles seem to be ancient
Only religion has remained brand new, religion
has remained simple as simple as the aerodrome hangars
It's God who dies Friday and rises again on Sunday
It's Christ who climbs in the sky better than any aviator

He holds the world's altitude record
Pupil Christ of the eye
Twentieth pupil of the centuries he knows what he's about,
And the century, become a bird, climbs skyward like Jesus.

He goes on:

> The important thing was that the Tower had a mass audience:
> millions of people, not the thousands who went to the salons and
> galleries to look at works of art, were touched by the feeling of a
> new age that the Eiffel Tower made concrete. It was the herald of a
> millennium, as the nineteenth century made ready to click over into
> the twentieth. . . . For the late nineteenth century, the cradle of
> modernism, did not feel the uncertainties about the machine that we
> do . . . for them, the 'romance' of technology seemed far more
> diffused and optimistic, acting publicly on a wider range of objects,
> than it is today.[26]

Conscious or unconscious, yet another machination, another cover-up, is
being perpetrated. It should now be clear that by 1912, in 'Zone',
'uncertainties' abound, technology prompts but a short-lived optimism
and the only thing that is consistently 'diffused' is the poetic persona.
Personality is split, voice is throttled – 'cou coupé', fragmented harbin-
gers, I suggest, of a more traditionally interpreted millennium,
apocalypse. While Hughes admits that 'after 1914, machinery was turned
on its inventors and their children',[27] the point of my analysis of 'Zone'
has nothing to do with prescience of the First World War.

The catastrophe intuited by Apollinaire in 1912, and picked up by
Alberti's 'voz, eléctrica', has more to do with the dawning of a realization.
There is but a loss of personal voice, a growing awareness of poetry's
superannuated, increasingly outmoded expression, receding before the
imminent explosion of impersonal machine voices. Apollinaire, let it be
recalled, was soon to state, 'one can foresee the day when, the phonograph
and the cinema having become the only "printed" matter in use, the poets
will have a liberty previously unknown'. But then?

The machine, at that point, becomes infernal, death of poetry, death of
the author. Already the attempt to possess, to control the machine age by
naming it in writing and in art, has been shown, I believe, to mask failure.
In Alberti's metaphor – even if the first and last pages of the record-book
are missing – the only record available now to the soul, the self, is that of
absence.

In a world of the machine, it is anticipated, there will be no other message than the medium alone. Yet it was Marshall McLuhan, writing in the 1950s at the very interstices of modernism and postmodernism though often overlooked now in the wake of Fredric Jameson's impact, who sought to isolate and describe an ethical imperative resistant to the totalizing machinations of mechanization:

> In cognition we have to interiorize the exterior world. We have to recreate in the medium of our senses and inner faculties the drama of existence. This is the work of the *logos poietikos*, the agent intellect. In speech we utter that drama which we have analogously recreated within us. In speech we make or *poet* the world even as we may say that the movie parrots the world. . . . What we have to defend today is not the values developed in any particular culture or by any one mode of communication. Modern technology presumes to attempt a total transformation of man and his environment. This calls in turn for an inspection and defense of all human values. And so far as merely human aid goes, the citadel of this defense must be located in analytical awareness of the nature of the creative process involved in human cognition. For it is in this citadel that science and technology have already established themselves in their manipulation of the new media.[28]

The medium of McLuhan is the literary critical discourse of the era of New Criticism in which, in 'cognition', we in turn might analyse creatively. For all its difference, terminologically, from Jameson's analysis of postmodernism, and however quaintly non-conformist a theology may be masked in the 'citadel' of 'defense of human values', McLuhan's project might be said to do for modernism what his successor has been described as seeking for its direct inheritor:

> Jameson's aim is to define the post-modern *Zeitgeist* – a daunting task, since one definition characteristic of the 'post-modern condition' is its lack of a sense of *Zeitgeist*, identity, or spirit of the age. Jameson manfully seizes these and other contradictions with both hands: his project is to root a rootless culture in its economic context and to historicize a phenomenon whose main effect is the waning of historical consciousness. . . . For Jameson, post-modernism represents a seismic shift in our very concepts of space, time and self. Modernism was the expression of the bourgeois subject (the grand *auteur*, the *Angst*-ridden individual). Post-modernism creates a new kind of decentred subject, 'a mere switching centre for all the networks of influence' (Baudrillard).[29]

In the light of this essay's examination of the street-level networks of the influence of technology on poetry, of bourgeois *Angst* on either urban (Apollinaire) or rural (Alberti) *auteur*, it may be that the distinctions to be made between modernism and its successor have become somewhat blurred. Concomitantly, the distance between a McLuhan and a Jameson may diminish. Neither, it seems, are embarrassed at the embracing of a theory, even a 'grand' theory, be it the *logos poietikos* which purports to inspect and defend human values, or Marxism, which has aspired to do no less. In a sense, each accepts the possibility of 'closure', of coming to conclusions in the cognitive absorption of history, of culture. How, though, do such activities differ from the poetry I have examined? Half a century before McLuhan, three quarters of a century before Jameson, the poets of the avant-garde at the same time assist and resist the completion of scientific and industrial modernization. In short, they both perform and require incompletion; mark out an ever-diminishing space in which the artist – and art – may function.

NOTES

1 Bill Bourne, Udi Eichler and David Herman (eds), *Modernity and Its Discontents, Voices*, from the Channel Four television series, Nottingham, Spokesman/Hobo Press, 1987, p. 93.
2 Ibid., p. 99.
3 Ibid., pp. 99–100.
4 Walter Benjamin, *Charles Baudelaire: A Lyric Poet in the Era of High Capitalism*, London, Verso, 1983, p. 37.
5 Ibid., p. 82.
6 Ibid., p. 170.
7 Dawn Ades, *Dada and Surrealism Reviewed,* with an introduction by David Sylvester and a supplementary essay by Elizabeth Cowling, London, Arts Council of Great Britain, 1978, p. 3.
8 Ibid., p. 17. The translation of 'Zone' (Appendix 1) is by Samuel Beckett.
9 'L'Esprit nouveau', a lecture given in the Théâtre du Vieux-Colombier in November 1917 and published, in revised form, as 'L'Esprit nouveau et les poètes' a year later in *Mercure de France*, 1 December 1918. The previously unprinted original text of this lecture is given in Margareth Wijk's *Guillaume Apollinaire et l'esprit nouveau*, Etudes Romanes de Lund, 36, GWK Gleerup, 1982. Paginated in romans I-XXI at the end of Wijik's Chapter 3, 'L'Esprit nouveau' will subsequently be referred to by title and roman in my text.
10 Quoted in Wijk, op. cit., p. 20. English translations by Bernard McGuirk unless otherwise stated. After a lengthy review of critical opinions on 'L'Esprit nouveau', she concludes:

> Nous avons d'abord pu constater que pratiquement toute la critique française (Breton, Billy, Pia, Adéma, Décaudin, Renaud et Oster) fait preuve d'une attitude plus ou moins négative vis à vis des idées

présentées sous cette rubrique. Par contre, presque tous les critiques d'origine étrangère (Friedrich, Davies, Steegmuller, Tzara, Zoppi et Balakian) voient dans ces textes des lignes importantes de développement. Je suis persuadée que les paroles sévères d'André Breton ont pesé lourd sur le destin de ce 'dernier testament' de Guillaume Apollinaire en France.

Firstly, we would claim that practically all French criticism (etc.) shows a more or less negative attitude towards ideas put forward under this heading. On the contrary, almost all foreign-based critics (etc.) see in these texts important lines of development. I am persuaded that the harsh words of André Breton have weighed heavily on the fate of this 'last will and testament' of Guillaume Apollinaire in France.

(Ibid., pp. 27–8)

11 Cited by Wijk, op cit., p. 17, from Breton's 'Ombre non pas serpent, mais d'arbre en fleurs', *Le Flâneur des deux rives*, no. 1, March 1954, Paris.

12 One notable exception is a recent article by Jeannine Kohn-Etiemble, 'Sur "Zone" ', *La revue des lettres modernes*, 15, 1980, pp. 79–93. In a predominantly stylistic analysis, particularly of the prosody of the poem in which she finds rhyme in all but 8–10 of the 155 lines and notes 'combien le vers prétendu prosaïque de "Zone" se détache difficilement de l'alexandrin' ('the extent to which the supposed prosaic line of "Zone" hardly departs from the Alexandrine'), Kohn-Ètiemble concludes:

Il me parait impossible de voir dans 'Zone' une forme qui, délaissant les structures 'dépassées' du rhythme, de la rime ou de l' 'image', innove à coup sûr dans un sens que dès 1912 préfigure le Surréalisme en gestation et, surtout, dans le sens de l'irrationalisme surréaliste.

I think it is impossible to see in 'Zone' a form which, leaving behind the 'outmoded structures' of rhythm, or rhyme or of the 'image', is undoubtedly innovatory in a sense which from 1912 prefigures Surrealism in the making and, above all, in the sense of surrealist irrationalism.

(Op. cit., p. 84)

13 'Carta abierta', Rafael Alberti, *Poesía* (1924–67), Losada, Buenos Aires, 1961, pp. 241–3. The translation provided in Appendix 2 is my own.

14 Une image n'est pas forte parce qu'elle est brutale ou fantastique – mais que l'association des idées est lointaine et juste. Le résultat obtenu contrôle immédiatement la justesse de l'association.

An image is not strong because it is brutal or fantastic – but because the association of ideas is distant and exact. The result obtained immediately controls the exactness of the association.

(Pierre Reverdy, 'L'Image', *Nord-Sud*, no. 13, March 1918)

See the facsimile edition, *Nord-Sud*, Revue Littéraire, Collection complète, edited by Etienne-Alain Hubert, editions Jean-Michel Place, 1980, unpaginated. (Wijk's reproduction of the title-page of 'L'Esprit nouveau', in Apollinaire's handwriting, shows that below the title, he had written 'accompagneé de Récitation de Rimbaud, Gide, Paul Fort, Fargue, Saint

Léger-Léger, Salmon, Divoire, Romains, Apollinaire, Reverdy, Jacob, Cendrars').

15 Reverdy, op. cit.

16 Ibid.

17 Michel Decaudin's invaluable annotated edition of the 'préoriginales' of *Alcools* in *Le Dossier d''Alcools'*, Droz, Geneva, Minard, Paris, 1965, is particularly illuminating on 'Zone'. It demonstrates the suppression of many of the more overtly personal, autobiographical references, such as the Joconda theft, from the final published version of the poem. I quote but one poignant and, here, relevant example of Apollinaire's self-censorship:

> Aujourd'hui je vais dans Paris les femmes sont ensanglantées
> (J'ai peur de tout leur sang)
> leurs menstrues coulent dans les ruisseaux, l'air est infecté
> L'haleine des femmes est fétide et leur voix est menteuse
> L'amour dont je souffre est une maladie honteuse
> C'est une enflure ignoble dont je souhaite d'être guéri
> Elle me tient éveillé jusqu'au matin dans mon lit
> Elle me fait mourir d'une voluptueuse angoisse
>
> (Op. cit., p. 78)

18 The seemingly endless debate over the possible influence of Blaise Cendrars' 'Les Pâques à New York' is adequately conveyed if by no means resolved in Marc Poupon's 'Apollinaire et Cendrars', *Archives des lettres modernes*, 103, 1969. Robert Couffignal, in ' "Zone" d'Apollinaire', *Archives des lettres modernes*, 118, 1970, juxtaposes 'Zone' with Dante's *Divina Comedia*. Cendrars's 'Les Pâques', Nerval's 'Aurélia', Rimbaud's *Une Saison en enfer*, Péguy's *Quatrains* and T. S. Eliot's *The Waste Land*, each time finding a Christian reading of descent into Hell, ascension to(wards) Heaven. It is a somewhat idiosyncratic study.

19 Arthur Rimbaud, *Une Saison en enfer,* Paris, Livre de Poche, 1972, p. 200.

20 See Rafael Alberti, *La arboleda perdida: Libros I y II de memorias,* Buenos Aires, abril 1959.

21 *Marinero en tierra*, Buenos Aires, Losada, 1961.

22 See especially Geoffrey W. Connell's 'A Recurring Theme in the Poetry of Rafael Alberti', *Renaissance and Modern Studies*, III, 1959, pp. 99–110. In his invaluable study *Spanish Poetry of the Grupo Poético de 1927*, Oxford, Pergamon, 1977, pp. 196–7, Connell writes of 'Carta abierta': 'In the confusion caused by the clash of old and new values *deshabitación* [disinhabitation] clearly threatens the poet (lines 49–60); but at this stage, he makes his decision and bravely aligns himself with the new values.'

23 A deliberately literal rendering of Alberti's own notion of 'deshabitación', pervasive in his poetry and used in the title of his play *El hombre deshabitado* (1931). The concept was a common one in the 1920s. Pablo Neruda, in *Residencia en la tierra,* entitles one of his poems 'El deshabitado' and Eliot's 'The Hollow Men' evokes a similar phenomenon.

24 The 'nortes ya difuntos' (now defunct Norths) are a reference to the loss of direction, by the compass-point, or the 'desnortamiento' of the Spanish sailor ('marinero').

25 Robert Hughes, *The Shock of the New*, London, BBC Publications, 1980.

26 Ibid. p. 11.
27 Ibid. p. 56.
28 H. M. McLuhan, 'Sight, Sound and the Fury', reproduced in *Literary Criticism: A Short History*, edited by W. K. Wimsatt and C. Brooks, New York, Alfred A. Knopf, 1969, pp. 75–76.
29 Simon Reynolds, 'The Way We Live Now', *The Observer*, 7 April 1991, review of Fredric Jameson, *Postmodernism or the Cultural Logic of Late Capitalism*.

APPENDIX 1

Zone

In the end you are weary of this ancient world

This morning the bridges are bleating Eiffel Tower oh herd

Weary of living in Roman antiquity and Greek

Here even the motor-cars look antique
Religion alone has stayed young religion
has stayed simple like the hangars at Port Aviation

You alone in Europe Christianity you are not ancient
The most modern European is you Pope Pius X
And you whom the windows watch shame restrains
From entering a church this morning and confessing your sins
You read the handbills the catalogues the singing posters
So much for poetry this morning and the prose is in the papers
Special editions full of crimes
Celebrities and other attractions for 25 centimes

This morning I saw a pretty street whose name is gone
Clean and shining clarion of the sun
Where from Monday morning to Saturday evening four times a
    day
Directors workers and beautiful shorthand typists go their way
And thrice in the morning the siren makes its moan
And a bell bays savagely coming up to noon
The inscriptions on walls and signs
The notices and plates squawk parrot-wise
I love the grace of this industrial street
In Paris between the Avenue des Ternes and the Rue Aumont-
    Thiéville

There it is the young street and you still but a small child
Your mother always dresses you in blue and white
You are very pious and with René Dalize your oldest crony
Nothing delights you more than church ceremony
It is nine at night the lowered gas burns blue you steal away
From the dormitory and all night in the college chapel pray
While everlastingly the flaming glory of Christ
Wheels in adorable depths of amethyst
It is the fair lily that we all revere
It is the torch burning in the wind its auburn hair
It is the rosepale son of the mother of grief
It is the tree with the world's prayers ever in leaf
It is of honour and eternity the double beam
It is the six-branched star it is God
Who Friday dies and Sunday rises from the dead
It is Christ who better than airmen wings his flight
Holding the record of the world for height

Pupil Christ of the eye
Twentieth pupil of the centuries it is no novice
And changed into a bird this century soars like Jesus
The devils in the deeps look up and say they see an
Imitation of Simon Magus in Judea
Craft by name by nature craft they cry
About the pretty flyer the angels fly
Enoch Elijah Apollonius of Tyana hover
With Icarus round the first airworthy ever
For those whom the Eucharist transports they now and then make
    way
Host-elevating priests ascending endlessly
The aeroplane alights at last with outstretched pinions
Then the sky is filled with swallows in their millions
The rooks come flocking the owls the hawks
Flamingoes from Africa and ibises and storks
The roc bird famed in song and story soars
With Adam's skull the first head in its claws
The eagle stoops screaming from heaven's verge
From America comes the little humming-bird
From China the long and supple
One-winged peehees that fly in couples
Behold the dove spirit without alloy

That ocellate peacock and lyre-bird convoy
The phoenix flame-devoured flame-revived
All with its ardent ash an instant hides
Leaving the perilous straits the sirens three
Divinely singing join the company
and eagle phoenix peehees fraternize
One and all with the machine that flies

Now you walk in Paris alone among the crowd
Herds of bellowing buses hemming you about
Anguish of love parching you within
As though you were never to be loved again
If you lived in olden times you would get you to a cloister
You are ashamed when you catch yourself at a paternoster
You are your own mocker and like hellfire your laughter crackles
Golden on your life's hearth fall the sparks of your laughter
It is a picture in a dark museum hung
And you sometimes go and contemplate it long

To-day you walk in Paris the women are blood-red
It was and would I could forget it was at beauty's ebb

From the midst of fervent flames Our Lady beheld me at Chartres
The blood of your Sacred Heart flooded me in Montmartre
I am sick with hearing the words of bliss
The love I endure is like a syphilis
And the image that possesses you never leaves your side
In anguish and insomnia keeps you alive

Now you are on the Riviera among
The lemon-trees that flower all year long
With your friends you go for a sail on the sea
One is from Nice one from Menton and two from La Turbie
The polypuses in the depths fill us with horror
And in the seaweed fishes swim emblems of the Saviour

You are in an inn-garden near Prague
You feel perfectly happy a rose is on the table
And you observe instead of writing your story in prose
The chafer asleep in the heart of the rose

Appalled you see your image in the agates of Saint Vitus
that day you were fit to die with sadness
You look like Lazarus frantic in the daylight

The hands of the clock in the Jewish quarter go to left from right
And you too live slowly backwards
Climbing up to the Hradchin or listening as night falls
To Czech songs being sung in taverns

Here you are in Marseilles among the water-melons

Here you are in Coblentz at the Giant's Hostelry

Here you are in Rome under a Japanese medlar-tree

Here you are in Amsterdam with an ill-favoured maiden
You find her beautiful she is engaged to a student in Leyden
There they let their rooms in Latin cubicula locanda
I remember I spent three days there and as many in Gouda

You are in Paris with the examining magistrate
They clap you in goal like a common reprobate

Grievous and joyous voyages you made
Before you knew what falsehood was and age
At twenty you suffered from love and at thirty again
My life was folly and my days in vain
You dare not look at your hands tears haunt my eyes
For you for her I love and all the old miseries

Weeping you watch the wretched emigrants
They believe in God they pray the women suckle their infants
They fill with their smell the station of Saint-Lazare
Like the wise men from the east they have faith in their star
They hope to prosper in the Argentine
And to come home having made their fortune
A family transports a red eiderdown as you your heart
An eiderdown as unreal as our dreams
Some go no further doss in the stews
Of the Rue des Rosiers or the Rue des Ecouffes
Often in the streets I have seen them in the gloaming
Taking the air and like chessmen seldom moving
They are mostly Jews the wives wear wigs and in
The depths of shadowy dens bloodless sit on and on

You stand at the bar of a crapulous café
Drinking coffee at two sous a time in the midst of the unhappy

It is night you are in a restaurant it is superior

These women are decent enough they have their troubles however
All even the ugliest one have made their lovers suffer
She is a Jersey police-constable's daughter

Her hands I had not seen are chapped and hard

The seams of her belly got to my heart

To a poor harlot horribly laughing I humble my mouth

You are alone morning is at hand
In the streets the milkmen rattle their cans

Like a dark beauty night withdraws
Watchful Leah or Ferdine the false

And you drink this alcohol burning like your life
Your life that you drink like spirit of wine

You walk towards Auteuil you want to walk home and sleep
Among your fetishes from Guinea and the South Seas
Christs of another creed another guise
The lowly Christs of dim expectancies

Adieu Adieu

Sun corpseless head

APPENDIX 2

Open Letter

(*The first page is missing*)

. . . There are fish which bathe on the sand
and cyclists who run through the waves.
I am thinking about me. School by the sea.
Childhood now in a boat or on a bicycle.

Free globe, the first balloon floated
over the spiral screech of the steamers.
Rome and Carthage walked face to face,
fleeting sailor-suits their sandals.

No one drinks in Latin when they are ten.
Algebra, who knows what that was!

Physics and Chemistry, my God,
if now the sun was being hunted by hydroplane!
... And the open-air cinema. Ann Boleyn,
I don't know why, in blue, walks along the beach.
If the sea doesn't uncover her, a policeman
dissolves her in the flower of his torch.

Gangsters in evening suits, at my eyes
are pointing their pistols. Arrested,
through cities of instant heavens,
they carry me off without soul, eyes only.

New York is in Cádiz or in El Puerto.
Seville is in Paris, Iceland or Persia.
A Chinese is not a Chinese. A pedestrian
can be white as easily as green and black.

Everywhere, you, from your rose,
from your immobile centre, without a ticket,
with mute tongue, you rule, king of all ...
And so the world is an album of postcards.

Multiplied you pass on the winds,
in the flight of the train and trams.
Not in you dies the lightning-flash which you think
but to a million moons from your lips.

I was born – respect me! – with the cinema,
Under a network of cables and aeroplanes.
When they abolished the carriages
of Kings and the Pope got into a motor car.

I saw the telegrams which rained down,
blue angel feathers, from the heavens.
The seraphic orchestras of the air
were held by the head-phones in my ears.

Of canvas and nickel, fish from the clouds,
bring down to the sea newspapers and letters.
(The postmen don't believe in mermaids
nor in the waltz of the waves, but in death.

And there are still bald spots on the moon
and weepy hair in books.

A snowy bustle, whitening
the shadows, commits suicide in the gardens.

What will become of my soul which some time ago
beat the continuous record for absence?
What of my heart which no longer skips,
pricked in the face of chance and accident?)

Explore my eyes, and, lost,
you will be wounded by anxieties of shipwrecks,
the heap of norths already defunct,
the single rolling of the seas.

Helmets of spark and gunpowder, horsemen
without soul and saddle amongst the wheat;
basilicas of debris, raised
spouts of fire, blood, lime, ashes.

But also, a sun on each arm,
The aviator dawn, golden fish,
on its forehead a number, a letter,
and in its mouth a blue letter, without stamp.

Messenger, – electric voice and tail –
of the acceleration of the stars,
of the limit of love, of the explosion
of the mechanical rose of the world.

(The last page is missing)

3

WYNDHAM LEWIS'S VORTICISM AND THE AESTHETICS OF CLOSURE

David Wragg

INTRODUCTION

Despite the existence of a respectable body of criticism, Wyndham Lewis remains a marginalized figure where the theorization of modernism is concerned. In this chapter I propose to take another look at his work by identifying his version of Vorticism (roughly 1913–1915) as a problematic and unstable form of aesthetic practice which can be related to a sense of epistemological crisis originating in his earlier thought. The nature of this crisis depends initially on our acceptance of Vorticism as a peculiar form of closure, which I have labelled 'objectivism', characterized by an opposition to what might loosely be described as an emphasis on the subjective in rival modernisms, most obviously the philosophy of Henri Bergson and the aesthetics of Cubism and Futurism. For the sake of an overview, this issue can initially be approached via Lewis's views in the late 1920s, before considering the situation of some earlier paintings, drawings and literary exegesis, ultimately as a function of his reception of Nietzsche.

The identification of the hegemonic 'Time-mind' in *Time and Western Man* (1927)[1] is keyed to the confrontation with Bergson. Essentially, Lewis considered that Bergson's philosophy had given up on objectivism, or a situation in which the distinction between mind and matter is fundamental to a grip on concrete reality, in favour of a 'pro-mental', or psychologistic, approach to perception. In *Time and Free Will* (1889)[2] Bergson had introduced the notion of 'real duration' (*durée réelle*), by which he meant to signify the temporal nature of psychic experience as something prior to our habitual tendency to privilege an organizational consciousness capable of foreclosing on an external world extended in space. It is this emphasis on the temporality of mental events which Lewis elevates to the status of a *Zeitgeist*. *Time and Western Man* is concerned to reveal the inadequacies of this situation, but as a work of philosophy it is by no means clear about Lewis's epistemology, not least because he tells us in a crucial statement that his arguments are mediated through his role as artist, and specifically as painter: 'whatever I, for my part, say, can be traced back to an organ; but it is the eye. It is in the service of vision that my ideas are mobilized.'[3] Such a proposition, grounded in the spatial form of painting, follows on from the theory of Vorticism, but it is also apparent, in a more embryonic way, in those early stories, later collected together and published with additional material as *The Wild Body* in 1927, which were written out of his experiences in Brittany during a period spent on the Continent after leaving the Slade School of Art in 1901.[4] By the beginning of the 1930s we find Lewis concentrating on a literary satirical method in his critique of what he saw as the pseudo-intellectualism of Bloomsbury in *The Apes of God*.[5] The pamphlet *Satire and Fiction*, first published in September 1930 in response to press reviews following a limited edition of this novel sets out Lewis's position as concisely as anywhere else:

… the great opportunity that narrative-satire affords for a *visual* treatment is obvious. To let the reader 'into the minds of the characters', to 'see the play of their thoughts' – that is precisely the method least suited to satire. That it must deal with the *outside*, that is one of the capital advantages of this form of literary art … *the eye* has been the organ in ascendant here. For *The Apes of God* it could, I think, quite safely be claimed, that no book has ever been written that has paid more attention to *the outside* of people. In it their shells, or pelts, or the language of their bodily movements, come first, not last.[6]

Lewis's Vorticism, short-lived but standing at the mid-point between 1901 and 1927, encompasses more than the BLAST manifestos and a few paintings and drawings. The objectivism found in *Time and Western Man* and *Satire and Fiction* has its correlative in a statement of the painter's position defined in the novel *Tarr*, which was in progress through Lewis's Vorticist phase:

… *deadness* is the first condition of art. A hippopotamus' armoured hide, a turtle's shell, feathers or machinery on the one hand: *that* opposed to naked pulsing and moving of the soft inside of life, along with the infinite elasticity and consciousness of movement … the second [condition] is absence of *soul*, in the sentimental human sense … This is another condition of art; *to have no inside*, nothing you cannot *see*. Instead, then, of being something impelled like an independent machine by a little egoistic fire inside, it lives soullessly and deadly by its frontal lines and masses.[7]

In the Vorticist period this should be counterposed to the Futurist emphasis on simultaneity, universal dynamism and the thrill of speed – the celebration of modernity as the flux of permanent activity, underwritten by Marinetti and more-or-less problematically subscribed to by Boccioni and the other Futurist painters. In *Blasting and Bombardiering* (1937) Lewis recalls an encounter with Marinetti, emphasizing once again the painter's use of line to map out a stable and solid reality. Lewis begins:

'. . . I loathe anything that goes too quickly. If it goes too quickly, it is not there.'

'It is not there!' he thundered for this had touched him on the raw. 'It is *only* when it goes quickly that it *is* there!'

'That is nonsense', I said. 'I cannot see a thing that is going too quickly.'

'See it – see it! Why should you want to *see*?' he exclaimed. 'But you *do* see it. You see it multiplied a thousand times. You see a thousand things instead of one thing.'

I shrugged my shoulders – this was not the first time I had had this argument.

'That's just what I don't want to see. I am not a futurist', I said. 'I prefer *one* thing.'

'There is no such thing as *one* thing.'

'There is if I wish to have it so. And I wish to have it so.'

'You are a monist!' he said at this, with a contemptuous glance, curling his lip.

'All right. I am not a futurist anyway. *Je hais le movement qui déplace les lignes.*'[8]

This emphasis on the visual is, then, an absolute priority or founding principle which Lewis's aesthetic tries to sustain, and in due course I will be raising questions about its deployment. But there is one other aspect of Vorticism which must be mentioned here, since its paradoxical or self-deconstructive configuration will also be important later. The pretensions of objectivism demand that the object-world be represented as a material fact, since Lewis was concerned to control the rival representative practices of Futurism and Cubism whose subjectivist epistemologies were considered to be based on the same confusions as Bergson when it came to the role of perception. For Lewis these representative practices were part and parcel of the general maelstrom of modernity which had somehow to be tamed, and he needed a concise theory which would locate the painter's eye in its objectivism. The crucial passage can be found in the following statement from 'Our Vortex' in BLAST 1, together with the clarification given by Lewis to Douglas Goldring after the latter had been puzzled by its meaning:

> The Vorticist is at his maximum point of energy when stillest
> The Vorticist is not the Slave of Commotion, but it's Master [*sic*]
> The Vorticist does not suck up to Life
> He lets Life know its place in a Vorticist Universe.[9]
>
> ... think at once of a whirlpool. ... At the heart of the whirlpool is a great silent place where all the energy is concentrated. And there, at the point of concentration, is the Vorticist.[10]

As far as the production of the artwork is concerned, this implies that painting's spatial form is used to represent the mind's command over the sensations bombarding it. But it is impossible to overlook the more general aspirations toward critical closure in these propositions. Tom Normand has recently argued that Lewis's project can ultimately be characterized as an absurdist realization of its impossibility,[11] but this still leaves plenty of room for debate about the theorization of such a move. If the Vorticist symbol of the cone, point upwards, signifies a transcendental consciousness capable of mastering contingency through art, it is equally obvious that the above formulations are paradoxical through and through, since the Vorticist production of artworks, and hence the Vorticist consciousness, is somehow brought forth by the very contingency it seeks to control. In the paintings and drawings, for example, such control is frequently sought not only through the depiction of the concrete modern world (including its cityscapes and the situation of the masses inhabiting them) but also through a critique of the representational practices of Cubism and Futurism which already mediate the real. Thus, it should be said at this point that Vorticism interests me here as a meditation on the capabilities and problems of representation, and this contention does, I think, become more understandable when Lewis's reception of Nietzsche is theorized.

With all this in mind the sense of epistemological crisis referred to earlier leads us to consider an autoreferential, even autocritical, dimension in Lewis's work. Although he has nothing to say about the paintings and drawings – despite noting the visual bias of Lewis's thought – the most theoretically adventurous study of Lewis to have emerged to date has been Fredric Jameson's *Fables of Aggression: Wyndham Lewis, the Modernist as Fascist.*[12] Detailed comment on Jameson's complex meta-narrative aspirations is beyond my present scope, but his suggestion that Lewis's productions can be deconstructed to reveal their contextual determinants is well worth further attention, since this permits us to give due weight to the discontinuities in Lewis's project – those moments when his texts unwittingly articulate a problematic or problematics to their own disadvantage. At the very least this guards against the risk, not avoided by some commentators, of positing a false coherence by reducing Lewis's precursive material to his own aesthetic signature. Theoretical justification for such a move should hardly be necessary given the present ambitions of critical practice, where the text/context issue is central to any analysis seeking to go beyond a narrow formalism. Having said this, it is not my aim simply to turn the tables by reading Lewis's work as a *mere* function of his precursors. The Althusserian formulation, given in *Fables*, that history 'is a process without a subject or a *telos*'[13] has to be considered in the light of Derrida's claim that a *situated* subject continues to intervene in history (or its representations). Sean Burke's recent book *The Death and Return of the Author* may be regarded as an attempt to situate those theories – he groups together Lévi-Strauss, Lacan, Althusser, Derrida, Barthes and Foucault – which 'have brought a concerted and epochal force to bear against the idea of an a priori [Cartesian] subject'[14] as examples of a misleading post-structuralist critical ethics. Burke argues that the unfeasibility of a transcendental subjectivity has been taken to extremes, and in a series of close readings he shows how the above-named critics are themselves either contradictory at key moments, or frankly ambivalent about the role of agency when it comes to textuality, the psyche, the episteme or whatever 'process' works against the idea of a founding or self-present consciousness. Derrida's comments on Rousseau in *Of Grammatology* are signal in this respect: 'His declared intention is not annulled ... but rather *inscribed* within a system which it no longer dominates'.[15] Thus, for Burke, 'Intertextuality, for example, as it has been formulated and put into practice, returns quite compliantly to notions of influence and revision'.[16] For present purposes I take this to mean that the mediation of *specific* contexts in Lewis's works gives his interventions particular shape and resonance without guaranteeing an intentional authority. It matters then, that Lewis read Nietzsche, because Nietzsche's aesthetic solution to the problem of philosophical modernity places Lewis's reception thereof in a particular modality as far as the issue of representation is concerned.

91

VORTICISM AND CRITICAL RECEPTION

Where the critical recuperation of Vorticism is concerned it will be convenient to identify three main positions. Those who seek to clarify Lewis's intention are often content to avoid delving into the deeper recesses of its epistemology. For example, Michael Durman and Alan Munton agree that Vorticism 'treats its materials with detachment and takes up a contemplative attitude towards them'[17] in the cause of the reflexive painting *Workshop* (1914–15), which shows 'the contents of the artist's own "workshop", or rather, the materials on which his imagination broods'.[18] As my own analysis of this picture reveals, the central question that must be asked concerns the way in which this reflexive dimension interacts with 'detachment', and this can only be addressed by a more thoroughgoing theorization of the text/context issue referred to above. Even on their own terms the remarks by Durman and Munton suggest an interactive process (the creative act, the brooding imagination) which stands behind its spatial resolution in paint. Opponents of this position, whether or not prioritizing the influence of Nietzsche, tend to stress the willed nature of Lewis's polemic as a form of creative and elitist individualism, triumphing over the ordered mentality which objectivism supposedly represents. Eric Svarny, while noting Lewis's 'classical detachment', nevertheless thinks that BLAST 1 more accurately represents:

> an anti-humanism which is not so much a purportedly metaphysical doctrine as a set of attitudes based on an implicitly Romantic glorification of the mystique of the artist and the power of the form imparting imagination, which is expressed through a self-conscious distaste for 'life' and a hostile stance towards the English public.[19]

As Svarny points out, Vorticism is constructed out of an art/life dichotomy, and there is a third, and to my mind more productive, position which attempts to negotiate the space between these poles. Paul Edwards maintains that Nietzsche was an important figure for Lewis, but warns that 'to imply that Wyndham Lewis was a purely Apollonian artist ... would be far from the truth',[20] on the grounds that the 'truth' of art is revealed in the problematic relationship between the Apollonian and the Dionysian. This is one suggestion worth holding on to, although I am tempted to disagree with Edwards's claim that by *The Art of Being Ruled* (1926) Lewis had rejected Nietzsche's ontogeneticism in favour of 'positivist truth' because the notion of positivism is dependent on aesthetic criteria in *Time and Western Man*, published the following year. Another critic to have spotted the paradoxical nature of Vorticism is Reed Way Dasenbrock, whose description of Vorticism as 'dynamic formalism'[21] tries to reconcile form and flux by suggesting that the flux is somehow present, gathered around the still point at the centre of the vortex and represented in the 'abstract' structure of its depiction, enabled by Lewis's use of an 'analytical' Cubist method. Dasenbrock suggests that Lewis employed Cubism's formal treatment of its subject-matter in order to critique both Futurist subject-matter *and* its identification through style with the experience of modernity it claimed to celebrate. But it seems to me that this suggestion only raises more fundamental questions about the intertextual nature of the exercise, and it is by no means clear how Lewis's visual method allowed him to disentangle himself from that experience if its representation is germane to the finished product. Two questions are immediately obvious. First, if a Vorticist painting represents a Futurist representation, what status does the object-world have in that representation? Second, to what extent can Cubism's 'concern with form' be regarded as a suitable vehicle for objectivism? These questions can only be addressed in stages.

Where Vorticist painting is concerned, the indispensible study remains that of Richard Cork, even if close inspection leads to more questions about the interaction between art and life.[22] Most obviously Cork is trapped by a desire to read Lewis's work as 'abstract' (or formalist) at the same time as he feels compelled to acknowledge its referential dimensions. The resulting unease is palpable at many points in the discussion, and, theoretically at least, it is always necessary to treat Cork's findings with some caution. While Cork's desire to rescue Vorticism from marginality in the annals of art historical enquiry must be respected, the then pervasive influence of Clement Greenberg's version of modernism[23] may have led him to try to establish the autotelic aspects of Lewis's work as a major criteria, and in this respect he echoes remarks made by Hugh Kenner in his 1971 essay in Walter Michel's catalogue of Lewis's works.[24] As Cork's own study abundantly demonstrates, a Greenbergian version of Lewis would be far too one-sided, not least because Lewis's aesthetic – despite being heavily committed to a visual priority – can never be reduced to the kind of painterly purity which Greenberg maintains is the defining characteristic of modernism. Thus, as far as Lewis is concerned, the term 'abstract' will only enter into the present discussion in one very specific context: that of T. E. Hulme's reception of Wilhelm Worringer's *Abstraction and Empathy*, which is relevant to the kind of political closure Lewis attempted through his art.

THE ASSUMPTIONS OF VORTICIST PAINTING

The closure attempted by Lewis in Vorticist painting can be theorized in terms of two traditions. The first of these is the ocularcentric priority found in the Renaissance. Lewis's admiration for the quattrocento is a matter of record, although those remarks made in retrospect in 1939 may have been designed to rationalize the conflicts at the heart of Vorticism. Describing himself '(1) a Revolutionary; and (2) a Traditionalist', he praises Mantegna's engravings because they embody a 'mechanical ideal' which embodies the 'spirit of the machine . . . the hard, the cold, the mechanical and the static'.[25] This can be connected up to his concept of 'Super-Nature', developed to counter the Freudian premises of Surrealism: '[Super-Nature is] nature transformed by all the latent geometries into something outside "the real" – outside the temporal order altogether.'[26] The linearity of Mantegna's engravings should be understood in terms of the *formal* severity which Lewis thought necessary to objectivism. At first sight it is true that Vorticist paintings, because of their engagement with Futurist and Cubist representational styles, appear barely related to the illusionistic principles of Renaissance painting, but closer inspection reveals some very interesting visual correspondences. This is most obvious when Lewis invokes recessionalism by including a vanishing point (although as we shall see there are also more oblique, and ultimately autoreferential, references in paintings which are based on grid-forms). In the paradigmatic Renaissance image the painter occupies a position such that, through the organization of recessional space, the view is a function of his gaze. According to Norman Bryson this is the 'Founding Perception', in which the world is objectified by a serene visual presence, recreated in due course when the spectator looks at the image:

> the gaze of the painter arrests the flux of phenomena, contemplates the visual field from a vantage point outside the mobility of duration, in an eternal moment of disclosed presence; while in the moment of viewing, the viewing subject unites his gaze with the Founding Perception, in a perfect recreation of that first epiphany.[27]

In Alberti's Euclidean model, the gridded surface interposed between eye and object which was used to map the world onto the canvas was effaced in the correspondence between the real and the represented.[28] Michael Baxandall has shown how Renaissance painting was situated in a general economy of recognition based on an ocularcentric priority, and this can be held to work against the possibilities of human narrative: in effect the temporal world of experience becomes frozen as quantitatively conceptualized space, predicated on an increasingly secularized scientific worldview composed of natural objects in mathematical relationship to each other.[29] The visual was a form of closure which parcelled up the heterogeneity of existence, confirming the world in its objecthood and establishing the connection between mind and matter. In this model the observing intellect enacts what Martin Jay describes as 'the surveillance and manipulation [by] a dominating subject'.[30] The scientific bias of painting should be emphasized: in sixteenth-century Italian academies drawing was established as a rational activity, where the control of line and the absence of colour served to place the emphasis on form.

It will already be appreciated that there is a significant theoretical correspondence between this situation and Vorticism's still point, and the connection is made stronger when we consider some further implications outlined by Martin Jay: for example, 'the withdrawal of the painter's emotional entanglement . . . in the name of an allegedly disincarnated, absolute eye . . . a reifying male look that turned its targets into stone'[31] can be applied to *Tarr*, which features a painter, Otto Kreisler, whose failure is partly due to his inability to carry on a disinterested sexual relationship with Bertha.

The second tradition is more closely connected to what we normally understand as avant-gardism, and facilitates further discussion of how Lewis used analytical Cubism against the grain of its own implications to depict the object-world of modernity. To begin with, Lewis's use of analytical Cubism (hereinafter simply 'Cubism') is *de facto* connected to the Renaissance in so far as Cubism marks the moment when the principle of fixed perspective was subjected to a radical visual critique emphasizing the contingent nature of the object-world. Thus, since Cubism invokes illusionism as its other we have to consider what it was that objectivism was seeking through Cubism. I think Lewis was attempting to reinstate painting's capacity to establish a world of fixed objects which guaranteed a fixed viewpoint. His problem was one of how to combine this with a critique of an avant-garde practice which was most blatantly critical of illusionism, without resorting to outmoded illusionistic conventions. The connection here may be the realism of Courbet, motivated as it was by a concern with the depiction of social realities. 'Realism' is a somewhat confusing term where nineteenth-century painting is concerned, in so far as the Impressionists were also concerned with truth-to-appearances as a reaction against the ideologies of Academic idealism. Broadly speaking, the more neutral phenomenalism of the early Impressionists is concerned with the play of light on the object, where all areas of the depicted scene are equally important because subject-matter is subservient to a pure opticality experienced by the painter's momentary glance.[32] This form of visuality might be thought relevant to Lewis, but its phenomenalism is something of a blind alley in the present context since Lewis's position does not luxuriate in any optical sensationalism. Nor does the inevitably subjective aspect of Impressionism – inevitable because the impression is derived from the transience of the painter's glance – chime with objectivism. Lewis regarded Futurism as the latest version of Impressionism, and his desire to read Futurism through Cubism is more of an attempt to re-establish a connection between the stationary eye, as the organ of the intellect, and the world of concrete fact. Cézanne is an important reference point here; although his disturbance of the picture plane adumbrates Cubism, his desire to structure his 'little sensations' before nature is arguably relevant to Lewis, for reasons which will become apparent. Courbet's Realism, concerned as it is with the world of class-based social fact, has some connection with literary naturalism. Zola's remark, made in a study of Manet, that 'All fields of knowledge, all human undertakings look for constant and definite principles in reality'[33] would have been understood by a Renaissance theorist such as Alberti; in this sense Realism suggests the continuity of tradition as far as the relationship between mind and matter is concerned.

Realism's depictions of the social were very much a response to economic, technological and social changes in material existence as a result of industrialization and the rise of modern capitalism. The issues here are extremely complex and cannot be discussed in any depth, but the main point to be emphasized is that the experience of modernity was one of dislocation. In an oft-quoted remark this experience is referred to by Marx in the Communist Party Manifesto: 'Constant revolutionizing of production, uninterrupted disturbance of all social conditions, everlasting uncertainty and agitation distinguish the bourgeois epoch from earlier ones. . . . All that is solid melts into air.'[34] It was this experience of modernity which led Baudelaire to the famous pronouncement in his essay 'The Painter of Modern Life' of 1863: 'Modernity is the transient, the fleeting, the contingent; it is the one half of art, the other being the eternal and immutable.'[35] Baudelaire's struggle to articulate the problems facing art in the nineteenth century is itself a product of the times, but it is relevant to the present discussion because we have on the one hand an attempt to take modernity into *account*, while on the other art is being asked to *preserve* itself. It will be recalled that the argument with Marinetti was configured in terms of an opposition to the insubstantiality of the Futurist flux that Lewis could not 'see'. Although the fact of modernity is here taken as a given, the mode of Marinetti's apprehension is dismissed because of its lack of detachment – Lewis was willing to concede the physical presence of the racing car 'more beautiful than the *Victory of Samothrace*'[36] but he was not prepared to concede its transposition into some kind of afflatus which elevated the flux into an aesthetic principle. This is why Cubism is so important to Lewis, although he attempted to disguise Vorticism's borrowings by detaching himself from what he saw as the Cubists' inadequacies.[37] What Lewis admired was Cubism's attitude to form because it gave him the means to achieve an avant-garde visual practice which could be adapted to go beyond an outmoded illusionist convention, while simultaneously retaining a grip on the object-world through a refutation of its disruptive effects on an ocularcentric tradition. But having said this we now come up against one of the central paradoxes of Vorticism, which, to my knowledge, has never been satisfactorily theorized. The problem is fairly easily grasped in terms of the question: what is it (or was it) about Cubism's attitude to form that Lewis could draw on in the cause of objectivism? Disappointingly, the various remarks about Cubism in and around BLAST 1 are inconclusive. Lewis's comments in 'The Cubist Room' (from the catalogue of an exhibition held late 1913 to early 1914) are rather gnomic, although he does refer to Cubism as 'superbly severe', following on from Cézanne (without being specific about what it is in the latter that interests him).[38] Later in the same piece he says that 'All revolutionary painting today [exhibits] an alienation from the photographer's trade and [the] realization of the value of colour and form as such, independently of what recognizable form it covers or encloses'[39] while in 'A Review of Contemporary Art' in BLAST 2 he tells us that

> Cubism means the naturalistic abstract school ... [whose paintings] have a large tincture of the deadness (as well as the weightiness) of Cézanne; they are static and representative, not swarming, exploding or burgeoning with life, as is the ideal of the Futurists. [40]

To some extent these (and other) comments are paradoxical: the appeal to 'form as such' is not a reference to autotelicism but a critique of Futurist principles, yet to describe Cubism as 'naturalistic abstract' simply begs the question of the relationship between the abstract (in the sense of the object's formalization) and the natural world being represented. Reading through Lewis's comments on Cubism at this time it becomes clear that he was, possibly for strategic reasons, unsure of how to particularize its significance, and critical recuperation is therefore faced with an interesting situation. For present purposes I will draw on Dasenbrock's assessment of what Cubism offers to Vorticism, not because I think it is entirely clear or correct but because it offers an initial possibility for what Cubist 'form' might mean for Vorticist objectivism. According to Dasenbrock, Vorticism signifies 'a deepened mode of representation *through* form'. Essentially, what he means by this is that Vorticism picks up on Cubism's 'more profound mode of realism' – the neo-Kantian truth which lies behind mere appearance – in order to 'paint and respond to the modern world' by means of 'a detached formal investigation' of it.[41] The introduction of neo-Kantianism is somewhat confusing so I will attempt to gloss Dasenbrock in more straightforward terms. His argument rests on the role of the intellect in the perception of the world. In effect, Cubism says that the world is made up of more than the stationary observer sees: for example, in the depiction of the object in a work like Picasso's *Portrait of Ambroise Vollard* (1909–10) the spectator is presented with its several discrete aspects as a result of the *knowledge* of how that object appears in space *and* time. The crucial point then, is that Cubist form (the fragmentation of pictorial space into discrete passages) signifies the mind's attempt to become aware of itself as it contemplates the object. Cubist painting is the record of an explicitly conceptual process; the *analysis* of an antecedent reality which still retains some connection to the intellectualism of painting as a mapping technique.

That this argument is distinctly problematic when adopted as a model for Vorticism will immediately be apparent, essentially because the mind assumes a more active role in perception than Lewis's critique of Bergson and the Futurists can afford to concede. However, I don't think Dasenbrock is saying or implying that Vorticism swallows Cubism whole. Rather, so the argument goes, Lewis identifies one specific quality of Cubism – its intellectual and analytical bias as evidence of detachment – and builds on that to critique the other Cubist premises. Cubism *per se* is no less guilty than Futurism in its subjectivist bias, but at least it has attempted to restore intellectual credibility to the act of perception through the distance from experience it maintains. In this model the result of Cubist looking – its production of static forms in accordance with the essentially spatial characteristic of painting – is antithetical to Futurism's eulogization of modernity, and by emphasizing the intellectual in Cubism Lewis can counter both Futurism and the more suspect aspects of Cubism itself. For Lewis, Cubism's comparative intellectual stability is a link back to an older form of perception in which the real was composed of tangible objects, arranged securely in space. An argument along these lines is certainly preferable to the comparatively untheorized advocacy of detachment favoured by Durman and Munton because it allows us to connect up intellectualism and social critique, at least if we understand the latter in terms of Courbet's well-known pronouncement that painting is an essentially *concrete* art and can only consist of the presentation of *real and existing things*. It is a completely physical language, the words of which consist of all visible objects; an object which is *abstract*, not visible, non-existent, is not within the realm of painting.[42]

From another angle the connection between Cubism and Realism can be appreciated if we remind ourselves of Gliezes and Metzinger's essay 'Du Cubisme' of 1912,[43] because it was this work that contained the claim that Cubism's emphasis on the act of perception can properly be understood in relation to Courbet. Put simply, the argument goes that Courbet is linked to Cubism in his concern for the truth of perception. As already explained, Cubist truth is very different in emphasis from that of the Realists, since its representational style is a critique of Realism's connection to the illusionistic assumptions of the Renaissance. But I want to argue that Vorticism's use of Cubism makes sense only if some connection can be established between the former's more theoretical repudiation of contingency and its critique of the social which is part and parcel of the manifestos and the paintings – failure to establish this connection reduces Vorticism's objectivism to a more abstract argument about perception as such. Though it has this component, the presence of the concrete is fundamental to the Vorticist intention because its existence as fact allows Lewis to stand at the still point of a vortex which otherwise sucks him up into its confusions about the nature and identity of the real.

T. E. HULME AND THE POLITICS OF ART

The foregoing situation is already quite involved but it cannot be fully understood unless we consider another ingredient in the armoury of closure. One of the major themes of *The Art of Being Ruled* concerns the problem of an authentic, if lonely, individuality contrasted with the 'disciplined well-policed herd-life'[44] desired by the mechanistic masses. Lewis's diagnosis of the condition of the masses has two components. First, he was concerned with those whose mental horizons were reduced by the alienation and false consciousness produced by the means-end rationality of industrial capitalism. In 'The New Egos' in BLAST 1, Lewis says that 'Dehumanization is the chief diagnostic of the Modern World',[45] and there are a number of images which attest to this fairly straightforward critique; for example, *Two Mechanics* of 1912 and *The Crowd* of 1914–15, which is a particularly interesting Vorticist depiction of the situation of the urban city-dweller. (This image is analysed in more detail below.)

99

The Wild Body stories also include similar references, most notably in the story 'Inferior Religions' of 1917, where Lewis introduces the 'fascinating imbecility of the creaking men-machines', telling us that 'The wheel at Carisbrooke [Isle of Wight] imposes a set of movements on the donkey inside it', before instantly expanding the metaphor with reference to a further one: the rhythms dictated by the fishing-boat industry are a 'scheme so complex, that it passes for open and untrammeled life'.[46] But this critique also has its essentialist aspects, and any interpretation of *The Crowd* would be incomplete without reference to T. E. Hulme's notion of 'original sin'.

In *Blasting and Bombardiering* Lewis suggests that Hulme might be the philosopher of Vorticism,[47] but it is crucial to understand Hulme's intellectual development if this remark is to be put into context. The situation here is obscured by Herbert Read's assemblage of essays in *Speculations* (1924) which makes it seem as though Hulme began as the antihumanist he only later became.[48] But once the correct order of the essays is established, the following situation can be sketched out. After being sent down from Cambridge in 1904 Hulme travelled in Canada and on the Continent before emerging as a Bergsonian disciple in London in 1907. Hulme recognized the relativist implications of Bergson – as he argues as late as April 1911 in 'Notes on the Bologna Congress': 'I am a pluralist. . . . There is no Unity, no Truth, but forces which have different aims, and whose reality consists in those differences. To the rationalist this is an absolutely horrible position.'[49]

But around this same date he seems to have abandoned this position, largely as a result of contact with Pierre Lassere's *La Romantisme Française*, published in 1907, and with the reactionary group *L'Action Française*, whose ideology can be traced back to the anti-humanism of Joseph de Maistre's objections to the ideals of the French Revolution.[50] *L'Action Française* promulgated a 'classical' authoritarian philosophy based on a belief that the Revolution could be understood in relation to the idea of human progress expressed in Romantic literature. In their view good art should depend on a hierarchy of values *limiting* human freedom. Hulme's essay 'Humanism and the Religious Attitude' criticizes humanism, which he dates to the Renaissance, for being primarily concerned with man's self-determination. Religion, in Hulme's peculiar understanding of the word, should not involve itself in questions of existence; rather, it should be redefined as 'a special region of knowledge, marked out from all other spheres of knowledge, [which is] the *Critique of Satisfaction*'.[51] For Hulme religion becomes the agent of social organization in the face of man's inherent imperfection. He wants to get rid of 'that bastard thing

Personality, and all the bunkum that follows from it'[52] because 'A man is essentially bad, he can only accomplish anything of value by discipline – ethical and political. Order is not merely negative but creative and liberating. Institutions are necessary'.[53] Hulme's revised views on art are expressed in this same essay in terms of a distinction between the vitalism of Renaissance humanism and the 'austerity . . . perfection and rigidity' of Byzantine art where 'Man is subordinate to certain absolute values: there is no delight in the human form, leading to its *natural* reproduction; it is always distorted to fit into the more abstract forms which convey an intense religious emotion'.[54] Hulme saw the later Cézanne as a step along the road to a new machine aesthetics because the latter, in his studies of bathers, had recreated the emphasis on form that distinguished the art of antiquity. A good deal of this was recycled from Wilhelm Worringer's distinction between empathetic and abstract art. Worringer's *Abstraction and Empathy* of 1908 is an extended exercise in historicization, but stripped to its essentials the argument runs as follows. Empathetic art is aligned with those forms of representation which are undertaken as a means to identify with life. The urge to abstraction, on the other hand, comes about when the subject experiences bewilderment in the face of the phenomenal world's heterogeneity. In this sense 'abstract' art confers a kind of security by taking

> the individual thing of the external world out of its arbitrariness and seeming fortuitousness, [of] externalizing it by approximation to abstract forms and, in this manner, [of] finding a point of tranquillity and a refuge from appearances.[55]

It should be noted here that 'abstraction' has nothing to do with formalism in the canonical (and misleadingly generalized) art historical sense. While the empathetic response will seek to copy the world of appearances, be they organic or non-organic, the abstractist tendency will concentrate on the essential quality of the thing represented – what Worringer calls its 'absolute value' – even when, as in Byzantine art, some degree of resemblance remains. In effect, the appearance of the object is mediated through its intellectualization as art. To abstract the object from life is to escape contingency by turning it into art: whereas the empathetic response uses art to celebrate life, the abstractist tendency uses art to signify detachment. Worringer's 'point of tranquillity' sounds similar to the Vorticist still point and could well have been an ingredient, via Hulme, in Lewis's opposition to the 'empathetic' ideas of Bergson and the Futurists.

It should be emphasized here that Hulme's views on religion have nothing to do with Christianity. Rather, we should consider his relationship to *L'Action Française* in terms of the political climate of the early twentieth century in England. As Alan Robinson points out in his fascinating study of the period,[56] Hulme's combination of aesthetics and politics can be seen as part of a concerted reaction to democratic trends, eventually focused by the Parliament Act of 1911, in favour of arguments on behalf of social stratification, borne out of a combination of Darwinism, eugenics and Nietzsche. Hulme was involved with *The New Age*, which became an important organ for the dissemination of these ideas; its editor, A. R. Orage, published books on Nietzsche in 1906 and 1907.[57] There is, for example, a close correspondence between Hulme's antihumanism and the views expressed in Anthony Ludovici's *Nietzsche on Art*, given that institutional closure acquires an aesthetic dimension in both.[58] Socially speaking, Ludovici and others read Nietzsche somewhat against the grain of a radical individualism to reach a situation in which self-actualized persons form an oligarchy ruling over the inert mass of the population.

Hulme's views on art, then, cannot be separated from his politics, but we must guard against simply accommodating Lewis to Hulme, and the situation is probably best glossed as follows. I think Tom Normand is essentially correct when he writes that Lewis and Hulme 'shared a radical conservatism, based on an elitism which flowed from a neo-Nietzschean and sub-romantic vision of the intellectual as privileged "seer" ',[59] except that I read Lewis's inheritance of Nietzsche as ultimately autoreferential. Lewis, even in retrospect, undoubtedly needed to assume some philosophical credibility for what was an overdetermined representational practice, but ultimately the fact that he placed art above philosophy, or at least attempted to engage with philosophical issues through art, obliges us to concentrate on the theme of representation as the key to his aesthetic value-system.

VORTICISM IN PRACTICE

I now propose to examine some Vorticist paintings to see how Lewis's objectivist spatial method operates in practice. I will be arguing in due course that Vorticism's representation of Futurist ideology invokes the latter's problematics to its own disadvantage, so I propose to approach the Vorticist intention here by looking at the kind of Futurist images that Vorticism was designed to counteract. I will concentrate on Boccioni for this purpose because he was both the leader and the most theoretically motivated of the Futurist painters. Boccioni's pre-Futurist work sees him trying to come to terms with a clash of interests, his positivist training under Previati being inimical to the Futurist aesthetic. The *Technical Manifesto of Futurist Painting*, largely authored by Boccioni and published in April 1910, contains the following passage – Lewis's encounter with Marinetti in *Blasting and Bombardiering* should be recalled:

The gesture which we would reproduce on canvas shall no longer be a fixed *moment* in universal dynamism. It shall simply be the *dynamic sensation* itself. . . . On account of the persistency of an image upon the retina, moving objects constantly multiply themselves; their form changes like rapid vibrations. . . . To paint a human figure you must not paint it, you must render the whole of its surrounding atmosphere. . . . Space no longer exists. . . . Our bodies penetrate the sofas on which we sit, and the sofas penetrate our bodies. . . . The time has passed for our sensations in painting to be whispered. We wish them in future to sing and re-echo upon our canvases in deafening and triumphant flourishes . . . our art is intoxicated with spontaneity and power.[60]

What Boccioni wanted to do was heavily influenced by Marinetti and the first manifesto. To some extent this manifesto, with its talk of 'great crowds excited by work, by pleasure, and by riot'[61] was attractive to Boccioni's Marxist sympathies, but this is overlaid by a quasi-symbolist aesthetic; not surprisingly the result is epistemologically confused. *The City Rises* (1910), originally called simply *Work*, is still concerned with the depiction of urban themes, although its style is some way removed from the earlier *Factories at Porta Romana* (1908). Boccioni said he wanted to create 'a great synthesis of labour, light and movement',[62] and the image derives from the observed facts of social life, filtered through the *impression* such an observation produces in the onlooker – this is particularly evident in the dominating foreground scene where a blur of men and horses produce an effect of energy and strain. Boccioni's aim in the *Technical Manifesto* was to 'put the spectator in the centre of the picture',[63] by which he meant that the communication of an impression, instead of some neutrally positivist reproduction thereof, was intended to break down the barrier between art and life. This is more marked in *The Street Enters the House* (1911), done in response to Severini's unfavourable comparison between the Futurists and the Cubists in the summer of that year (although Boccioni had not actually seen any Cubist work at that stage of his career). There is an obvious attempt to present the scene from several different viewpoints, even if a broadly recessional perspective still governs it: the woman spectator on the balcony, who doubles for the actual spectator, is merged with the central area of the building site and a horse has 'escaped' from its proper location as part of the observed scene. Two other women are visible on balconies left and right, and it may be that these three onlookers are one and the same person. In his explanation of the work as part of a catalogue entry at its exhibition in February 1912 Boccioni explained that 'the picture must be the synthesis of *what one remembers and of what one sees*',[64] but at the same time he is severely critical of Cubism's analytical treatment of the object because this is intellectual in method and static in result. Boccioni had certainly read Bergson by this time, and it is tempting to see his theoretical struggles as a response to Bergson's ideas about the interaction of mind and matter.

If Lewis's *Workshop* is a response to this situation it is probably best approached through a slightly earlier image. The watercolour *Composition* (1913) is one of several which *r*epresents (or, perhaps more accurately, re-represents) the urban landscape of the Futurists. It therefore depicts the kind of *experience* signified by *The City Rises* and *The Street Enters the House*. This is achieved by a series of fragmented and intersecting planes, confusing to the eye and impossible for the mind to resolve into a coherent whole. Apart from the obvious reference to a building at bottom centre, other bits of building might be made out; for example, there is a maroon rectangle at top left of centre which might have a black 'side', and some of the other rectangles might be windows. But the sensation of movement generated by the blurred outlines of *The City Rises* could not be more different from Lewis's frozen treatment of the scene, and neither do the pseudo-Cubist interpenetrations of *The Street Enters the House* function in the same kind of way. This is not simply a matter of the more blocky demarcations of the picture space, assisted by the containment of colour areas, in *Composition*. The absence of human figures is particularly interesting. Whereas in the Boccioni paintings the presence of figures and spectators-in-the-picture identifies the actual spectator with the experience of the represented one, the only position available to the spectator of *Composition* is the external 'stilled' one of the objectivist painter. Note too that in common with several other images of this period the picture is roughly held together by intersecting diagonals which pay homage to a vanishing point, even though this reference sits uneasily with the general impenetrability of the central passage, where an awkward block of clashing forms affronts the eye.

At this stage of the argument I am reading *Composition* in terms of Lewis's Cubist-derived pictorial methodology, discussed above. Looking at a range of analytical Cubist images (say those produced by Picasso and Braque between about 1908 and 1912) a certain type emerges: characterized by the use of facet planes, all these pictures present objects which are more-or-less recoverable from their depiction as a function of the Cubist glance. If, for example, we take Braque's townscape *Céret: Rooftops* of 1911 (this image is chosen because its subject-matter can more easily be compared to Lewis's urban themes than the Cubist theme of still-life which he derided) we find that the solidity of the walls, gables and rooftops is severely compromised by the various acts of looking that the image represents. The title helps, of course, and so do the small dark rectangles of the windows, the chimneys, the trees or shrubs dotted about, and the repetitive and superimposed pattern of the roofs (although it is by no means clear how many roofs we are looking at, since a number of roof shapes may signify one single roof looked at from a number of spatial and temporal locations). The scene consists of a view through an open window (marked by two verticals) whose framing capacities are already placed in doubt. As with *Composition*, the image retains a diagonal reference suggestive of a vanishing point which, together with the move from dark to light tones, helps to create a problematic sensation of depth appropriate to the critique of an illusionist view across an intervening space. But Lewis's image is immediately marked out as different in emphasis. As already mentioned, this is largely achieved by the strict linear demarcations of the various pictorial passages, assisted by the use of clashing colours, which is far removed from the homogeneous effect of the Braque. This generates the massivity of *Composition*, lifting, or 'abstracting', the facet planes out of their fluid interrelation to produce the desired stability and stillness.

Coming to *Workshop* via *Composition* helps us to appreciate the former's further rationalization of the latter's engagement with Futurist modernity. Lewis continues his portrayal of the urban metropolis by depicting a series of fenestrations, but the overall effect is far calmer and more organized than in *Composition*, due to the lighter tonal palette and because the clamour around the middle of that picture now seems, via the repetition of tilted pyramidal shapes, to have a more structural purpose, in relation to a displaced centre. A suggestion that the blue patch occupying this centre may denote an area of blue sky glimpsed above tall buildings is inferentially supported by *New York* (1914).[65] But the most obvious reason for including it would seem to be that it functions as a centre around which the Futurist cityscape revolves, and the fact that the picture has an unmistakable recessionalist appearance can once more be related to the underlying correspondence between Vorticism and Renaissance ocularcentrism. It could be argued that Lewis has made his intentions explicit in this respect via the title if this is read in conjunction

Plate 3.1 Wyndham Lewis, *Workshop* (1914–15), reproduced by permission of
The Tate Gallery, London. © Estate of Mrs G. A. Wyndham Lewis. By permission.

with the theory of Vorticist objectivism in BLAST 1; the work now acquires an extra resonance in that it depicts the Vorticist intention in operation. This is achieved by the manipulation of two spectatorial positions: the one internal to the image at its centre, which signifies the Vorticist in the process of drawing energy from the forms swirling around him; the other external to the finished picture which establishes the work's 'deadness' as a result of that process.

This particular reference to Renaissance methods is not common to all Vorticist pictures however, and Lewis's experimentalism resulted in variations on the theme of objectivism. In keeping with his thesis, Cork regards *Plan of War* (1914) as predominantly formalist. I take it from his remarks in an essay written to accompany the exhibition of Lewis's war art at the Imperial War Museum in 1992 that this is one of the readings Paul Edwards does not want to exclude. But understandably, given the title, he clearly prefers the suggestion, made by Lewis's friend Frank Rutter in 1922, that the image contains military references: the left-hand block representing the components of an army turning to attack its opposite number.[66] Normand thinks this picture can be related to *Red Duet* whose 'series of black and grey splinters ... are arrayed, for all the world, like armies on a battlefield'.[67] It seems reasonable enough to regard both works as 'abstractions' of battle, since war is the ultimate breakdown of social order and signifies in particularly acute form the kind of reversion to instinctual behaviours that Lewis's ratiocinations were designed to oppose. Thus, these diagrammatic methods are perfectly in keeping with objectivism, and in their relatively direct representation of an event may well be the most simplified statements of the complex Vorticist aesthetic. The connection with *Composition* and *Workshop* is certainly felt in so far as we are looking at an artwork whose content has been subjected to formal restraint. The depiction of 'serried ranks' involves a complex ironization of the 'rationality' necessary to modern industrial warfare, although there may also be some distant connection to the Renaissance in so far as Lewis's tendency to map out his subject-matter into more-or-less vertical bands (*Red Duet*) or massive blocks (*Plan of War*) recalls the mathematicization of the object-world which characterized a general economy of means at that time.[68]

The final work under discussion is *The Crowd* (1914–15). This large canvas is particularly interesting because it brings together a number of themes. There are two obvious contexts to begin with. First, we should have in mind Marinetti's alliance of technology and revolutionary fervour in the first Futurist Manifesto:

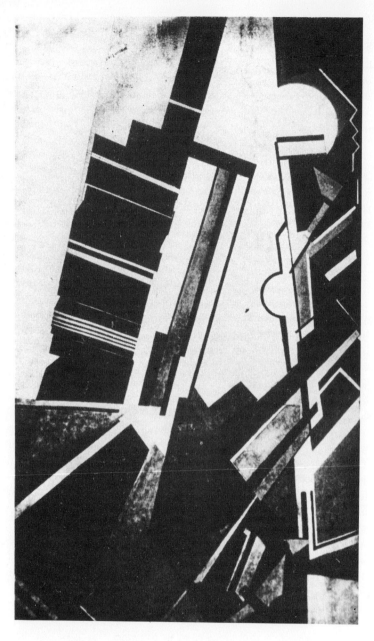

Plate 3.2 Wyndham Lewis, *Plan of War* (1914). © 1981 by the estate of Mrs G.
A. Wyndham Lewis by permission of the Wyndham Lewis Memorial Trust.
Reprinted from *Blast* with permission of Black Sparrow Press.

We will sing of great crowds excited by work, by pleasure, and by riot; we will sing of the multicoloured, polyphonic tides of revolution in the modern capitals; we will sing of the vibrant nightly fervour of arsenals and shipyards blazing with violent electric moons; . . . and the sleek flight of planes whose propellers chatter in the wind like banners and seem to cheer like an enthusiastic crowd.[69]

Second, there is Lewis's story 'The Crowd in Master' In BLAST 2, which clearly expresses the opposition between the artistic self and the other of the masses:

THE INDIVIDUAL and THE CROWD: PEACE and WAR. . . . Death is however, only a form of Crowd. It is a similar surrender . . . . The Crowd is an immense anasthetic toward death. . . . Duty flings the selfish will into this relaxed vortex. . . . Wars begin with this huge indefinite Interment in the cities.[70]

Taking these contexts at face value appears to leave us with a fairly convincing interpretation. 'The Crowd Master' is set in the London of 1914, but the fact that Lewis has given the large figures at bottom left a French tricolour suggests that the location represented by his painting is Paris (or that he fears that the events in Paris might occur in England). Lewis was in Paris during the protests of 1908, and the painting may include a recollection of his early unease in the face of collective unrest. The figures at bottom left lose their individuality as they appear to pass through a kind of doorway to emerge as the mass of interlinked red cyphers, some waving red flags, whose progress continues up the picture space before disappearing into a treadmill at top right (this last can be paralleled with the Carisbrooke wheel mentioned earlier). The painting is another of Lewis's cityscapes, complete with fenestrations and girders, which help to generate a feeling of claustrophobia – with the letters ENCLO Lewis has even managed to be specific on this point while enjoying a pun on the Cubist's use of found material in their 'synthetic' stage. For present purposes *The Crowd* combines three major themes. First, although it has less of a purely visual resemblance to analytical Cubism than *Composition* or *Workshop* it continues Lewis's attempts to find a perfect marriage of form and content by using the severity of the modern city as a structural device. Second, this is obviously connected to a desire to counteract the Futurist's representation of the city as the glorification of modernity, together with the distorted sense of progress resulting therefrom. Third, the influence of Hulme's ideas of political

Plate 3.3   Wyndham Lewis, *The Crowd* (1914–15), reproduced by permission of
The Tate Gallery, London.
© Estate of Mrs G. A. Wyndham Lewis. By permission.

closure through art is undoubtedly present in the denial of humanism and its belief in the perfectibility through self-determination of the human subject.

TOWARDS AUTOREFERENTIALITY: LEWIS, NIETZSCHE AND THE EARLY WILD BODY

Presented in this way, the works discussed above appear to substantiate the forms of closure central to Lewis's Vorticist aesthetic. They appear to rest on an aesthetic epistemology arrived at as a result of a masterful engagement with alternative forms of art and philosophy, undertaken to establish the mind's necessary connection to a modern world, where the threat to the rational intelligence can be grasped as an objective fact. But I now want to suggest that this is only one side of the story, and that the radical individualism which powers Lewis's creative impulse works to unsettle this position by foregrounding the act of representation itself.

The BLAST manifestos contain abundant evidence that Vorticist theory carries a strong individualist charge. We have already seen that 'The Crowd Master' contrasts individualism with collective action, and by extension the only form of authentic art will be that created by those who can occupy the still point of the vortex in order to sustain a detached perspective on events. But Lewis was well aware that his art was borne out of the events he critiqued. In BLAST 1, for example, he writes that

WE NEED THE UNCONSCIOUS OF HUMANITY – their stupidity, animalism and dreams.

We believe in no perfectibility except our own.[71]

These statements suggest that Lewis did, in fact, crave a form of self-transcendence through art at the same time as he was obliged to acknowledge its enablement through structural opposition between self and other. Normand offers the valuable suggestion that Lewis's need for 'the unconscious of humanity' has its precedent in Nietzsche's *The Birth of Tragedy* (1872), where the encounter with tragic drama brings about a renewal of self.[72] I agree that the influence of Nietzsche has been undervalued but I want to extend the debate by arguing: (1) that Lewis inherited via Nietzsche a profound unease about the epistemology of his objectivist position; (2) that this manifests itself in some of his earliest work; and (3) that Vorticism was the putative solution to this dilemma. Recalling my Introduction above, the argument here depends on reading Nietzsche, together with the Enlightenment problematic his 'aestheticist' solution was intended to go beyond, as something of an absent presence in Lewis's

111

work. To be sure, Lewis was aware of Nietzsche as early as 1907, but it is likely that it took him some time to digest the implications of his reading.[73] It is therefore entirely possible that his work acquires another dimension as an intensification of Nietzsche's deliberations on the possibilities and limitations of art, consequent on the much larger problematic of the relationship of self to other which can be traced back to the Enlightenment, and specifically to Kant's attempt to bridge the gap between self and other by means of the category of the aesthetic.

The version of Nietzsche I am concerned with here is the 'aestheticist', or ontogenetic, one presented by Alan Megill in *Prophets of Extremity: Nietzsche, Heidegger, Foucault, Derrida* (1985). Megill's Nietzsche is firmly associated with the sense of cultural crisis which began in the latter half of the nineteenth century, and which is figured by 'the dominant metaphor of the abyss: the metaphor of humanity stranded in a world without God or any other absolutes on which we can depend'.[74] Seen in this light, *The Birth of Tragedy*'s ruminations on the role of the aesthetic adumbrate Nietzsche's later and more radical doubts about metaphysical thinking, resulting in the will-to-power and the purely assertive 'philosophy' of *Thus Spake Zarathustra* (1883–92). Megill argues that Nietzsche was responding to a tension inherent in the central premises of the Enlightenment. The rationalization of the object-world in the name of science goes hand-in-hand with the construction of a science of society, but this occurs in an atmosphere of self-legitimation predicated on the notion of individual freedom. In other words, there exists a contradiction between ideas of determination (science) and ideas of freedom (morality) – in the first case everything is objectified in the name of a Newtonian cause and effect, while in the second the human subject must necessarily escape these limitations in order to decide on an appropriate *conduct*. Initially Kant kept these two issues separate, with the *Critique of Pure Reason* of 1781 being concerned with questions of empiricism, while the *Critique of Practical Reason* of 1788 occupies itself with questions of morality. But the *Critique of Judgement* (1790) attempts to deal with the subject/object problem by suggesting an autonomous realm for the aesthetic, which somehow bridges the gap between the cogito and the inert external world of matter. The details of Kant's argument do not concern us here; the important point is that Nietzsche's response to Kant is fundamental to crisis thought, not simply because *The Birth of Tragedy* is centrally concerned with the aesthetic as a mediator between different realms of experience, but because the later, ontogenetic, Nietzsche insists that the aesthetic transcends the subject/object division, together with its attendant moral dilemmas. This radical move, prefigured by the famous remark in *The Birth of Tragedy* that 'Only as an aesthetic product can the world be justified to all eternity'[75] insists that interpretation is all we have if we want to escape the aporia created by Kant. Megill draws our attention to the many statements of this position; for example, in fragment 560 of *The Will-To-Power* where Nietzsche says that the idea that 'things possess a constitution in themselves quite apart from interpretation and subjectivity' is an 'idle hypothesis'.[76] Even more crucially where Lewis is concerned there is a case, suggested by Megill's arguments with John T. Wilcox's version of a rationalist Nietzsche,[77] for regarding even this later Nietzsche as concerned with the epistemological possibilities in Kant, since this allows us to refer the radicality of ontogeneticism back to its origins, and thus to keep the subject/object problem alive *within* the ontogeneticist move. In the same passage in *The Birth of Tragedy* in which he writes of the aestheticist move Nietzsche also refers to the artist's resemblance to 'the uncanny fairy tale image which is able to see itself by turning its eyes [so that] he is at once subject and object, poet, actor and audience'.[78]

In a basic sense *The Birth of Tragedy* is concerned with art's superiority to science, in so far as the former is capable of rescuing man from the tyranny of the conceptual, and particularly the turn away from Socrates' own insight that culture is founded on instinct. The Socratic search for truth (producing what Nietzsche calls the culture of 'theoretical man') actively blocks off the source of its own creative powers, which are fundamentally unknowable. Once this is realized, argues Nietzsche, science will turn back into art, bringing about a more healthy relationship between intellect and instinct. Hence the importance of the Apollonian and the Dionysian in Nietzsche's schema. The relationship between the Apollonian and the Dionysian can be regarded in several ways, but two features are especially important here. First, there is a correspondence between the visual and the form-giving in Apollo, as opposed to the non-visual and the formless in Dionysus. Second, Nietzsche also regards Apollo as the god of illusion – illusion being necessary because without it rational man could not bear the reality of the instincts, centred on his bodily desires. As Terry Eagleton succinctly puts it: 'The body ... figures in effect for Nietzsche as the unconscious – as the submerged sub-text of all our more finely reflective life.'[79] The epistemological problems of *The Birth of Tragedy* centre on this relationship between Apollo and Dionysus – mind and body – because it is never clear how the passage from one to the other is to be negotiated. Yet it is apparent that the realm of the aesthetic suspends questions about this relationship – or to put it another way: one of art's creative functions is to contain the movement from one domain to another by insisting on the constructional nature of reality.

Lewis's Wild Body stories, which began to be published by Ford Madox Ford (then Ford Herman Hueffer) in *The English Review* of 1909, witness the development of a quite complicated satiric phenomenalism which is ultimately predicated on the same kind of objectivist intention we have already encountered. What initially interests us is the introduction of a narrator, Ker-Orr who mediates between the observing intellect and the body in which it is housed: 'This forked, strange scented, blond-skinned gut-bag, with its two bright rolling marbles with which it sees, bull's eyes full of mockery and madness, is my stalking horse. I hang somewhere in its midst operating it with detachment.'[80]

Ker-Orr is presented as a 'soldier of humour' (a phrase Lewis was using by 1911),[81] whose militant activities are concerned with protecting himself from the effect of the Wild Bodies, based as they are on those Breton peasants encountered by Lewis during his time spent in France after leaving the Slade. Ker-Orr's campaigns are dedicated to the aestheticization of combative encounters, where laughter achieves the necessary distance from experience: 'Everywhere where formerly I would fly at throats, I now howl with laughter. That is me.'[82] But the internal evidence suggests that in the early stories Lewis is considerably less sure of his distance from his subject-matter, and there is no reason to disagree with Bernard Lafourcade's view that they evidence a considerable fascination with the primal energies of peasant culture.[83] In those fragments which have become known as the Quimperlé Diary or Breton Journal we find a description of the carnivalesque release from conventional restraint, at the same time as the observing Lewis admits that his status as artist already makes it other. Some of Lewis's syntax in this piece is confusing but the following is clear enough:

> There fêtes are essentially *orgies*. [The peasants] pay their supreme tribute to Fate . . . they come here and fling all to the winds, leave themselves bare, make a bonfire of what the intelligence tells us is most precious. . . . The artist, in his defiance of Fate, has always remain'd a recluse, and the enemy of such orgaic participation of life, and often lives without knowing this emotion felt in the midst of its wastefulness.[84]

In 'Some Innkeepers and Bestre' (published June 1909) Lewis is impressed by Bestre's ungovernable and mysterious ability to provoke his clientele, including a 'well-known painter', to the point of violence, when 'the desire to give the blow is as painful as the blow received'.[85] Lewis then asks:

Has Bestre discovered the only type of action compatible with artistic creation, assuring security and calm to him that holds the key of the situation, in a certain degree compelling others to accept your rules? But Bestre is perhaps alone in the possession of such a physique as is his.[86]

In these two passages Lewis seems to be carrying on a debate with himself about the sources of artistic inspiration, and this explains the interest expressed elsewhere in the activities of mediation. The story 'Les Saltimbanques' (published June 1909) consists of a reflection on the circumstances of a travelling circus from Arles. These performers regard the 'vast beast' of the public with near-contempt because it fails to see through their rituals to the 'miserable existence' which is their lot, and one can read this as a comment on the role of the artist whose business it is to satisfy the public's insatiable appetite for illusion. As well as more general sociological components indicating Lewis's preoccupation with the relationship between the observer and the mass, the story contains passages which are prophetic of Lewis's later externalist method of word-painting. Consider these two descriptions: the first comes from a miniature portrait of the showman; the second is a depiction of his wife who berates the audience for being tight-fisted:

His eyebrows were hidden in in a dishevelled frond of hair. The only thing he could look at without effort was the ground, and there his eyes were usually directed. When he looked up they were heavy – vacillating painfully beneath the weight of their lids. The action of speech with him resembled that of swallowing: the dreary pipe from which he drew so many distressful sounds seemed to stiffen and swell, and his head to strain forward like a rooster about to crow. His heavy under-lip went in and out in a sombre activity.

While delivering this harangue, her attitude resembled that seen in the London streets when women are quarrelling – the neck strained forward, the face bent down, and the eyes glowing upwards at the adversary – or in this case on the people in front – and one hand thrust out in a remonstrative gesture. And the body is generally screwed round to express the impulse of turning on the heel in disgust and walking away, while the face still confronts whoever is being apostrophised, and utters its ever-renewed maledictory post-scriptums.[87]

The visual bias cannot be mistaken. To some extent these are caricatures, but there is something missing. Caricature works when the person depicted has some *quality* emphasized; at such moments we recognize the distortion as a reflection of what the original characteristic signifies *in essence* – the caricature 'captures' its original 'to a tee'. But Lewis's descriptions are somehow blind to the essences which would otherwise give rise to them – instead they function as *quantified* descriptions of bodily processes which signify nothing beyond the mere fact that they have been observed. In effect Lewis has manufactured a double distance by controlling the thematization of mediation via a phenomenalist descriptive process. Yet this attempt at an Apollonian marriage of form and content is clearly predicated on an equal interest in the forces which make them necessary in the first place. The public has its own collective behaviour because 'The brute in us [i.e. the spectators] always awakens at the contact of a mob of people'. Describing the circus tent as a tabernacle dedicated to 'the many-headed beast', Lewis goes on:

> [the performers] felt their anger gnawing through their reserve, like a dog under lock and key, yet maddened by this other brutal presence. . . . Whenever they met one of these monsters – which was on average twice a day – their only means of escape was by charming it with their pipes, which never failed to render it harmless and satisfied.[88]

These references to the public constitute a foretaste of the attitudes Lewis would, under the influence of Hulme, explore in *The Crowd*, although at this time he was embarking on a series of paper sketches which supplement the more obvious iconographies of these stories. However, there is one seminal drawing which does deal with the theme of mediation, and this is *The Theatre Manager* of 1909. The image consists of a group of figures, including a naked female, clustered round a desk, behind which sits the manager poring over what is presumably a script. A number of Lewis's works of this period are overdetermined and this one is no exception, with its apparent references to Dürer's *Four Witches*, Leonardo's grotesques, primitivism and the *mise-en-scène* of the theatre popular with Degas and Toulouse-Lautrec, where Degas's English advocate Walter Sickert may be the connection.[89] (Lewis became a member of the Camden Town Group, formed around Sickert and Lucien Pissarro in 1911). Possibly relevant here would be the truncation of the scene (see the woman on the extreme left and the figure on the extreme right who might be in contact with someone or something beyond the picture space), implying (as in Degas) the portrayal by an observer who has caught a particular moment in an ongoing narrative. However, the primitivist references can be connected to the position mapped out for the Wild Body

Plate 3.4 Wyndham Lewis, *The Theatre Manager* (1909), reproduced by permission of the Victoria and Albert Museum, London. © Estate of Mrs G. A. Wyndham Lewis. By permission.

stories if we agree that the accentuation of otherness goes hand-in-hand with an interest in 'uncivilized' modes of being. Equally significant is the reflexive nature of the image, as the manager is separated from life (the nude) by the text on his desk. (There is also a hint – again through the nude – of the theme of art and sexuality, explored in *Tarr*, which was in progress by 1908). It is very tempting to read this image as the visual equivalent of the epistemological meta-narrative informing the early Wild Body stories, establishing early on that Lewis was unsure of how to manage the relationship between the Apollonian and the Dionysian in his role as artist.

Lewis's experimentalism in the years leading up to Vorticism is too complex to be glossed here, but one major project deserves to be mentioned in the present context. *Kermesse* (originally called *Creation*) was a canvas nine feet square depicting three dancing figures from a peasant carnival, which was exhibited at the Allied Artists salon in the summer of 1912 before being lost. In his attempt to describe something of the sense of energy it conveyed Roger Fry actually referred to its 'Dionysiac mood'.[90] The painterly intertext was probably Rubens's *La Kermesse*. Rubens is targeted in BLAST 1 because he merely 'IMITATED life [and] traced the sprawling and surging of it's animals hulks [*sic*]';[91] seen in this light the work signifies an 'abstract' approach to the human form. The pseudo-Cubist style can be regarded as prefigurative of the kind of Vorticism seen in *Composition* and *Workshop*. The theme is undoubtedly energy, but energy formally controlled by a schematization of bodily elements and by the rigid demarcation of the picture plane into compositional areas – this last is particularly noticeable in a study for the larger work called *The Dancers*, which is clearly held together by an intersection of diagonals somewhere around the centre of the image. Both these pictures refer to the aesthetic sublimation of forces whose thematization is inseparable from the artwork.

THE PAINTINGS RE-EXAMINED

Having introduced the idea of autoreferentiality I now want to go back to *Workshop*, *Plan of War* and *The Crowd* to see how our critical recuperation might be affected as a result of the shift of emphasis away from closure and towards the idea of Vorticism as a species of crisis thought. We can begin here with the paradoxical nature of the vortex itself, which has to accommodate both an Apollonian stillness – the point at which the aesthetic product emerges – and the Dionysian impulses which are crucial to creativity. For Lewis, these impulses are primarily found in the peasant carnival and the proto-artistry of Bestre. But recalling Normand's suggestion that Lewis sought a renewal of self through cathartic encounters with the other, it becomes possible to see how this then becomes transmuted into an engagement with the subjectivist philosophy of Bergson and the representational practices of Cubism and Futurism – hence the attempt to master these others for the sake of a grip on the object-world, guaranteed by those references to Renaissance ocularcentrism, which are otherwise called into question. Such a transfer of values is, as I see it, entirely typical of an overdetermination resulting from basic insecurity about the subject/object relationship originating, via Nietzsche, in Kant's aporetic aesthetic solution to the problem of Enlightenment modernity.

Looked at in this light the first problem for closure concerns its reliance on Cubism, and, through Cubism, Futurism. The fact that Cubism and Futurism are so *present* in Vorticism defers this closure into the representational problematics of those styles, for it is impossible to ask questions of Vorticism without also asking questions about the representational values on which Vorticist objectivism depends. In the most obvious way this means that Vorticism cannot but help invoke the problematics of Cubism and Futurism. For example, even assuming that Vorticism does somehow extract the 'analytical' component of Cubism in order to foreclose on Futurism, this cannot but refer to the problematic meeting of Marinetti and Boccioni in the latter's depictions of the object-world. The entirely necessary reliance of Vorticism on Futurism for its depiction of this object-world means that Boccioni's work becomes the subtext or the palimpsest of *Composition* and *Workshop*, and, as already pointed out, the difficulty he experienced in synthesizing Futurism with Previati's scientific divisionism then assumes its own problematic as a debate about the status of the real. And if this problem seems clear enough in *Composition*, what is the further effect of the self-confessed reflexive dimension in *Workshop*? In his attempt to construct a double viewpoint (the spectator-in-the-picture who occupies the still point of the depicted vortex, and the spectator who stands outside the finished picture) does not Lewis emphasize the temporality entirely proper to the provisionality and experimentalism of a work-in-progress? This merely intensifies the question of Vorticist epistemology because such a gesture seems to admit that we cannot separate out the end result from the sources of its inspiration.

Turning to Vorticism's employment of Cubism we find more difficulties. For Lewis's 'analytical' method, together with his references to a vanishing point, raises in a particularly acute way the whole theoretical question of Vorticism's delimitation as a bounded practice, whose centripetalism is the token of a transcendental critical consciousness. For it is obviously crucial to objectivism that the spectator recognizes both Vorticism's visual references to Cubism and Futurism *and* the difference which permits it to distinguish itself from them. But this raises, in typically deconstructive fashion, the question of how the essential can be distinguished from the marginal. If we take Vorticism to function as the distillation or abstraction of some essential property of Cubism (i.e. its 'analytical' bias) then its remaining properties must be considered redundant, to be consigned beyond its frame of reference. But in fact, Vorticism has to refer to Cubism *in toto* in order that those other properties can be properly identified, otherwise what is essential and inessential to the Vorticist version of Cubism can neither be painted nor theorized. In short, Vorticism literally frames the essential quality of Cubism only by *including* all those redundant/improper/inessential aspects as part of its tableaux, and once it does this it opens itself up to the corrosive effects of those other aspects, including the temporal assumptions of the Cubist glance. Thus, the very necessity of Vorticist painting (the visual recognition of Vorticism as distinct from Cubism) implicates the possibility of an alternative way of seeing (the Cubist glance as opposed to the Vorticist gaze) which must be rendered scandalous if detachment is to succeed. And once this is allowed, the control of Futurism which the analytical aspect of Cubism is supposed to facilitate also gives way to that spectator whose situation in the centre of the picture represents the anathematized Futurist moment, powered as it is by modernity's unsettlement of the old stabilities. At the very least, what we are left with is a shuttling between possible viewpoints; an undecidability occurring at the very moment when Vorticism's maximum *visibility* is supposedly ratified at the still point.

In the situation now facing us, any adherence to a Vorticist spatial model will be problematic, and this proves to be the case when we turn to *The Crowd*. In terms of a Vorticist representational practice this painting is unusual in relying for its political message on an explicit narrative dimension. In general, Vorticist images eschew narrative because of its temporal implications, but once again the situation is far from clearcut. In the works discussed thus far we have seen how Lewis seeks to close down the temporal implications of Cubism and Futurism by recourse to the most obviously spatial (because intellectual) characteristic of the former, but it has also been shown how this leads Lewis, at the very least, into undecidability. True, as soon as we speak of a narrative dimension in Cubism and Futurism we run into a number of problems which are not effaced by simply eliding temporality and narrative in those movements. (For example, the relativism of the Cubist glance is not the same as a narrative if the latter is understood in terms of the representation of theme, while Futurist thematics – the temporal activity of a building site in the two Boccioni's analysed above – is transcended in Marinetti by the pure present of 'universal dynamism' or 'simultaneity'). But the real problem here is the long-standing historical issue of the depiction of narrative in painting. Wendy Steiner devotes a chapter of her book *Pictures of Romance* (1988)[92] to this issue and her findings are well worth summary examination. The most important point to note in the context of Vorticism is the anti-narrative thrust of Renaissance ocularcentrism (already touched on above). The Renaissance did contain a transitional period when the various medieval methods for depicting different time-events in one image (basically the simultaneous presentation of temporally distinct scenes) were only slowly giving way to the absolute spatial imperative of ocularcentric ideology based on the concept of a 'realism' which was true to the laws of illusionist perspective. But the eventual conclusions could not be escaped, and when Alberti and Leonardo were attempting to define an approach to narrative they did so in spatial terms. Indeed, according to Jack Greenstein, Alberti's use of the term 'istoria' (Latin: *historia*, Greek root: 'to see or to know') was transplanted uncritically from other forms of artistic discourse, including allegorical modes, into painting.[93] The contradiction is obvious enough in a work like Titian's *Three Ages of Man*, which unites the consequential but temporally separated moments of childhood, courtship and death in a single landscape scene. To an extent, these difficulties are also apparent in the hugely influential theories of Lessing, which argue for the distinction of painting and poetry along spatial and temporal lines. W. J. T. Mitchell's deconstruction of Lessing's demarcations shows how unstable they are,[94] but it remains a fact that the assumption of painting as *immediately* visual, rather than delayed through literary syntagm, became taken for granted. Steiner concludes:

> In a painting with vanishing point perspective and chiaroscuro, the assumption is that we are observing a scene through a frame from a fixed vantage point *at one moment in time*. Nothing could be more foreign to Renaissance realism than the juxtaposition of temporally distinct events within a single visual field . . . in the gradual transition from medieval to Renaissance conventions . . . the fate of narrativity in painting is apparent.[95]

The narrative properties of *The Crowd* are clear enough from the depiction of a temporal sequence beginning with the figures at bottom left and ending with the cyphers in the treadmill, but the work's metonymic possibilities are enhanced if we see it as a further mediation of the Futurist city, for here the entire issue of modernity is re-presented as a properly temporal matter: what the image finally seeks to control is its own contingent situation resulting from the experience of capitalism's inexorable progress, overlaid by the representative problematics which are a response thereto. Incidentally, Lewis's depiction of buildings may also have a historical context in a transition from the temporal to the spatial, where Renaissance examples show rooms as dividers of the picture space in order to present different episodes in a narrative.[96] In Lewis's picture the progression of the machine-men is ordered through architectural enclosures so that the reduction of individuality is seen to be a process engendered by the cramped conditions of the metropolis.

It seems typically paradoxical then, that Lewis should complicate the kind of pictorial closure he has thus far tried to establish by going against the grain of his own stated aims. But this is only the beginning of the autoreferential possibilities on *The Crowd*. *Workshop*'s use of grid-forms parallels their appearance in a number of Lewis's works of 1914–15 (see for example, *New York*, *Composition* (1915) and the sketches *Composition III*, *Composition VI*, *Composition VIII*) and, as we have seen, *The Crowd* deploys them both as denotational element and structural device. This leads us back to an issue which has been bubbling under during the present discussion. For if Lewis's use of Cubism and Futurism now seems far more concerned with the issue of representation, would this not also be true of his use of Renaissance references? With my general trajectory in mind, Norman Bryson's comments on ocularcentrism are particularly interesting in so far as they contribute to the meta-theoretical argument about intentionality. In *Tradition and Desire*, Bryson deconstructs Alberti's theory of the 'centric ray' to show how a vanishing point depends on a reversal. Already installed in the image which gathers itself at the vanishing point is a perspective looking back at the painter, fanning out beyond his one-eyed location and relativizing his gaze.[97] The point is similar to the one made in the essay 'The Gaze in the Expanded Field', which seizes on a passage from Sartre's *Being and Nothingness*, where the entry of another person into the park which until that moment had been 'the watcher's solitary domain' radically decentres the observer:

> Before, all the perspective lines had run in from the horizon towards the watcher ... now another perspective opens up. ... For the intruder himself stands at his own centre of things, and draws towards and into himself everything he sees, the watcher self is now a tangent, not a centre, a vanishing point, not a viewing point, an opacity on the other's distant horizon. Everything converges on this

intrusive center where the watcher *is not*.[98]

Aside from the particular problems of a Sartrean existentialism, the attack on a transcendental critical consciousness which this reading can be held to represent is tied to the exposure of ocularcentrism as conventional, depending on the effacement of the representative process. With this in mind we can turn to BLAST 2, where Lewis differentiates between the ordinary spectator's habits of looking and the artist's 'capacity for impersonal vision' before continuing:

A Vorticist, lately, painted a picture in which a crowd of squarish shapes, at once suggesting windows, occurred. A sympathiser with the movement asked him, horror-struck, 'are not those windows?' 'Why not?' the Vorticist replied. 'A window is for you actually A WINDOW: for me it is a space, bounded by a square or oblong frame, by four bands or lines, merely.'[99]

These comments must be carefully evaluated. Lewis does not say that he is not painting windows, and neither is this an argument for the pure formalism which Cork and others regard as the key to Vorticist abstraction (in the loose sense of the term). Instead, the 'squarish shapes' have a function beyond the denotational which can be understood with reference to 'a space, bounded by a square or oblong frame'. If we look beyond Lewis's use of grid-forms for structural ends, the idea of window-as-transparency recalls its Renaissance function as an aid to representational accuracy. As already mentioned, Alberti's perspectival method (derived from Euclid) used a gridded surface interposed between eye and object in order to map out the spatial locations of the scene. Around the turn of the sixteenth century Leonardo was referring to the ocularcentric nature of perspective in terms of 'seeing a place or object behind a pane of glass, quite transparent, on the surface of which objects that lie behind the glass are to be drawn'.[100] The precise formulations of this process are quite complex and need not detain us here; what is important is that the 'veil' is an entirely necessary, though finally invisible, component in the connection between eye and object. It seems to me then, that given the repeated invocation of the Renaissance perspective in Vorticism, Lewis's use of grid forms may well have an unexpected autoreferential dimension.

The important essay 'Grids' by Rosalind Krauss has some relevance to this argument, although it should be pointed out immediately that I am making rather tendentious use of it. Krauss's principle point – that the apparent consanguinity of the twentieth-century 'discovery' of the grid and 'the space of [modern] art [which is] autonomous and autotelic'[101] –

is best dealt with in relation to ongoing arguments about the value of Greenbergian modernism, but a couple of points remain interesting in the present context. First, the idea that the grid has a history – Krauss says it functions as a 'mythic' structure which contains the rival claims of science (from the Renaissance to neo-Impressionist treatises on physiological optics) and the anti-materialistic or transcendentalist values attached to its use by modernists from Mondrian and Malevich to Reinhardt and Rothko – is very useful since it permits to see its appearance as a more-or-less unconscious manifestation of the long narrative of representational practice. Second, during her discussion of Symbolist art Krauss points out that the grid which appears there so often as a depicted window is 'simultaneously transparent and opaque'; transmitting light but also reflecting like a mirror which 'freezes and locks the self into the space of its own reduplicated being'.[102] Naturally enough, this latter point is tied to the notion of self-transcendence through autotelicism, but there is enough here to theorize Lewis's problematic use of the grid. Krauss thinks that the appearance of the grid in Mondrian *et al.* marks 'a trauma that must be repressed'[103] because the twentieth-century transcendentalists cannot afford to acknowledge its scientism. This idea can be adapted in Lewis's case because in his pictures the 'trauma' consists of a doubt about the role of the representational, where the Renaissance grid as an aid to the phenomenal accuracy which guarantees the necessary connection between the eye and the world now comes to signify a renewed concern with the act of representation itself. I am suggesting then, that pictures like *Workshop* and *New York*, together with those related drawings seemingly neutrally entitled 'Composition this-or-that', record, with an explicitness latent in all those other works referring to a vanishing point, a degree of concern about the issue of representation which is coterminous with Lewis's involvements with Futurism and Cubism and which can be traced back, through *The Theatre Manager* and the Wild Body stories, to a Nietzschean-inspired sense of epistemological crisis.

With all these comments in mind how are we finally to regard *Plan of War*? I have left this work until last because it seems to be a much more effective demonstration of the Vorticist spatial method than the other productions discussed above. It does, of course, possess a narrative dimension in that its references to war depend on the whole history of man's inhumanity to man, about to be unleashed in its first fully industrialized form in the Great War. But in so far as Lewis has not in this case thought it necessary to get himself involved with Cubism and Futurism this painting is devoid of the immediate intertextual clutter the other works rely on for their effect. Its abstractist diagrammaticism seems to offer a real alternative to *Composition* and *The Crowd* because it achieves the kind of spatial purity they cannot attain. At such moments we come close to believing that we are looking at the result, rather than the process, of Vorticism's paradoxical theory. Close ... but not quite. For if, in order to recognize this success, we are obliged to refer to an unstable theory whose dual purposes – the closure of a transcendental critical consciousness predicated on a ocularcentric priority, and a Nietzschean creative individualism with all it entails – are somehow held in suspension before the problematics they articulate, Plan of War is indubitably tied into those problematics and cannot be read as the 'essential' or echt Vorticist artwork whose realization consigns the other 'failures' beyond its boundary. Here, as elsewhere, Vorticism is intertextual above all.

As a movement, Vorticism came to an end with the Great War. But the kind of closures attempted by Lewis continued, giving rise to the satiric literary practice referred to in the passage from *Satire and Fiction* quoted in the Introduction above. Dasenbrock has argued that the 'play' *Enemy of the Stars*, which first appeared in BLAST 1, can be construed as the most radical attempt to establish a Vorticist prose, based on a verbless para-tactical style, whose image-units are disruptive of the temporal flow of syntagma.[104] If the external literary method adopted for *The Apes of God* is less radical in this respect, the rewritten version of 'Bestre', which appeared in 1922, contains passages which are clearly related to a Vorticist programme:

His very large eyeballs, the small saffron ocellation in their centre, the tiny spot through which light entered the obese wilderness of his body; his bronzed bovine arms, swollen handles for a variety of indolent little ingenuities . . . His tongue stuck out, his lips eructated with the incredible indecorum that appears to be the monopoly of liquids, his brown arms were for the moment genitals, snakes in one massive twist beneath his mamillary slabs, gently riding on a pancreatic swell, each hair on his oil-bearing skin contributing its message of porcine affront . . . On reaching the door into which he had sunk, plump and slick as into a stage trap, there he was inside – this greasebred old mammifier – his tufted vertex charging about the plank ceiling – generally ricochetting like a dripping sturgeon in a boat's bottom – arms warm brown, ju-jitsu of his guts, tan canvas shoes and trousers rippling in ribbed planes as he darted about – with a filthy snicker for the scuttling female, and a stark cock of the eye for an unknown figure miles to his right: he filled this short tunnel with clever parabolas and vortices, little neat stutterings of triumph, goggle-eyed hypnotisms, in retrospect, for his hearers.[105]

Lewis's purpose with this astonishing snapshot-accumulation style would seem to be twofold: each description can be appreciated as a discrete and static image, before the images are connected up to present an 'abstract' account of what is essential to Bestre's person and activities. This is a virtuoso display of word-painting designed to make writing draw attention to itself as a form of *seeing*, as a specific demonstration that the objectivist ideology of painting, signalled with reference to 'ribbed planes' and 'clever parabolas and vortices', can be made to work even against the narrative movement of linguistic signs. The problem – and this is also true for any reading of *Enemy of the Stars* which seeks to make sense of a content beyond the purely demonstrative – is that the reader cannot be prevented from encountering the passage as a *process*; in the end the accumulation itself carries a temporal movement in order that the composition has some connection to the thing it describes. Ian Duncan's comment that Bestre is like the other Wild Body characters who are 'odious simply because they are other than the narrator . . . the language invades and controls them, they become mere objects of its terminologies'[106] is accurate in so far as this outlandish use of metaphors converts something unknowable into something aesthetically determined. But in the end all this virtuosity draws attention to itself as an attempt to rework earlier problematics, based on a fascination with the sources of artistic creativity.

Lewis's virtuoso writing is, of course, a mark of his separation from mass culture, with its degraded and ritualistic versions of aesthetic experience – a fact that Hugh Kenner, for one, has identified more than once. As late as *A Sinking Island* (1987) we find that the 'unique eloquence' of Lewis's early style is capable of discerning comment on art from Uccello to Cézanne, in contrast to Roger Fry and Clive Bell who, 'in making unfamiliar art assimilable implied that all art was alike ... in conferring aesthetic ecstasy'.[107] This kind of elitism follows Lewis in sending up the pseudo-elitism of Fry and Bell, but it nevertheless depends on the disclosure of truths unavailable to ordinary mortals.[108] The issue of disclosure is, in fact, central to Vorticist epistemology, particularly in BLAST 1, which is rarely coherent when pressed, an irony redoubled by its obvious satires on the typologies of newspapers, which can again be regarded as a dig at synthetic Cubism. Even the 'explanation' of the theory of the vortex given to Douglas Goldring depends on the kind of instant recognition which suggests that explanation is really unnecessary and that the rationale of Vorticism will be self-revealing. But if the image of the whirlpool asks us to take this metaphor as an invocation of the intelligence occupying the still point, we are still struck by Lewis's need to find a more commonplace vehicle for the disclosure of Vorticism. The significance of this kind of procedure, which depends for its effect on the privileging of metaphor's immediacy above the more contingent nature of metonymy, is not lost on either Jameson or, in a different context, Paul de Man, both of whom have been determined, though for rather different reasons, to refute any idea of communicative structures depending on a notion of a transcendental consciousness.[109]

CONCLUSION, OR MORE PROBLEMS WITH CLOSURE

This essay has examined a good deal of material in attempting to specify the grounds for an autoreferential Lewis, based on the impossibility of remaindering either one of two powerful but contradictory drives: on the one hand the achievement of a critical consciousness which is capable of foreclosing on contingency; on the other, the problem of aesthetic mediation as itself a form of that consciousness. I have also argued that this situation is a particularly modern one, if we date modernism back to the Enlightenment and to Kant's philosophical response to its central problematic. I am therefore arguing for a certain type of reception which sees Lewis's art as a species of crisis thought. Another reading which begins to explore this line of enquiry appeared fairly recently. Toby Myrthen advances a thematic interpretation of *Enemy of the Stars* as a postmodernist 'novel' in which the end of philosophy is dramatized. According to Myrthen, the two main characters of Arghol and Hanp represent 'the ideological poles of individuality and collectivism'.[110] The self-sufficiently intellectual Arghol rebuts Hanp, who then murders him before committing suicide in his loneliness. Lewis's gloomy diagnosis of the contemporary situation is that both 'the representatives of higher culture' and 'crude materialism'[111] have failed to find a workable solution to the problems of existence. According to Myrthen, the character of Arghol is particularly interesting since he is described in the opening lines of the play as being in 'AN IMMENSE COLLAPSE OF CHRONIC PHILOSOPHY'. Myrthen shows how Arghol figures for a bankrupt Left Hegelian humanism (represented in the text by the radical egoism of Stirner) 'that marks itself off specifically from its relation both to the transcendentalism of Hegel himself and the materialist collectivism of Marx.' *Enemy of the Stars* is thus a work of art whose thematic concretization 'becomes the most appropriate *philosophical* expression for a philosophical argument' (original emphasis).[112] In Myrthen's view Lewis refuses to take up the option of the will-to-power and is thus left to advocate a 'position' outside the dialectic of individual and collective, which, read philosophically, situates him as a precursor of Derrida's ruminations on the 'non-site' of deconstruction.

This reading of *Enemy of the Stars* is clearly undertaken to establish Myrthen's claim that Lewis was moving away from his abstractist painterly methods towards a more self-conscious literary style in which his spatial aesthetic could be transcended, and the extent of my disagreements with this argument will be obvious from the foregoing – I think we need to recognize that Lewis's spatial aesthetic continues to be bound up with its critique. In any event, to posit such a 'non-site' might be thought to misread Derrida's (and Nietzsche's) own situation within a history of metaphysics whose deconstruction does not simply destroy its horizon, or the notion of intentionality which arises within it. But the obvious question raised by all this is the one referred to by Donald Marshall, in his Preface to Stephen Melville's *Philosophy Beside Itself*, when he says:

> The taste for 'modern' writers justifies itself on the principled ground not of their achievement of critical consciousness, still less of their solving the antinomy between possibility and impossibility, but their awareness that that antinomy is inescapable. Are we to take this awareness as a triumph of critical consciousness because it is an awareness, or as a defeat, because it is an awareness of an inescapability?[113]

Arguably, and with the autobiographical last novel *Self Condemned* in mind, this question can be seen to hang over Lewis's entire *œuvre,* but it also has a more generally applicability where the economy of critical recuperation is concerned. For if Lewis's is a highly mediated response to the conditions of modernity, can criticism go beyond the problematic relationship between fact and value which his work represents? This suggests a return to Jameson's own meta-critical project if we regard Vorticism as allegorical of those more recent critical practices, going under the guise of 'post'-Marxism, which have grappled with the textualist versions of deconstruction in search of some objective conditions beyond the representational. It would have been interesting to see how Jameson would have theorized Lewis's visual art in *Fables of Aggression*; as it is he claims that we can read through Lewis's narrative strategies to discover their 'objective preconditions' deriving from 'the objective configurations of the political history of pre-1914 Europe' before they are mutated to form a new 'narrative apparatus' in the post-war works.[114] As previously remarked, Jameson's methodology has too many ramifications to be debated here, but it is clear that his rationalization of Lewis is undertaken to counter the destructive effects of the textualist version of deconstruction, which in Jameson's version of events should not be confused with a more Macherean analysis of the semi-autonomy of materials which are textualized in the aesthetic artefact. The methodology in *Fables* is indebted to Jameson's theory of the 'political unconscious', and it is there that we find the claim that

hermeneutic or interpretative activity has become one of the basic polemic targets of contemporary post-structuralism in France which – powerfully buttressed by the authority of Nietzsche – has tended to identify such operations with historicism, and in particular with the dialectic and its valorization of absence and the negative, its assertion of totalizing thought.[115]

Jameson's post-structuralist Nietzsche is troubling because he threatens the security of a Marxism which must now deal with the charge that its situation within the horizon of metaphysical thinking produces those oscillations between realism and idealism which are an inescapable fact of critical awareness. Jameson's attempt to colonize the insights of deconstruction, ideological analysis, psychoanalysis and narrative theory is born out of the important essay 'Metacommentary', where we are told to 'observe our own [critical] struggles and patiently set about characterizing them',[116] and is undertaken to re-establish the meta-narrative supremacy of a Marxist account of history, where incoherent or discontinuous aesthetic products can be understood with reference to a final signified. At the heart of this conundrum lies Jameson's need to take account of the intractable problem of the interaction between the object, its circumstances of production, *and* the frames of its critical reception. Or to put this another way, if Lewis's reading of history is a specifically textual activity (i.e. his productions are meditations on the issue of representation) how does Jameson manage to read through the various texts and subtexts of Lewis's aesthetic practice to find the material substrate which underpins them? This is a vital question because, in so far as Jameson's approval of Macherey aligns him with a deconstructive mode of thought, it raises the question of whether Marxism can identify deconstruction as part of the problem. Ultimately, claims Jameson, the achievements of both Lewis and post-structuralism are subject to the same kind of blindness about their origins, and in this sense the real subtext of *Fables* is the kind of direct statement produced in his gloss of Lukács in

Marxism and Form of 1971:

> [The bourgeois] relationship to the objects that they produce, to the commodities, the factories, the very structure of capitalism itself is a contemplative one, in that they are not aware of capitalism as a historical phenomenon . . . They can understand everything about their social environment (its elements, its functioning, its implicit laws) except the sheer historical existence of that environment itself: their rationalism can assimilate everything but the ultimate questions of purpose and origin. In this sense, capitalism is itself the first thing-in-itself, and the primal contradiction upon which all later, more specialized and abstract dilemmas are founded.[117]

The central remaining question, then, concerns the coherence of Jameson's notion of the political unconscious, since it would allow us to see Lewis, together with all the ingredients of his vortex, as expressions of the objective social contradictions on which his aporia is founded. The real problem for our acceptance of Jameson lies in the somewhat elusive epistemology of his notion of history. His assertive statement that 'One does not have to argue for the reality of history: necessity, like Dr. Johnson's stone, does that for us'[118] leads us to consider what such necessity might be and to whom it might belong. Jameson's book has generated much discussion in theoretical circles which I am unable to summarize adequately here. However, of particular interest to the present reading of Lewis is the argument advanced by my present editor, to the effect that Jameson appears to be stranded between a model of vulgar materialism and its 'textual' alternative which sees the referent disappear behind a revealed subtext whose status seems to assume a further mediation. Jameson is

> caught in this epistemological dilemma because of the way in which, under the influence of Sartre and Lacan, he sets up an unbridgeable gap between Knowing and Being, arguing on the one hand that all knowledge or reality is categorically determinate, but on the other that reality as such is an ontological realm beyond the category and therefore inaccessible to it.[119]

If this is correct, it would seem that Jameson does not escape the net of deconstruction, and that his reading of Lewis, for all its productive theorizing, also doubles a certain problematic in its object by remaining enmeshed within the deconstructive textual economy whose Nietzschean aestheticism is corrosive.

NOTES

1 Wyndham Lewis, *Time and Western Man*, London, Chatto & Windus, 1927.
2 Henri Bergson, *Time and Free Will: An Essay in the Immediate Data of Consciousness*, London, Allen & Unwin, 1971. A useful account of Bergson in context appears in Sandford Schwartz, *The Matrix of Modernism: Pound, Eliot and Early 20th-Century Thought*, Princeton, Princeton University Press, 1988.
3 Lewis, op. cit., pp. 7–8.
4 Wyndham Lewis, *The Wild Body: A Soldier of Humour and Other Stories*, London, Chatto & Windus, 1927. This is now republished as Wyndham Lewis, *The Complete Wild Body*, edited by Bernard Lafourcade, Santa Barbara, Black Sparrow Press, 1982. This edition includes all the relevant material, including the original versions of the stories, together with notes by Lafourcade on the history of their composition and publication.
5 Wyndham Lewis, *The Apes of God*, London, Arthur Press, 1930.
6 Wyndham Lewis, *Satire and Fiction*, preceded by 'The History of a Rejected Review' by Roy Campbell, Arden Library, 1985, p. 46.
7 Wyndham Lewis, *Tarr*, edited by Paul O'Keefe, Santa Barbara, Black Sparrow Press, 1990, pp. 299–300. This edition synthesizes the three original editions of the novel (the serialization in *The Egoist* from April 1916 to November 1917, an American version published by Alfred A. Knopf in June 1918, and the first English edition published by the Egoist Press in July 1918) and should be the text consulted by scholars henceforth. It permits any of these three editions to be recreated and thus facilitates the examination of Lewis's various innovations in context. There is also an important essay on the novel's compositional history by O'Keefe which shows the 'inadequacy of viewing Tarr as a coherent whole, rather than as a series of layers built up over seven years and several periods of revision', p. 382. Begun around 1908, the novel's theme was adjusted in stages with the figure of Tarr added later, indicating Lewis's attempts to arrive at an objectivist position.
8 Wyndham Lewis, *Blasting and Bombardiering: An Autobiography (1914–1926)*, London, John Calder, 1982, pp. 34–5.
9 Wyndham Lewis (ed.), BLAST 1, originally published June 1914, rpt. Santa Barbara, Black Sparrow Press, 1981, p. 148.
10 Quoted in Richard Cork, *Vorticism and Abstract Art in the First Machine Age*, London, Gordon Fraser (vol. 1), and Berkeley, University of California Press (vol. 2), 1976, p. 254.
11 Tom Normand, *Wyndham Lewis the Artist: Holding the Mirror up to Politics*, Cambridge, Cambridge University Press, 1992. See especially Chapter 5: 'A Jest too Deep for Laughter.' In so far as it manages a better theorization than Cork (see note 10), Normand's is a notable attempt to cover the major issues, focusing on the political aspects of Lewis's visual art from its earliest manifestations through to the 1930s.
12 Fredric Jameson, *Fables of Aggression: Wyndham Lewis, the Modernist as Fascist*, Berkeley and Los Angeles, University of California Press, 1979. Jameson quotes Lewis's remark about his visual priority (see note 3) on p. 122.
13 Quoted, ibid., p. 12.

14 Sean Burke, *The Death and Return of the Author: Criticism and Subjectivity in Barthes, Foucault and Derrida*, Edinburgh, Edinburgh University Press, 1992, p. 107.

15 Quoted, ibid., p. 141.

16 Ibid., p. 155.

17 Michael Durman and Alan Munton, 'Wyndham Lewis and the Nature of Vorticism'; in Giovanni Cianci (ed.), *Wyndham Lewis: Letteratura/Pittura*, Palermo, Sellerio editore, 1982, p. 104.

18 Ibid., page 112.

19 Eric Svarny, *'The Men of 1914': T.S. Eliot and Early Modernism*, Milton Keynes, Open University Press, 1988, p. 25.

20 Paul Edwards, 'Wyndham Lewis and Nietzsche: "How Much Truth Does a Man Require?" ', in Cianci, op. cit., p. 209.

21 Reed Way Dasenbrock, *The Literary Vorticism of Ezra Pound and Wyndham Lewis: Towards the Condition of Painting*, Baltimore, John Hopkins University Press, 1985, p. 36.

22 Cork, op. cit. A consideration, via the index, of a few of those passages where Cork uses the term 'abstraction' will be enough to indicate the problems here.

23 Clement Greenberg's theory of autotelic modernism is so well known, and writings about it are so voluminous, that any references here can only scratch the surface. One might begin with Greenberg's succinct essay of 1965, 'Modernist Painting', which now appears in Francis Frascina and Charles Harrison (eds), *Modern Art and Modernism: A Critical Anthology*, London, Harper & Row, 1982, pp. 5–10. Basically Greenberg's position rests on the idea that modern, or avant-garde, painting is defined by the strict attention to its own existence as painting, purged of all other artistic means and references.

24 See Hugh Kenner, 'The Visual World of Wyndham Lewis', in Walter Michel, *Wyndham Lewis: Paintings and Drawings*, London, Thames & Hudson, 1971, which reproduces nearly eight hundred of Lewis's works. Kenner claims that '[Lewis's] pictures are quiet: that is their first law. Theirs is a static world ... Lewis [turned] the nature of painting back in upon itself [presenting] us with pictures which are *about* their necessary condition of silence and immobility' (pp. 20–1).

25 Walter Michel and C. J. Fox (eds), *Wyndham Lewis on Art: Collected Writings 1913–1956*, pp. 339 and 341.

26 Ibid., p. 332.

27 Norman Bryson, *Vision and Painting: The Logic of the Gaze*, Basingstoke, Macmillan, 1983, p. 94. In the context of my claims for Lewis's reception of Nietzsche which follow, Bryson's discussion of Titian's *Bacchus and Ariadne* is particularly interesting, with its reference to the painter's control of 'the disorderly, rhythmical, dionysian vision of the dancers' (p. 95).

28 For a brief discussion of this procedure see Lawrence Wright, *Perspective in Perspective*, London, Routledge & Kegan Paul, 1983.

29 See Michael Baxandall: *Painting and Experience in Fifteenth-Century Italy*, Oxford, Oxford University Press, 1974. For example, Baxandall shows how painters and merchants were schooled in the same methods in order to quantify the observed world by a means of stock reductions to mathematical proportions – see the remarks on gauging beginning p. 86, and especially pp. 88–9: 'In both cases there is a conscious reduction of irregular masses and voids to combina-

tions of manageable geometric bodies.'

30 Martin Jay, 'Scopic Regimes of Modernity', in Hal Foster (ed.), *Vision and Visuality: Discussions in Contemporary Culture*, Seattle, Bay Press, 1988, p. 10.

31 Ibid., p.8

32 This was at least the central aim of the early Impressionists, facilitated by painting out of doors at the scene (although the finished work was often arrived at in the studio). But it does not, of course, exclude a recuperation of their work as selective of particular subject-matters – see, for example, Meyer Schapiro's famous essay 'The Nature of Abstract Art', first published in *Marxist Quarterly*, vol. 1, no. 1, 1937, where he identifies the depiction of bourgeois leisure as coterminous with the informality of Impressionism's 'neutral' phenomenalist glance.

33 Quoted in Linda Nochlin, *Realism: Style and Civilization*, Harmondsworth, Penguin, 1971, p. 41.

34 The most obvious recent context for this remark is Marshall Berman, *All That Is Solid Melts Into Air: The Experience of Modernity*, London, Verso, 1983. See also David Harvey, *The Conditions of Postmodernity*, Oxford, Basil Blackwell, 1989. Harvey begins his discussion of 'Modernity and Modernism' with Berman, via Baudelaire (see note 35).

35 Charles Baudelaire, 'The Painter of Modern Life', in *The Painter of Modern Life and Other Essays*, translated by J. Mayne, London, Phaidon, 1964, p. 12.

36 Umbro Apollonio, *Futurist Manifestos*, London, Thames & Hudson, 1973, pp. 22 and 21.

37 See 'Relativism and Picasso's Latest Work' in Lewis, BLAST 1, pp. 139–40. Lewis's main point seems to be that Picasso's avant-garde works – and particularly the still-life productions – are essentially trivial because they do not concern themselves with the important themes of Vorticist paintings.

38 Lewis, 'Room III: The Cubist Room', in Michel and Fox, op. cit., p. 56.

39 Ibid., p. 57.

40 Wyndham Lewis, BLAST 2 (War number), Santa Barbara, Black Sparrow Press, 1981, p. 38.

41 Dasenbrock, op. cit., pp. 34–6.

42 Quoted in Nochlin, op. cit., p. 23.

43 Albert Gleizes and Jean Metzinger, 'Du Cubisme', in R. L. Herbert (ed.), *Modern Artists on Art: Ten Unabridged Essays*, Englewood Cliffs, New Jersey, Prentice-Hall, 1964.

44 Wyndham Lewis, *The Art of Being Ruled*, London, Chatto & Windus, 1926, p. 35.

45 Lewis, BLAST 1, op. cit., p. 141.

46 Lewis, *The Complete Wild Body*, op. cit., p. 315.

47 See Lewis, *Blasting and Bombardiering*, op. cit., p. 100, where he writes:

> All the best things Hulme said about the theory of art were said about my art. … We happened, that is all, to be made for each other, as critic and 'creator'. What he said should be done, *I did*. Or it would be more exact to say that I did it, and he said it.

48 T. E. Hulme *Speculations: Essays on Humanism and the Philosophy of Art*, edited by Herbert Read, London, Routledge & Kegan Paul, 1987. Page numbers are identical to the 1924 edition. Note that Read's chronology for the

essays is largely back to front. See also *Further Speculations*, edited by Sam Hynes, University of Minnesota, 1955, which draws on material mostly originating from the *New Age* between 1909 and 1921. A very useful account of Hulme in context is given in Michael Levenson, *A Genealogy of Modernism: A Study of English Literary Doctrine 1908–1922*, Cambridge, Cambridge University Press, 1986. For the implications of Hulme's Bergsonianism see Richard Shusterman, 'Remembering Hulme: A Neglected Philosopher–Critic–Poet', *Journal of the History of Ideas*, vol. 46, no. 4, 1985, pp. 559–76.

49 Hulme, *Further Speculations*, p. 26.
50 For these references together with an account of Hulme and *L'Action Française* see Svarny, op. cit., pp. 17ff.
51 Hulme, *Speculations*, p. 23.
52 Ibid., p. 33.
53 Ibid., p. 47.
54 Ibid., p. 53.
55 Wilhelm Worringer, *Abstraction and Empathy: A Contribution to the Psychology of Style*, London, Routledge & Kegan Paul, rpr. 1963, p. 16.
56 Alan Robinson, *Poetry, Painting and Ideas, 1885–1914*, London and Basingstoke, Macmillan, 1985. His chapter 'The New Classicism', pp. 90ff. is directly relevant.
57 See Robinson, op. cit., p. 95.
58 In *Nietzsche on Art*, Ludovici refers to an anti-realist Ruler-art which supposedly marked the apogee of Greek civilization, exemplified in the statue of King Kephrën, where we find

> that autocratic mode of expression which brooks neither contradiction nor disobedience; the Symmetry which makes the spectator obtain a complete grasp of an idea; the Sobriety which reveals the restraint that a position of command presupposes; the Simplicity proving the power of a great mind that has overcome the chaos in itself and has reflected its order and harmony upon an object.

See Robinson, op. cit., p. 99.
59 Normand, op. cit., p. 65.
60 Apollonio, op. cit., pp. 27–9.
61 Ibid., p. 22.
62 See the letter to Barbantini dated September 1910 in G. Ballo, *Boccioni: La Vita e l'Opera*, Milan, Il Saggiatore, p. 220.
63 Apollonio, op. cit., p. 28.
64 See 'The Exhibitors to the Public', in Herschel B. Chipp, *Theories of Modern Art: A Source Book by Artists and Critics*, Berkeley, Los Angeles, University of California Press, p. 296.
65 My point here is that *Workshop* may be linked to *New York* as far as that city had to face the problem of getting light to ground level as buildings became taller and taller. This problem was only partially solved by the 'step-back' method of construction.
66 See Paul Edwards, *Wyndham Lewis: Art and War*, London, Lund Humphries, 1992, p. 27.
67 Normand, op. cit., p. 76.
68 See note 29.

69 Apollonio, op. cit., p. 22.
70 Lewis, BLAST 2, op. cit., p. 94.
71 Lewis, 'Long Live the Vortex!', in BLAST 1, op. cit., p. 7.
72 Normand, op. cit., p. 81.
73 The first reference to Nietzsche occurs in a letter of 1907 from Lewis to his mother – see W.K. Rose (ed.), *The Letters of Wyndham Lewis*, London, Methuen, 1963, pp. 36–7. Both Normand (op. cit.) and Edwards ('Wyndham Lewis and Nietzsche', op. cit.) speculate on Lewis's appreciation of Nietzsche at this time, although as it stands the matter remains inconclusive. It could be, for example, that by 1907 Lewis had imbibed something of Nietzsche's early philosophy without actually having read it. Edwards suggests (p. 203) that Lewis's self-confessed interest in a 'militantly vitalist' philosophy before the First World War derived from Nietzsche as well as Bergson, although he is careful to guard against taking Lewis's later reminiscences at face value.
74 Alan Megill, *Prophets of Extremity: Nietzsche, Heidegger, Foucault, Derrida*, Berkeley and Los Angeles, University of California Press, 1987, p. xiii.
75 Friedrich Nietzsche, *The Birth of Tragedy and The Genealogy of Morals*, New York, Doubleday Anchor Books, 1956, p. 42.
76 Quoted in Megill, op. cit., p. 86.
77 See Megill, op. cit., pp. 85–6. Megill points out that Wilcox's argument for a rationalist Nietzsche is forced to concede the many antinomies in his thought, with the result that, according to Wilcox, Nietzsche was searching for some undiscovered marriage of the cognitive and the non-cognitive – what Wilcox calls the '*trans*-cognitive'.
78 See note 75.
79 Terry Eagleton, *The Ideology of the Aesthetic*, Oxford, Basil Blackwell, 1990, p. 235.
80 Lewis, 'A Soldier of Humour', in *The Complete Wild Body*, op. cit., p. 18.
81 See Lafourcade's introduction to this story, ibid., p. 16.
82 Ibid., p. 17. Lewis's theory of laughter was probably initially indebted to Bergson. See Henri Bergson, *Laughter: An Essay on the Meaning of the Comic*, London, Macmillan, 1911. For the connection between Bergson and Lewis one might begin with Geoffrey Wagner, *Wyndham Lewis: A Portrait of the Artist as Enemy*, London, Routledge & Kegan Paul, 1957.
83 See Lafourcade's valuable essay, 'The Taming of the Wild Body', in Jeffrey Meyers (ed.) *Wyndham Lewis: A Revaluation*, London, Athlone Press, 1980, pp. 68–84.
84 Lewis, *The Complete Wild Body*, op. cit., pp. 194–5.
85 Ibid., p. 229.
86 Ibid., p. 231.
87 Ibid., pp. 238 and 244.
88 Ibid., pp. 237–8.
89 Some of the intertextual dimensions of this image are explored by Cork, op. cit., pp. 10–11. He also thinks that Lewis may have heard about Picasso's crucial painting *Les Demoiselles d'Avignon*, even if he had not actually seen it. It is more likely, however, that Lewis was unaware of what Cubism would mean to him at this date.
90 Quoted in Cork, op. cit., p. 42.
91 Lewis, 'Futurism, Magic and Life', in BLAST 1, op. cit., p. 132. Rubens is

contrasted with Leonardo who 'MADE NEW BEINGS, delicate and severe'.

92 Wendy Steiner, *Pictures of Romance: Form against Context in Painting and Literature*, Chicago, University of Chicago Press, 1988.

93 Ibid., pp. 25–6.

94 W. J. T. Mitchell, *Iconology: Image, Text, Ideology*, Chicago, University of Chicago Press, 1986. See Chapter 4, 'Space and Time: Lessing's *Laocoon* and the Politics of Genre', pp. 95–115.

95 Steiner, op. cit., pp. 23 and 41.

96 Ibid., p. 37.

97 Norman Bryson, *Tradition and Desire: From David to Delacroix*, Cambridge, Cambridge University Press, 1987, p. 77.

98 Bryson in Foster, op. cit., p. 89. The discussion in question can be found in Jean Paul Sartre, *Being and Nothingness: An Essay on Phenomenological Ontology*, London, Methuen, 1957, beginning with 'The Look', p. 252, and especially p. 255, where Sartre says: 'The appearance of the Other in the world corresponds to a decentralization of the world which undermines the centralization which I am simultaneously effecting.'

99 Lewis, 'A Review of Contemporary Art', in BLAST 2, op. cit., p. 44.

100 Wright, op. cit., p. 87.

101 Rosalind Krauss, *The Originality of the Avant-Garde and Other Modernist Myths*, Cambridge, Mass., MIT Press, 1987, p. 10.

102 Ibid., pp. 16–17.

103 Ibid.

104 For Dasenbrock's discussion see his chapter 'Lewis's *Enemy of the Stars* and Modernism's attack on Narrative', op. cit., pp. 127–51. A revised, and less syntactically radical, version of Lewis's text was issued in 1932 together with an explanatory essay 'Physics of the Not-Self'. All now appear in Alan Munton (ed.), *Collected Poems and Plays*, Manchester, Carcanet, 1979.

105 Lewis, *The Complete Wild Body*, op. cit., pp. 78–9.

106 Ian Duncan, 'Towards a Modernist Poetic: Wyndham Lewis's Early Fiction' in Cianci, op. cit., p. 84.

107 Hugh Kenner, *A Sinking Island: The Modern English Writers*, London, Barrie & Jenkins, 1988, pp. 137–8.

108 On the issue of Kenner's elitism see David Fite, 'Kenner/Bloom: Canonmaking and the Resources of Rhetoric', *Boundary 2*, Spring/Fall 1988. Fite considers that Kenner's subscription to the rarefied values of critical discourse are indicated in sentences which, at their most impressive, 'are meant to *intimidate* by the very torsion of their form on the page; such syntax refuses kinship, suggests the superiority of the intellect whose perceptions it enacts' (p. 141).

109 Jameson argues, via a suitably strenuous reading of the story 'Cantleman's Spring Mate', that Lewis's presentation of metaphor disguised as metonymy, whether intended or not, achieves

> a demystification of the process of creation itself, an implicit repudiation of that valorization of metaphor, from Aristotle to Proust, as the 'hallmark of genius', a fundamental subversion of that still organic aesthetic ideology for which the very essence of the poetic process consists in the perception, or better still, the invention of analogies.

(p. 29)

Lewis's story now appears in C.J. Fox and R.T. Chapman (eds), *Unlucky for Pringle: Unpublished and Other Stories*, London, Vision Press, 1973.
In *Allegories of Reading: Figural Language in Rousseau, Nietzsche, Rilke, and Proust*, New Haven, Yale University Press, 1979, Paul de Man takes that passage from Proust's *A la recherche du temps perdu* in which Marcel, using the solitude of his room as a metaphor for the mind, feels himself able to invoke the immediate presence of summer by the analogical means of some buzzing flies. By so doing, argues de Man, Proust asks the reader to bypass this tropological move in the interests of sharing Marcel's experience. De Man's deconstruction of this move is not easily glossed in a few words, but the upshot is that the metaphor of the room depends for its effect on the several operations of metonymy, and thus the passage's celebration of the 'self willed and autonomous inventiveness of a subject' (p. 16) is autoreferential of its grammatical contingency. One of the images in this respect is the hand held still amidst a running stream – a remarkable resemblance to the theory of the vortex and its 'clarification'.

110 Toby Myrthen, 'Wyndham Lewis: Between Nietzsche and Derrida', *English Studies in Canada*, vol. 16, no. 3, September 1990, p. 341.

111 Ibid., p. 342.

112 Ibid., p. 344.

113 Stephen Melville, *Philosophy Beside Itself: On Deconstruction and Modernism*, Manchester, Manchester University Press, 1986, pp. xii-xiii.

114 Jameson, *Fables of Aggression*, op. cit., p. 11.

115 Jameson, *The Political Unconscious: Narrative as a Socially Symbolic Act*, London, Methuen, 1981, p. 21.

116 Jameson, 'Metacommentary', now in *The Ideologies of Theory: Essays 1971–1986: Volume 1, Situations of Theory*, London, Routledge, 1988, p. 4.

117 Fredric Jameson, *Marxism and Form: Twentieth Century Dialectical Theories of Literature*, Princeton, Princeton University Press, 1971, pp. 185–6.

118 Jameson, *The Political Unconscious*, op. cit., p. 82.

119 Steve Giles, 'Against Interpretation? Recent Trends in Marxist Criticism', *British Journal of Aesthetics*, vol. 28, no. 1, Winter 1988, p. 75.

4

KURT MERZ SCHWITTERS: AESTHETICS, POLITICS AND THE NEGENTROPIC PRINCIPLE

Mike Johnson

Merz signals a challenge in a double sense – to become sensitive to the Merz approach and to constitute ourselves as an object of analysis. The art event provokes us to compare and mirror personal data with global and cosmic phenomena, and with collective archetypal experiences of the mythic world. Merz is based on the experience of the totality and the connectedness of ourselves with this totality. Schwitters emphasizes the counterbalancing effects of art. Whenever the individual or society is unbalanced, for instance by too much emphasis on politics or consumption, the art event becomes treatment for the disease. Only the connection with total knowledge of world functions allows this therapeutical viewpoint.

(Friedhelm Lach)[1]

A writer does not regard his works as means to an end. They are an end in themselves; so little are they 'means', for himself and others, that he will, if necessary, sacrifice his own existence to their existence.

(Karl Marx)[2]

INTRODUCTION: SCHWITTERS, AESTHETICS, AND POLITICS

Picture a comedy sketch by *Monty Python's Flying Circus*, featuring famous painters from several centuries; they are taking part in a bicycle race. Hear the ever more frenetic commentator, as he rattles off competitors' names. In short, unfold a typical 'Python' mixture, in this case one which ridicules both the excessively serious tone of television art programmes, by using the style of a programme on sport, and yet also pokes fun at the banality to which programmes on sport descend. Near the end of the kerfuffle, the commentator mentions 'our own, our very own, Kurt Schwitters'. I was very surprised when I first saw the sketch I have asked you to imagine, for Schwitters was apparently being referred to as British. Subsequent to the 'Python' show I checked this fact in an encyclopaedia of art at the local library and discovered, as I should have expected from the zany 'Python' team, that Schwitters was actually German (though it later transpired that he had spent some time in Great Britain). From this appropriately playful and somewhat contradictory start grew my continuing fascination with Kurt Schwitters's art and poetry.[3]

Schwitters (born 1887) lived briefly in Scotland, and in England, for several years during and after the Second World War (being offered British citizenship on the day before he died, in 1948). His art and life are congruent to many of the ludic antics of the short-lived Zurich Dada (in whose penumbra much of the best 'Python' lives), and a degree of convergence in attitude is readily apparent.[4] They shared many influences and Schwitters continued to correspond with several of the original Dadaists well after the Zurich group had disintegrated and/or metamorphosed into other Dada strains. His precise relationship to Dada is complex and many of the ideas I discuss here may also be traceable in the diverse activities that Dada gave birth to. Although he was a friend of several early and later Dadaists, and is generally considered to be Dada-like, Schwitters is principally accredited with establishing a one-man movement called 'Merz'.

Merz paintings were assemblages (strictly speaking, bricolages) constructed from materials discarded by others, which Schwitters found by chance. Similarly, Schwitters created poems out of casually overheard snippets of conversation and banal clichés, amongst other elements. Through his Merz artefacts, Schwitters attempted to develop an extensive and consistent aesthetic theory, a teleology which was quite at variance with early Dada. Schwitters's more serious side, if I may characterize it thus (for he always retained sparks of playfulness), did not overtly embrace ideological and/or (party-)political affiliation. Such affiliation is, though, precisely what characterized Dada in the wake of its move to Berlin and, eventually, the direction it took in Paris, via surrealism, as explored by Helena Lewis.[5] In fact, Schwitters was rejected for membership of communist Berlin Dada by Richard Huelsenbeck. (The recent Channel Four documentary on Dada and surrealism, *Europe After the Rain*, maintains that Huelsenbeck took an aversion to Schwitters on account of 'his bourgeois face'!)

Peter Bürger[6] claims that Dada, as one movement in what he calls the 'historical avant-garde', was concerned with overturning the institution of art, an aim both furthering, and continuing alongside, direct political allegiance. He suggests that Dada set about attaining this goal by attempting to topple the central pillars of the art institution, which supported the values of the *status quo*. Dada denied the existence of good or bad taste and rejected obedience to established aesthetic preconditions and norms. The Dadaists were not concerned with principles of aesthetic judgement, but rather their artefacts sensuously embodied a critique of bourgeois cultural conventions. Dada experimented with an inspirational, radically alternative perspective on man, mediated through artefacts and performances.

By interrogating the situation of aesthetics with regard to other cultural activities, Dada (anti-)art began to involve itself with what Bürger terms 'life praxis'. The notion of a culture's life praxis embraces its various interpenetrating systems and values, the institutions that maintain and propagate these, and the way they effect or otherwise contour the lives of citizens. For the Dadaists, as I have said, institutionalized aesthetics were implicated in capitalism's value system, which meant reifying workers as mere functionaries toiling at the behest of mechanical principles (exemplified in Henry Ford's automobile assembly lines from 1913 onwards). These dehumanizing forces were perceived as going hand-in-hand with values that had contributed strongly to the causes of the First World War. The reification of reason and rationality as inevitably promoting human progress and emancipation was questionable. If anything, the converse was perceived as being the case for Dadaists, who noted the numerous examples of the inhuman irrationality of Western(ized) man.

So-called Enlightenment, twisted into striking a pose alongside capitalism's modes of production, had ultimately led to a chaos of inhuman conditions. Zurich Dada certainly rejected all notion of art as a kind of soothing balm for, or escape from, such chaos. Dada delighted in shock, surprise and irreverence, which were themselves goads that embodied this sense of chaos. Dada thereby continuously teased the bourgeoisie of Switzerland, and the many *émigrés* (like themselves), who were passing the dreadful war in a neutral haven. According to Bürger, then, the Dada aesthetic had ceased to be a means of providing pleasure for individual (bourgeois) consumption, and could begin to have revolutionary consequences for life praxis.

Schwitters himself did not entirely divorce the aesthetic from other cultural projects, indeed, he recognized the inevitability of cultural interpenetration; in terms of artefacts, aesthetic pleasure was neither more nor less important or significant than shock and discomfort. At best, the same artefact would yield both of these simultaneously. Merz artefacts, therefore, did not attempt to espouse a determinate ideological or political message, going about their cultural engagement in a manner rather different from Bürger's characterization of Dada. Instead of trying to topple the institution of art, Schwitters sought to open up and extend aesthetic parameters within art itself. His Merz aesthetic not only embraced Dada's concerns for life praxis, it also attempted to embrace new principles for realizing the sublime through artefacts; if this was a paradoxical desire, so much the better.

Schwitters worked at his Merz aesthetic constantly; he 'was absolutely, unreservedly, 24 hours-a-day PRO-art. His genius had no time for transforming the world, or values, or the present, or the future, or the past', according to Hans Richter, an associate Zurich Dadaist.[7] Schwitters 'pro-art' stance would seem to be diametrically opposed to Dada's anti-art stance, but notwithstanding Richter's characterization, I shall tentatively explore and speculate upon alternative frames of reference within which Merz poems and assemblages might be critically read and realized.[8] I shall contend that Schwitters wanted to represent the chaotic totalities of the twentieth century, but that interwoven with this, he also wanted to generate artefacts that might lead towards the transformation of human powers.

Richter's comment about Schwitters's non-political nature is not un-controversial, and John Elderfield has claimed that 'he was outspoken in his distaste for Nazism'.[9] Schwitters did concede, too, that his Merz artefacts incorporated what was 'to some extent a social viewpoint'.[10] Nevertheless, further support for a claim that he was non-political could be extrapolated from reference to historical facts concerning Schwitters's life: at the rise of Nazism he moved to Norway from his native Hanover; thence, upon the invasion of Norway, he escaped to Britain (where he was interned, almost until the end of the war). After leaving Nazi-controlled Europe, Schwitters not only never saw his wife again, as she died of cancer in 1944, but he also lost almost his entire financial resources, including his house in Hanover (which was destroyed, ironically, by an Allied air-raid). His third and final 'Merzbau', what might nowadays be called an environment, was taking shape in the Lake District when he died. Although impoverished and extremely ill, suffering from the effects of a stroke, Schwitters laboured to complete his work, which was to have saturated a large barn. Schwitters certainly fulfilled Marx's requirement, cited in my second epigraph, of an artist being prepared to sacrifice himself for his art.[11]

To conclude this opening section on Schwitters's aesthetics and politics, and to further problematize doubts about his commitment of changing life praxis, let me refer to Terry Eagleton's comments concerning the inhuman brutality of the twentieth century. 'In a condition in which the powerful run insanely rampant', writes Eagleton, 'only the powerless can provide an image of that humanity which must in its turn come to power, and in doing so transfigure the very meaning of that term.'[12] I shall propose that Schwitters, an extreme example of dispossessed powerlessness, sought uninterrupted space and time to represent, through Merz, an aesthetic paradox; the potential representation of the sublime, although clearly an end in itself, can also be a means. The importance to him of the continuing development of Merz meant that it could not be abandoned; the political realities of Nazi Germany thus forced upon Schwitters a certain course of action. Merz artefacts became a means that might transform the way power had been used to produce disastrous manifestations. If Lach's claim in my opening epigraph is correct, these speculations I enter on here might provide a tentative basis upon which later artefacts, by other artists, might also be critically read and realized.[13]

MODERNITY, MARX, MERZ

The frame of reference or critical matrix I shall commence with, in order to pursue points I have raised in my first section, is one initially stimulated by Marshall Berman's notion of 'modernity'.[14] Not only currents of (avant-garde) modernism, but also an explicit engagement with the effects of modernization can be traced in Merz artefacts. The modernization of Western(ized) culture had particular effects upon men and women, which permeated all manner of cultural activity and changed the very perspectives within which relationships, events and processes were viewed; capitalism's metamorphic effects are, of course, still extant. Berman claims that, under capitalism:

> there is a mode of vital experience – experience of space and time, of the self and others, of life's possibilities and perils – that is shared by men and women all over the world today. I will call this body of experience 'modernity' ... modernity can be said to unite all mankind. But it is a paradoxical unity, a unity of disunity; it pours us all into a maelstrom of perpetual disintegration and renewal, of struggle and contradiction, of ambiguity and anguish. To be modern is to be part of a universe in which, as Marx said, 'all that is solid melts into air'.[15]

This paradigm of perpetual change, where turbulence creates and destroys, only to create again (only to destroy again, *ad infinitum*...) can be seen as the experiencing of a gigantic, perverse mechanism. I say mechanism, because man-made devices of various kinds are the major instruments exciting the maelstrom. To underline what I said earlier, it seems incontrovertible that the forces of industrialization have a tendency to try and make human responses more and more automatic (as with Ford's production lines). The perverse mechanism, though, at least purports to bring about capitalist ideology's revamped Enlightenment promises of progress, human emancipation and democracy. It is supposed to transport men and women towards utopia-just-over-the-next-hill, but there is a feeling for many that capitalism has cross-threaded itself and swerved out of control; the mechanism is whirling, but not serving human desires.[16]

Under the principle and increasing sway of mechanisms, as utilized by capitalist industry, changes have been constantly occurring. Innovations leading to greater prominence (or decline) in one cultural area inevitably cause transformations in others; the crucial issue for Marxism is the fact that changes in economic power cause changes in political power. No one discipline or process of culture, though, can be hermetically sealed off from, or confidently claim itself to be exclusive of, any other, and even quite minimal changes in one aspect of life praxis can have unforeseen repercussions in another. Following Berman, I shall be starting with an economics-based argument and will gradually bring in the aesthetic dimension of culture, to see how aesthetics might stimulate a radical transformation in capitalist modes of production and perception, helping to serve, rather than deny, human desires.

In the mid-nineteenth century, Marx began explicitly to expose the exploitation that bourgeois capitalist processes engendered. The bourgeoisie own the means of production and live upon the surplus profit generated by the labour power of the proletariat, whom they exploit. However, 'at the same pace that mankind masters nature, man seems to have become enslaved to other men and to his own infamy'.[17] Marx's attack on the 'infamy' of the bourgeois class includes the implication that the very forces that enslave the proletariat also degrade the owners of production. 'More than any other mode of production, (capitalism) squanders human lives, or living labour and not only flesh and blood, but also nerve and brain.'[18]

There was, for Marx, less and less of a convincing singular or well-integrated set of principles locatable as a determinate framework within which human desires might be consummated. Self-realization (self-determination) was being sacrificed to mechanical processes, whilst the religious dimension had been devalued as merely anodyne, according to

Marx, who infamously derided religion as the 'opium of the people'. Marx felt that the religion of his day had ceased to be a cultural pursuit that might serve to reconcile man and nature and had, instead, become a supporter of the debilitating and enslaving *status quo* (rather similar, in fact, to what Dada later claimed for the institution of art). The evolving industrial landscape had become relatively unconnected to natural rhythms such as daylight and seasonal variation; moreover, interpersonal relationships had become subsumed under what Marx termed 'naked interest', that is, a standardized (de-)valuation and transmogrification of human lives into economic counters was masking and disfiguring authentic human relationships. 'All that is solid melts into air', then, could be taken to mean that the organizing principles that sustained the ideology of Western(ized) culture were no longer of unquestionable worth.

Money had become if not the sole, then by far the overriding, yardstick against which human relationships and interactions were measured; money supposedly represented the value of labour, but had itself become abstracted, represented by a signifier, for example coinage or an entry in a ledger. Money incessantly refers to something else against which it may be exchanged, but this is, in turn, only of differential value against something else… and so on. The replacement of many long-established principles of life praxis was concomitant with the rise of the signifier 'money' as primary arbiter of value. Transient values of consumerism emerged, based on an artificial system that transmuted all activity into an endlessly deferred chain of abstractions. Berman comments:

> in this world (modernity), stability can only mean entropy, slow death, while our sense of progress and growth is our only way of knowing for sure that we are alive. To say our society is falling apart is only to say that it is alive and well.[19]

Making and breaking, stumbling and tumbling forward into ceaseless change had become an ideology in itself, but it put the bourgeoisie in a paradoxical position; they would have liked a determinate measure of stability in society so as to maintain their status, yet they could not even asymptotically move towards the condition of stasis, given the inherent dynamics of capitalist cultural development.

Marx, of course, expected that the proletariat, whom he thought were destined to suffer ever greater exploitation by the mechanisms of capitalism, would remove the bourgeoisie. This would initially cause apocalyptic chaos, but thence the logic of communism would triumph, its image of humanity as one reconciled with nature providing a new and just set of integrated cultural principles. The capitalist mode of production was highly successful in manufacturing material goods in excess of basic needs (food, clothing, shelter). However, the sensuous physical and/or psychic needs of women and men, in terms of aesthetics, were not being addressed, but were merely being continually deferred, parallelling the situation of monetary valuation. The result was to additionally debilitate the workers and owners of production alike, for consumerism merely provided commodities that were endlessly absorbed, rather than artefacts that absorbed and provided genuine aesthetic experiences.[20]

Merz artefacts are an attempt to come to terms with the capitalist espousal of churning mechanisms, by turn stabilizing and destabilizing all manner of cultural interactions. They do not attempt to represent a definitive vision of stability, an end-state utopia, that could be used as a model to guide capitalism into serving all men and women (which would lead to entropy, as Berman claims). Instead, Merz artefacts embody ways in which the maelstrom of capitalism might be threaded through with a principle that could inform the maelstrom's prodigious energies. Indeed, I shall attempt to read Merz artefacts as complex aesthetic information mechanisms that represent principles whereby modernity's cogs might be metaphorically retooled to liberate human desires.[21]

In the very processes that brought about mass production there was the dormant germ of an aesthetic that might engender a condition of reflexive contemplation, through the cultural contexts inherent in new kinds of artefacts. The Merz aesthetic, which attempted to break down artistic boundaries and become truly multidisciplinary, is analogous to the interpenetration of cultural activities that modernity's make-and-break turbulence was making ever more explicit. As Schwitters wrote:

> my aim is the total work of art [*Gesamtkunstwerk*], which combines all branches of art into an artistic unit. I have pasted together poems from words and sentences so as to produce a rhythmic design. I have on the other hand pasted up pictures and drawings so that sentences could be read in them. I have driven nails into pictures so as to produce a plastic relief apart from the pictorial quality of the paintings.[22]

Schwitters further reveals that:

> at the end of 1918, I realized that all values only exist in relationship to each other and that restriction to a single material is one-sided and small-minded. From this insight I formed Merz, above all as the sum of individual art forms.[23]

The genesis of the Merz aesthetic occurred during the First World War.

Schwitters, a pacifist, had avoided the call-up into the German forces by feigning imbecility and, as he claimed, by bribing doctors; Schwitters clearly recognized that money, as an arbitrary medium of exchange, had a multiplicity of uses, including subversive ones. Instead of fighting, Schwitters worked as a graphic artist in the Wülfel ironworks, and it was here that Merz began to inform his life.[24]

Writing of his experience at the ironworks from 1917 to 1918, Schwitters observed 'there I learned to love the wheel, and came to realize that machines are also abstractions of the human mind. Since that time I have loved to combine machinery with abstract painting to create a total work of art.' [25] At the same time, Schwitters's aesthetic praxis continued to develop from a variety of inputs, especially the Expressionist magazine *Der Sturm*, which was the model for his own *Merz* magazine wherein he published his aesthetic theory.

It is not coincidental that 'Merz' originally came from a cut-up of the German word 'Kommerz' (commerce), first incorporated into an assemblage, *Das Merzbild* (*The Merz Picture*) in 1919; Schwitters consistently engaged with material that was discarded by extremely wasteful capitalist processes, which ultimately characterized the entire system. Not only men and women were leading wasted lives, but the actual processes themselves were invalidated precisely because they failed to recognize their own prodigality. Merz artefacts imply that no experience, no relationship, event or process was necessarily unimportant for self-realization (and, on the other hand, they were not necessarily of importance either). Merz assemblages were constructed from randomly collected waste, the jetsam of mechanized culture (non-human-worked materials are rarely used). A non-exhaustive list of elements Schwitters incorporated would include: wire; wood; cigar butts; fragments of toys; postcards and letters; in fact, anything that Schwitters chanced across during his perambulation through his native Hanover might be utilized (whilst in Norway, his work has elements of Norwegian origin, when in England the material changes, reflecting Schwitters's environment again). The analogy between the dog-eared clutter he found so fascinating, and the flotsam-lives of women and men under capitalism, is a compelling one.

THE KOTS PICTURE: SCHWITTERS'S SCATOLOGICAL SUBLIME

One of Schwitters's most powerful assemblages, which bears out what I have claimed above, is *Das Kotsbild* (*The Kots Picture*) of 1920.[26] *The Kots Picture* does not actually contain pieces of machinery, but it is an

Plate 4.1 Kurt Schwitters, *Das Kotsbild,* (1920), reproduced by permission of
The Sprengel Museum, Hanover.

index of mechanization, including the fact that its compositional elements have been machine-made. Initially, the assemblage might appear to consist of completely random juxtapositions, with a few lines added, almost as if it were one of Dadaist Hans Arp's chance pictures. Indeed, the assemblage never shakes off this aleatory possibility; it may be precisely that, a scattering of cuttings, and any attempt to bring these into a semblance of order could be futile. Nevertheless, I shall attempt a critical reading and bear the mockery of Schwitters's ghostly laughter.

In *The Kots Picture*, the reader is presented with pictures of men and women taken from what seems to be a fashion catalogue, though none of the images is complete. Many of the fragments have been rotated and at least one is upside-down, if compared to the general orientation of the book from which my illustration is taken. Most of the elements seem to have been cut by a knife or scissors, that is, they have been trimmed for the picture, rather than torn out, or left in the condition in which they were originally found. This strongly suggests that the assemblage has been meticulously arranged.

There are several German words and phrases, which also appear to come from a catalogue. Elderfield[27] translates the more prominent ones thus: 'Bezugsschein' is German for a goods order, or ration card; 'Frauenberufe' is German for women's professions; 'Hundehalsbänder' is German for dog collars; 'Preisang(abe)' is German for price quotation; and 'Sämischgares Rindleder' is German for chamois-dressed cowhide. 'Kot' is the German word for excrement or filth, so that an alternative English translation of the title of the assemblage could be *The Picture of Excrement* or, perhaps, *The Filthy Picture*. Kot might also translate as dung, however, which could suggest *The Fertilizer Picture*, which might, in turn, connote fecundity. Additionally, 'Kotzen' is German for vomit, thus the *The Sick Picture* might also be a suitable title, alluding to a sick society. These alternative titles offer the critical reader a plenitude of initial interpretations for the assemblage. However, I wish to concentrate upon the elements of the composition in formal terms, giving relatively less space to semantic possibilities.

The formal arrangements of the assemblage, the rhythms within and between its shapes, lines, angles, tonal variations and the proximity of one element to another, combine in such a way as to order the primary visual impact of the artefact. [28] For example, the bold border to 'Frauenberufe' connects two other elements, 'Kots' and the piece of paper with 'Hundehalsbänder', by virtue of proximity and the fact that their borders are parallel. 'Kots', in turn, connects the trio to the Polish banknote, which also lies parallel. A realization of the assemblage's form might, therefore, usefully continue with the Polish banknote, which occupies a prominent position established by the fact that it has been placed on top of the planes of which the bold 'Kots', 'Frauenberufe' and 'Hundehalsbänder'; are lower elements. The bottom left-hand corner of the banknote is actually very close to the geometric centre of the assemblage and is also directly above the 'o' of 'Kot', which as befits its eponymous status, is the word with the largest lettering in the piece.

The top left-hand corner of the banknote connects to the discernible circumference of a circle, which extended also passes through the 'o' of 'Kots', establishing further relationship between these two elements. The top right-hand corner of the banknote points to, perhaps, the most complete large image of what appears to be a catalogue model, drawing her into the cluster. The bottom right-hand corner extends beyond the Merz's frame, as if the banknote is attempting to delinquently exceed any merely formal limitation placed upon it. The banknote has the greatest surface area of any single element and it is the most complete, missing only a tiny corner and being slightly obscured by the name 'Anna Blume'.

Three images in the top half of the assemblage seem to radiate from a point within the banknote: the model close to the number '260000'; the figure presumably wearing the shoes above 'Bezugsschein'; and the model pierced by the top right-hand corner of the banknote. That is, if lines are produced approximately along the central axes of their bodies, they meet at the edge of the dark centre circle of the banknote. A line drawn through the central axis (along the spine) of the little dog in the lower right-hand corner, also meets there. This point could, therefore, legitimately be claimed to be a centre of formal energies in the assemblage.

Pursuing this perspective further, the assemblage can almost be seen to revolve around a point within the density of the Polish banknote, for the actual centre of the entire assemblage is locatable at roughly the point where the 'M' of Anna Blume meets the bottom of the number 1 on the banknote. A circle inscribed about this focus will touch the edge of the circle Schwitters has added and pass through the 'o' of 'Kots'. Schwitters's circle also meets an incompletely circular form just below 'Bezugsschein' and a group of dark semicircles under the banknote. This circular principle informing the assemblage, then, interconnects the parallels that link 'Kots', the banknote and those components below, and the radial axes that pass through the banknote. (I again stress that I am taking these various elements as geometric forms, whilst neglecting their (former) cultural values.) No other area of the assemblage displays such a recognizably integrated order as this interpenetration of circle and line, such that this group of items seems to be foregrounded against others. Not only does the assemblage contain mechanically produced items, then, but the formal structure, with these strong circular, parallel and diagonal elements, connotes a blueprint or technical drawing, perhaps the wheels and axles of a mechanism, not unlike those that would have been produced at the Wülfel ironworks.

In addition to, or rather interpenetrating with, its formal properties are the 'Kots' picture's semantic possibilities, each of whose elements sensuously serve as a nodal point for a multiplicity of energies. The images and words, which refer to consumer culture, provide fascinating possibilities of interpretation. For example, the repeated face of the man who is minus the top of his head might be meant to signify that he is two-faced, or empty-headed, or both. In a kind of visual pun, the man's face is echoed by the two faces on the banknote, which are looking at similar angles to the scalped man. That these images are turned one way and the other adds to the rotational principle I have already suggested. The woman in the top right-hand corner appears to be squinting sideways at both the money and at the empty-headed man, as if her gaze flickers from one to the other. Indeed, few of the pairs of eyes in the assemblage seem to match the direction of gaze of other pairs. For example, those on the money look outwards, the model next to '260000' looks to her right, whilst the (bourgeois?) couple strolling in the park have their backs to the reader, which may signify their indifference to anything but themselves. This inconsistency, or the suggestion of a plurality of perspectives, added to the fragmented nature of the images, may suggest that mere furtherance of the circulation of money makes life unfocused. A culture that espouses such behaviour has no integral vision; there is no rhythm of continuity perceivable in the money-mad splurge of capitalism.

Additionally, as I have said, the circumference that encircles much of the banknote also passes through 'Kots', which may accentuate notions of the random circulation of money as filthy. Furthermore, the corner of the banknote pointing to the model's heart and the fact that the inscribed circle also passes through 'Frauenberufe' may imply that if love (the heart) is centred upon money, then this masks and disfigures a fundamental factor in what it is to be human. The dissipation of capitalism leads to inhuman prostitution (prostitution, perhaps, being seen as the oldest profession of women, this does cause a frisson of sexist embarrassment; it was probably the oldest men's profession too). Even the deepest, most personal of human relationships, the act of love, can become a commodity, whereas the true measure of love is its paradoxical immeasurableness. (I consider further aspects of love in my later discussion of a Merz poem.) Consistent with my reading, the eagle caged in at the centre of the banknote may be interpreted as implying that man has sacrificed nature to money. This is added to by the fact that the little dog, who looks up to the model (its mistress?), is prevented from being with her by the money; 'Hundehalsbänder' is crossed out, a metaphor for the fact that we should not have restraints to natural affection. A realization, combining the above, could proceed along these lines: nature has been trapped; we cannot establish genuine relationships, for money and the things money buys separate us from each other; money, devoid of human principles, is excremental and, in Freudian terms, linked to the death drive, that is, entropy. However, if we recognize the aesthetic possibilities of mechanisms, serving man not money, a rhythmic integrity might be discovered that enhances natural relationships via the erotic bringing together of events and processes. These include the recuperation of all manner of waste material from the improvident capitalist grind. Paying aesthetic attention to elements of mechanical production may serve as a kind of psychic fertilizer and can promote the growth of self-realization.

I neither wish to claim that the above is a correct reading of *The Kots Picture*, nor would I claim that it is in any way the only one or succeeds in being all-inclusive. I have not incorporated the upside-down image, for example. However, it does combine some of the strongest sensuous elements, both visually and verbally, of the assemblage. Sensations are excited by rhythms that the act of contemplation realizes; incremental (a false antonymic pun on excremental) visual and verbal interrelationships and, possibly, sensations of smell, taste and touch may be evoked by the Merz materials. Visual movement along parallel lines and a change of levels, going forward and back, up and down and across the surfaces, from one element to another, are demanded by the assemblage, imparting kinetic and rhythmic pleasure.

The formal laws of art generate rhythms of integrity for the artefact; by extension, these laws might also provide a basis upon which a culture should be maintained. No process, event or relationship should be wasted as if it were a meaningless experience, no one aspect of culture is superior to any other; but man is lost without the guiding principle of aesthetics.[29] As an object of contemplation and absorption, the Merz artefact can be seen as a point through which the entire cultural realm might be realized and co-ordinated (as my reference to 'intertextuality', below, will further amplify). At any one time, a particular realization may dominate, but other readings are always waiting to push themselves into the foreground. The excess of meanings might almost be seen as a kind of 'surplus value' produced by the information mechanism. This is analogous, perhaps, to the profit-making of capitalism, but in this case no one is exploited. My proportioning of the assemblage ties in with the notion that artefacts sensuously embody their meanings, that is, they do not provide a philosophical statement 'this thesis invites such-and-such an antithesis', but they contain a mediated set of possibilities that only aesthetic activity might engage with.

Schwitters insisted that 'art is a spiritual function of man, which aims at freeing him from life's chaos (tragedy). Art is free in the use of its means in any way it likes, but is bound to its laws and to its laws alone.'[30] He also noted that 'self-absorption in art, is like service to the divine in that it liberates man from everyday cares'.[31] In constructing his assemblage, then, Schwitters felt himself to be involved in a transcendental activity. Only the right combination of elements and the rhythm that shapes and is shaped by them, will permit the artist to experience the liberation from chaos that brings this sense of transcendence or, as I term it here, the sublime. The artist is neither Hegelian slave to, nor master of, such aesthetic energies, but rather a partner in their exploration and unfolding.

In Kantian terms, the sublime is an awesomeness, a limitlessness beyond coherence; the sublime is that which cannot be represented by man.[32] However, the Merz scatological sublime is not a humbling experience, dwarfed by awesomeness, like Kant's; Merz thrives on paradox, there is neither a final exhaustion nor non-exhaustion of this sublime, but commitment to the aesthetic process is endlessly required in order to realize an artefact's potential sublimity. Each surface of *The Kots Picture* insists upon its formal construction and yet, simultaneously, contains a semantic depth or width; these properties generate ripples of negotiable exegesis, transactions waiting to be engaged with. That the various metaphoric and metonymic, or selective and combinative configurations respectively, may present contradictory realizations is part and parcel of the Merz sublime. The actual material elements exciting this sublime are far from conventional, but in their paradoxical down-to-earthness lies the fundamental extension of aesthetic parameters that Schwitters aimed for. (There is additionally, of course, a degree of shock tactics in the very notion that rubbish might be the genesis of the sublime.) The indeterminacy of the Merz artefact provides intersections of cultural interpenetration to endlessly pursue, to be ever more absorbed by. The Merz artefact, then, can generate transcendence effects, which may last as long or as short as the time spent in contemplation.

Following my reading of Eagleton's characterization of the Marxist sublime, I believe that Merz can be critically read as providing a model congruent to Marx's integral desires. Eagleton contrasts the symmetry and proportion Marx preferred, with 'bad' sublimity, 'an unstoppable metonymic chain in which one subject refers itself to another and that to another, to infinity'.[33] For Marx, aesthetics and politics overlapped, both being predicated upon the need for principles of human liberation. Aesthetics and politics were only valid cultural pursuits if and when they were enabling men and women to realize their potential, that is, finding rhythms that could be used for individual and collective emancipation. 'The condition of communism could be envisaged only by a process which has all of the sublime's potentially infinite expansiveness, but which nevertheless carries its formal law within itself.'[34] What is most important, then, is finding a rhythm of interpenetrative relationships, within and between processes. This requires that 'if the aesthetic is to realize itself it must pass over into the political, which is what it secretly always was.'[35]

I shall argue in my next section that the rhythms that might lead to human emancipation, in the interpenetrative disciplines of aesthetics, politics and life praxis in general, can be seen to generate a 'negentropic principle' within and between individuals, the larger culture that they are part of and the fundamental forces of the universe. That is, they need order to sustain themselves, together with a sense that cultural pursuits are of benefit in the widest sense. Artefacts, as I claimed earlier, might indeed be realized as embodying tentative models of cultural integrity and continuation; they may represent ways in which a transformation of power could begin to serve the entire spectrum of human activity. To explain more fully what I mean by negentropy, a journey into the world of information theory is necessary.

INFORMATION, NOISE AND NEGENTROPY

Entropy is a much debated concept, with implications for a number of disciplines, including aesthetics, biology, cosmology and politics. Berman's modernity model, for example, touches upon entropy (= 'slow death') in relationship to the endless (re-)organization of energy in capitalism's interconnecting cultural networks and patterns. Jeremy Campbell [36] embraces the diversity of entropy's applicability under general principles of information theory and I shall use him as my source of explication.

Entropy, in one frame of reference, is the tendency for enclosed systems to move, over a period of time, from a state of order to a state of disorder (chaos). Anyone who regularly does housework will appreciate how chaotic the domestic situation can become in a matter of days, if order (vacuuming, general tidying up and so on) is not injected into the house system. This new or restored order demands the expenditure of energy. What is disorder for some, though, may be order for others; the average child's room may seem chaotic, but he or she often manages to find things searched for, that is, the child probably has an (albeit imprecise) internal model of where things are likely to be. This is congruent to Wolfgang Köhler's assertion that '(disorder) is not the absence of all order, but rather the clash of uncoordinated orders'.[37] In this context, models provide organizing principles whereby co-ordination might be established. Entropy can, therefore, also be seen as a state proportional to the amount of energy needed to realize a co-ordinated order from disorder.

Organizing principles inform structures and facilitate the efficient flow of energy, directing where and how it might be used most effectively. Without the flow of energy, there can be no information; information thus equates to structured energy as agent of negentropy, reinforcing the primary organizing principles. An illustrative example of biological negentropy would be the unlocking of energy by a tree, via the organizing principle of photosynthesis, in order to use sunlight; the tree grows larger and can thence increase its capture of information. Noise, on the other hand, is energy which lacks organization, it is without structure, containing no contribution to negentropy. Hitting a tree with an axe imparts energy to it, but it is not energy that the tree can absorb, or otherwise utilize. In this case, precisely the opposite effect to positive feedback can be envisaged, for noise increases entropy dramatically, damaging the tree's organization.

In cosmological terms, entropy is aggrandized as the 'Second Law of Thermodynamics', and is considered to demonstrate the existence of a metaphoric 'arrow of time'; universally, no less than domestically, order moves to disorder. However, the mere existence of organisms creates problems for the concept of entropy, for all life contravenes the arrow of time, at least for a while. Eventually, though, fauna and flora succumb to the arrow of time; they grow old and fail to maintain negentropic processes. In this sense, death is the ultimate entropic state for the organism, which no longer has any organizing principles. The mechanical analogue to the above is the fact that mechanisms always waste a proportion of the energy that drives them, in the form of heat and noise. As a mechanism ages it becomes less efficient, so the amount of heat and noise lost in its activities increases. Eventually, a mechanism ceases functioning unless it is efficiently maintained. Neither mechanisms, nor living organisms, nor the cosmos as a whole, can escape entropy, but entropy can be postponed, perhaps indefinitely. Extending this, analogically, it could be claimed that unless a culture is efficiently maintained, such that energy and power are used providently, it condemns itself to relatively swift entropic cessation. Information, in human terms, is more usually thought of as something to do with communication between a writer and reader (speaker and listener, transmitter and receiver), but the same general rules apply. Campbell asserts that 'in communications parlance, noise is anything which interrupts the integrity of a message'.[38] My biological example of negentropic processes can still be used as a provisional analogy to human communication, for the realization of a message could be modelled as the organization of a co-ordinated structure. Further information increases the complexity of the structure, which feeds back to extend the organizing principle still more. However, in order to increase negentropy the medium of communication should contain 'redundancies' in excess of, but integral to, the information being communicated; this basically means that grammars are incorporated in acts of communication, to help separate information from noise.

In visual terms, traditions of perspective and proportion are aesthetic grammars that man has utilized. In terms of (verbal) language, rules of spelling, syntax, punctuation and so on act as grammatical buoys that help to channel the energy of communication such that it becomes information. Language is also replete with phrases that act similarly to redundancies, setting up expectations of how and when the information will proceed or conclude. The limits within which further information might be realized are set by the probability or expectation raised by previous elements of information. For example, 'The cat sat on the . . .' sets up a probability that the next word will be 'mat'. Indeed, if the next word turns out to be 'map' the final 'p' might well be realized as an error or noise, so strong has the conventional probability of 'mat' been established; and even if not realized as an error, 'map' has a high degree of indeterminacy.[39]

There appears, though, to be an aporia at the core of information theory, in that indeterminacy actually increases information. Campbell asserts 'a message conveys no information unless some prior uncertainty exists in the mind of the receiver about what the message will contain. And the greater the uncertainty, the larger the amount of information conveyed when the uncertainty is resolved'.[40] 'The cat sat on the map' has greater information potential than 'The cat sat on the mat', then, but 'aaa cee hhm no pst ttt' (the same letters but in alphabetic order, and retaining a semblance of the original spacing) approaches closer to information's apotheosis; 'm   ttoh a p   ae   shtctna   e' gets closer still. . . . This indeterminate fecundity has a delightful piquancy; on the one hand noise

155

is apparently complete absence of information, whereas on the other it tends towards the highest negentropic process! Campbell claims that 'the message will not be impossible, in the sense that it violates grossly the rules of grammar or meaning; otherwise it could not be called information at all'.[41]

The crux of information theory's aporia, then, is 'what is to count as the violation of grammatical rules?' and, related to this, 'what are the limits to the realization of a message as either information or noise, sense or nonsense?' The fulcrum of co-ordinate resolution in this balance of order and disorder is the critical reader's mind, his or her psychic matrices or frames of reference. Rudolf Arnheim suggests that the creation of order is a built-in phenomenon, a 'field process'[42] in the human (and animal) brain, such that information is always searched for.

The interpenetration of form and content in Merz artefacts, for example, should be realized within a modernist matrix that tries to discover the grammar inherent in the piece. In other words, the reader actualizes rhythms informing and integrating its elements. Indeed, Lach suggests that:

> the ideal public that Schwitters dreamt of was an unconditioned public, without any conception of what was to follow and without pretentions, preoccupations, prejudgements, codifications, norms, clichés, automatizations – a public that did not know the great restraints of redundancy, of repetition, of predetermined expectations.[43]

In my earlier realization of *The Kots Picture*, I suggested formal grammars that were latent in what initially appeared to be a random presentation of images and words. Similarly, to realize the message 'The cat sat on the map' from 'm ttoh a p ae shtctna   e' would involve establishing a grammar that transformed the random noise into information. However much it may be the most likely one, though, 'The cat sat on the map' is only one possible realization of the jumble, just as my realization of *The Kots Picture* retained a multiplicity of different readings. These readings not only stand on their own, to an extent, but also create tensions that act upon alternative readings, or as I claimed earlier, rhythms between the various realizations are set up. These rhythms, sensuously inherent in Merz artefacts, embody a critique of mechanized culture, where no one organizing principle can stand on its own or will suffice to promote negentropy.

Focusing the above from the cosmic, through the biological and the cultural, to the personal, I could point out that Schwitters was fond of announcing that 'Schwitters = Merz'. Hence Schwitters, by extension everyone else, and, indeed, culture as a whole, was neither more nor less than a kind of Merz construct, an epiphenomenal effect that resulted from interpenetrative energies that flowed within and between numerous, random causes. This would appear to be a quite specific recognition of what has been termed 'intertextuality'. For Julia Kristeva, intertextuality is 'the transposition of one or more systems of signs into another, accompanied by a new articulation of the enunciative and denotative position'.[44] By overlapping or transposing one sign system with another, such as the verbal and the visual, the artefact, as a signifying practice, can be realized in more than one way. All signifying practice is 'a field (in the sense of space traversed by lines of force) in which various signifying systems undergo . . . transposition'.[45] For the reader, a word or phrase may allude to all manner of memories, such as the common stock of conventions, or to personal intimacies; these intersect and involve more than one sensuous response. For example, the image of the little dog in *The Kots Picture* might excite an olfactory, tactile or aural response (in Steve Giles's case, the song 'How Much is that Doggy in the Window?' came to mind).

Another way of putting this would be congruent to the surface and depth/width relationships that contemplation realizes, as with my reading of *The Kots Picture*. The reader, then, is not motionless, as a still point around which everything else spins, but is a moving element no less than any other. Kristeva additionally asserts that:

> establishing a sign system calls for the identity of a speaking subject within a social framework, which he [*sic*] recognizes as a basis for that identity. Countervailing the sign system is done by having the subject undergo an unsettling, questionable process; this indirectly challenges the social framework with which he had previously identified, and it thus coincides with times of abrupt changes, renewal, or revolution in society.[46]

To dovetail the above references to Kristeva with my previous exploration of information theory, then, the transmitter selects from a mix of discourses in his or her aesthetic creation, whilst the receiver is expected to organize the information within approximately the same grammar. However, the transactional aspects of intertextuality, in the sense Kristeva conceives it, would suggest that the receiver is highly unlikely to realize perfectly what the transmitter sends, due to cultural mismatching, that is, they inevitably have different backgrounds and experiences; artefacts are bound to be realized disparately.

The aesthetic drive not only aims to discover and to connect with grammars that might sensuously represent the relationship between individual man and woman, and culture (and nature), but it can additionally situate the complexities of physical and psychical energy that make up the individual ever 'in-process', to use Kristeva's phrase. Reality for any individual, then, is the interpenetration and interference of grammars that separate information and noise, and the rhythms within and between them that the mind (informed by cultural grammars) tries to integrate into a completeness. Self-realization, by way of aesthetic absorption, produces a rhythm through which others may, in turn, begin to negentropically realize themselves, contemplating the principles that organize an artefact's form and content. This is a culturally transfiguring kind of power, the power to motivate others towards realizing their own resources, which Eagleton's Marx would surely approve of.

EVE BLOSSOM HAS WHEELS

The example of Schwitters's Merz poetry I consider here, to further explore the Merz aesthetic, engages with human relationships at their most immediate. Love is a mixture of pleasure and pain, of anxiety and carefreeness, interwoven in a complex emotional figure. Love is most certainly an end in itself in terms of self-realization, but it is also a means in that it is predominantly the basis for continuation of the human species. Love, the genesis both of becoming fully human and of the procreative process, certainly has an extremely complex grammar. Additionally, loving another, with or without procreation taking place, is a fundamental human desire. Indeed, the notion of loving one's fellow man in the wider sense, for all its hackneyed repetition throughout the centuries, could still be seen as a revolutionary one in a world where such love is in short supply.

However, Marx's 'naked interest' implies that, under capitalism, even love had become subject to mechanical, unreflexive responses (and had possibly become a commodity, as I mentioned in my analysis of *The Kots Picture*); love, too, is a matter of economics and cultural convention to a degree. However personal it may seem to be, love is a process subject to the interferences of cultural life; the notion of loving someone is at least partially constructed from a variety of intertextual sources, even if the basis is founded upon natural parent–infant and childhood relationships.

The methodology of Schwitters's love poem 'An Anna Blume' is entirely consistent with his assemblage techniques. Elderfield notes that 'Schwitters collected scraps of conversation and newspaper cuttings just as he collected scraps of paper and other materials; it was out of these "banalities" as he called them, and his own delight in verbal nonsense, that "An Anna Blume" was composed'.[47] The original German version of 'Eve Blossom has Wheels' appeared in *Der Sturm* in August 1919 and I reproduce here Schwitters's own translation of it, completed when Schwitters had settled in England. For a time Schwitters enjoyed a degree of popular acclaim and financial gain from the success of the poem in Germany, and interestingly enough two different banknotes in *The Kots Picture* appear to meet under Anna Blume!

Eve Blossom has Wheels

O thou, beloved of my twenty-seven senses,
I love thine!
Thou thee thee thine, I thine, thou mine, we?
That (by the way) is beside the point!
Who art thou, uncounted woman,   5
Thou art, art thou?
People say, thou werst,
Let them say, they don't know what they are talking about.
Thou wearest thine hat on thy feet, and wanderest on thine
      hands,
On thine hands thou wanderest   10
Hallo, thy red dress, sawn into white folds,
Red I love eve Blossom, red I love thine,
Thou thee thee thine, I thine, thou mine, we?
That (by the way) belongs to the cold glow!
eve Blossom, red eve Blossom what do people say?   15
PRIZE QUESTION: 1.   eve Blossom is red,
                        2.   eve Blossom has wheels,
                        3.   what colour are the wheels?
Blue is the colour of your yellow hair,
Red is the whirl of your green wheels,   20
Thou simple maiden in everyday dress,
Thou small green animal,
I love thine!
Thou thee thee thine, I thine, thou mine, we?
That (by the way) belongs to the glowing brazier!   25
eve Blossom,
eve,
E-V-E,
E easy, V victory, E easy,
I trickle your name.   30

Your name drops like soft tallow.
Do you know it, eve,
Do you already know it?
One can also read you from the back
And you, you most glorious of all,   35
You are from the back as from the front,
E-V-E.
Easy victory.
Tallow trickles to strike over my back!
eve Blossom,   40
Thou drippy animal,
I
Love
Thine!
I love you!!!!^{48} 45

In this extraordinary poem Schwitters reorganizes, and thereby reener-
gizes, sentimental and/or hyperbolic clichés exchanged in human
relationships. Clichés act as redundancies that may help establish a shared
grammar, but in many ways they are a mechanical use of language; they
can be merely noise, and carry a weak intertextual charge. Nevertheless,
Schwitters has, paradoxically, made prattle an important element in his
poem. Once again, the notion that nothing should be wasted, nothing
should be entropically abandoned, informs Schwitters's work. Indeed, to
condemn platitudes outright would itself be an automatic response. All
words carry graphic, phonetic and semantic energies, that is, they are
visual shapes and verbal sounds, as well as bearers of meaning. The
arrangement of formal properties, though, also bears a content in their
rhythm of relationships and this can reinforce or negate, or otherwise play
with, the more conventional notion of meaning.

The name 'Eve' is a habitual archetype of woman and may connote
the first of her kind. Her surname, 'Blossom', is an endearment passed
between lovers, and it also accentuates the allusion to the Garden of Eden,
a blissful, natural setting for the beginnings of human love. Even within
this prototypical matrix, however, may be seen a foreboding of ill, for in
the traditionalist view Eve tempted Adam and they were expelled from
Eden. Further complicating the natural setting is the fact that Eve Blossom
'has wheels'; how on earth can or should this be reconciled or accommo-
dated within the matrix that has set the poem in the Garden of Eden? Is
this nonsense or sense? Indeed, should the surreal image of a woman with
wheels be realized as anything other than being akin to an oneiric

curiosity, ripe for psychoanalysis? Alternatively, given that the search for order is inevitable, according to Arnheim, can the critical reader fail to try and grammatically wrest the noise into information?

One possible reading is that Schwitters is attempting to establish the fact that mechanisms and man are not oppositional, but complementary. This is consistent with comments from Schwitters cited earlier and it also extends to my references to the gradual mechanization of man in the twentieth century. Mechanisms are not inherently anti-human, seeing one's lover as a mechanism may not be reifying him or her, but instead recognizing his or her balance and integrity in relation to the unfolding of human culture. Eve Blossom and the lover's response to her have been shaped by the energies of culture (and nature), but an aesthetic appreciation of her qualities can, in turn, feed back into those energies.

The multiple repetitions of 'I love thine' have considerable uncertainty in information theory terms, for the expectation of a noun phrase is frustrated. They may, of course, be perceived as mere noise, or against this, could be seen as rhythmic, nodal points through and/or around which the poem is built (in formal graphic/phonetic terms and in semantic ones). The phrase punctuates the poem, occurring in lines 2, 12, 23, 42 – 44 and, in a slightly changed form, it concludes the poem. The critical reader's problems of finding a matrix for 'I love thine' may be meant to be associated with the clumsiness of a lover trying to express uncertainties about Eve Blossom. 'Who art thou, uncounted woman' (line 5); 'Thou simple maiden in everyday dress' (line 21); and 'And you, you most glorious of all' (line 35) conflict with each other. One moment Eve's great virtue is her multifariousness, the next it is her simplicity and, finally, it is seen in her apotheosis as a superior amongst women; these tensions may suggest that the lover is actually insincere, or perhaps he is trying to convince himself, as much as the loved one, about his feelings. (I shall assume a male–female relationship, as the poet is male, but a realm of interesting readings could be stimulated by alternative pairings.)

It is not possible to know whether Schwitters is actually celebrating, or ironizing, or paradoxically switching between these perspectives on the man's attitude to love and lover. In this case, the problem that arises with expressions of affection is an acute one; where can a reader find an Archimedean point from which to decide whether he approves, or is contemptuous of, or is indifferent to, the almost nostalgic yearning for the loved one to be unique in some way (to have what could be termed an aura)? Aesthetic use value, to briefly engage with Benjamin's model, is culturally shared and resides in the aura that adheres to the artefact, but without an aura objects merely have a shallow exchange value. As with

MIKE JOHNSON

artefacts, so too with human relationships; to love someone is to be profoundly absorbed in their life, to be symbiotically shaped by, and to shape, their rhythms. Grammars, then, have to be found that guide attempts to realize the bosh and banalities that Schwitters may be using in order to convey the rhythms of love. The dichotomies between sense and nonsense, between what is information and what is noise, must in some way be dissolved and yet simultaneously held, so as to meld content and form within and between rhythms that are dynamically maintained. I would argue that any definitive resolution is impossible, that is, overlapping and shifting, expanding and contracting matrices must be continuously encountered.

In 'Eve Blossom has Wheels' the thrice repeated 'Thou thee thee thine, I thine, thou mine, we?' (lines 3, 13 and 24) is a poetic device, each time following 'I love thine', which serves several purposes. As Elderfield says:

> divided into three sections (each opened by a hyperbolic declaration of love), that tell of the poet's devotion to Anna Blume, of her appearance, and of her animal sexuality, the poem is in fact a structured, linguistically complex ode to the beautiful in the banal. In short, it is both ironic and idealistic, both avant-garde and bourgeois, like Schwitters himself.[49]

The alliteration on 'th' is not necessarily an attractive one, sounding rather like a lisp, which perhaps alludes to a degree of imperfection accompanying these pronouncements of love. Schwitters exaggerates it, however, accentuating the fact that language has a multiplicity of indeterminate possibilities; even an impediment may be of inestimable value.

These lines break conventions of syntax, too, denying an important element of information theory's notion of redundancy; what is information and what is noise? How important is the especially poignant, archaic twist of 'thee', 'thine' and 'thou' in English? Is it a return to, or yearning for, older traditions and values? (English has no contemporary equivalent to the informal German 'du'.) 'Th' is a difficult phoneme for many native German speakers and there is just a hint that Schwitters was trying out his new environment's language. He may well have been tasting the 'pothibilitieth' that English held for him as a poet.

The above repetitions additionally connote the cyclical nature of wheels, ever returning to the same place, before grinding on. Nature, too, has cyclic properties, such that mechanical and organic rhythms may not be realized as oppositional, but complementary. At the same time, the repetitions add a leitmotif that may either support a realization of triviality, or in a reading quite opposite to this, suggest that only multiple repetitions can generate negentropy. Every time the line is repeated it is followed by sentences that are similar to each other:

'That (by the way) is beside the point!'

'That (by the way) belongs to the cold glow!'

'That (by the way) belongs to the glowing brazier!'

A move from a point, through a cold glow, to a hot glowing force is expressed, that is, an increase in energy. These lines also get progressively longer, such that two properties of language, semantic and graphic, work together. Against this, the information mechanism could be perceived as running down, on the path towards maximum entropy: 'Red is the whirl of your green wheels' (line 20) suggests speed and great usage of energy, whereas the later line: 'Your name drops like soft tallow' (line 31) suggests a slow, viscous process, its destiny stasis. Schwitters is playing with the semantic properties of words and playing with his readers at the same time. Is it possible to adequately represent emotion, or not?

The possibility, playing against the impossibility, of communicating emotion is highlighted further by the absurd, almost syllogistic, form of lines 16–20 (which also change the graphic shape of the poem, not being justified on the left):

PRIZE QUESTION: 1. eve Blossom is red,
2. eve Blossom has wheels,
3. what colour are the wheels?
Blue is the colour of your yellow hair,
Red is the whirl of your green wheels.

This ludicrous question and answer, followed by the lover's expression of his confused state, exemplifies the indeterminacy of the poem, in fact. The movement along the visual spectrum of Eve's various colours, almost from one extreme to the other, could be interpreted as the poetic representation of the lover's perception; he is bewildered by the interference of intertextual play through his mind, even in a comparatively simple act of observation, as different psychic matrices (visual, verbal, kinaesthetic) collide. These lines might also suggest that any attempt to be logical about love is bound to fail, for the object of study is ever-changing. Only a mediated representation of emotion as in the poem, which must thence be aesthetically engaged with, is adequate for the task.

That Eve Blossom has wheels could be considered to be an extreme violation of sense, then, but it could alternatively fetch in metaphoric and metonymic connections, and/or a swing and swerve from one to the other, a continuous back and forth motion, that may realize a more complex and profound sense. The palindromic nature of 'E-V-E' accentuates this notion of movement, being reinforced by the 'E's seeming to revolve around the axis of 'V' (for Victory – a triumph against entropy). In the poem, Eve is invariably written entirely in either lower or upper case, underlining the reversible/circular nature of the name's symmetry. In fact the poem, as a permanent record of love's search for grammars of the negentropic principle, opens up the twenty-seven senses of its opening line, as it were, for each sense is multiplied at its uncertain interface with other senses. Grammars integrate and/or conflict, as rhythms of relationships emerge and submerge. Aesthetic absorption in a Merz artefact transcends the ordinary sensory range and facilitates the reaching of a new sublime.

CONCLUSION: FROM MERZ MODERNISM TO POSTMODERNISM

Reading and realizing the information mechanism of a Merz poem or assemblage, I have claimed, is analogous to discovering a grammar that can be extended into twentieth-century life praxis. The artefact acts as a microcosmic model of the totality of interpenetrating and/or paradoxical relationships, events and processes that men and women experience. The indeterminacy of Schwitters's artefacts, therefore, represents the turbulence of modernization that has led to industrial capitalism's constant changes; the modernity of their form and content, and the way these interpenetrate, represent the fact that in spite of (or, perhaps, increasingly because of) mechanization, no one organizing principle will suffice if Western culture wants to defer entropy. Notions of progress, self-realization and general human desires must constantly be reflexively examined and re-adjusted, in order to meet the integral life praxis of the whole of culture.

Another way of putting the above is to claim that Merz artefacts embody a negentropic principle. However, in order to realize or otherwise discover this, the reader has to aesthetically engage with their potentialities. Schwitters has put in his order and rhythms, but because of the play he has necessarily included, the critical reader must begin the negentropic task anew. Perhaps a reader will only chance upon something approximating to a correct reading (if, indeed, there is one). As Lach says, in my opening epigraph, aesthetics is the 'treatment for the disease' and, additionally, highlights pathological symptoms.

The negentropic principle that should inform the interpenetration of aesthetics and politics is not so much analogous to the growth of a tree, according to which information leads to further growth whereas noise stunts, but is that which is shared by all trees. In biological terms these are the negentropic processes of the natural life-forces, in cultural terms it could be considered to be shared grammars of interpenetration, endlessly combining and recombining cultural energies, ever shaping and being shaped. As I have shown, the concept of entropy inextricably connects the individual, culture, nature and cosmos, therefore the smallest reversal of entropy has immeasurable consequences. The role of love, as a contributory factor to the negentropic principle, is fundamental to the full realization of what it is to be a human being. Love of another individual, of one's fellow man and a loving attitude to natural and cultural processes in general, could serve as the basis for the necessary human responsibility and sensitivity that the delaying of entropy demands. If love becomes a commodity, serving the mere circulation of money, its vital, dynamic energies are lost.

Natural life processes are diverse and self-regulatory, non-wasteful and, on the widest scale, balanced. Western culture, however, although heterogeneous, is extremely wasteful, there is no grammatical balance to delay the relatively rapid onset of entropic decay; negentropy cannot be sustained. Most especially, there is the bad sublimity of the exchange factor of money, flawed because it does not subsume itself under the negentropic principle.

I have tried to elucidate the fact that the self, for Schwitters (=Merz) is an epiphenomenon moving through fields of information and noise, ever open to new energies. Kristeva parallels Schwitters when she speculates that the integrated human organism, in-process, is represented by, or is analogous to, an artefact which he or she, creates (and/or reads and realizes); the artefact thenceforth may be reflected upon to generate still further rhythmic representations of self-realization. There are no absolute grounds for deciding the precise status of either Merz artist or artefact, and the critical reader, in encountering manifestations of the latter, is also decentred by a mediated, moving experience.

Huelsenbeck saw 'Eve Blossom has Wheels' as merely being bourgeois play to no practical (political) purpose, but I hope I have made a sufficient case to now claim that Huelsenbeck misinterpreted Schwitters's commitment to, and desires for, negentropic ways of seeing and being (and despite espousing Communism, Huelsenbeck may have misinterpreted Marx too).[50] Whether an artist or poet is political depends upon how one chooses to interpret the term, on how one sets bounds to what is to count as a political action.

Indeed, to make a more general point, whenever boundaries are set, whatever definitions of such-and-such are made, there will always be some element that is not included. This latter mode of thinking equates to the post-structuralist position of Jacques Derrida, who claims that deconstruction is covertly manifest in all texts, waiting patiently for the critical reader:

> the poetic or the ecstatic is that in every discourse which can open itself up to the absolute loss of its sense, to the (non-)base of the sacred, of nonmeaning, of unknowledge or of play, to the swoon from which it is reawakened by the throw of the dice.[51]

Schwitters's work should be seen overtly to embody possibilities of deconstruction, for the playful, aleatory indeterminacy of Merz can be realized as generating 'ecstatic' rhythms. Within and between oppositions such as organic/mechanic, solemnity/play, sense/nonsense and means/ends, Merz artefacts dramatically exemplify a post-structuralist sublimity, one of play, uncertainty and chance, via absorption leading to transformation. In the negentropic principle that may be realized via aesthetic absorption, then, is a new sublime, a sublime that rejoices in the perpetuation of information's possibilities. At the same time, this new sublime embraces the paradox that all information may be mere noise.

If postmodernism can be characterized, according to Ihab Hassan, as including elements of Dadaism, openness, play, chance, deconstruction, intertextuality and indeterminacy, Merz as an example of modernism is actually well on the road to being postmodernist.[52] That is, the so-called postmodernist paradigm shift is in evidence in certain modernist artefacts. If the precise date of modernism's ascent is highly problematic, the same is even more certainly the case for postmodernism. Poets and artists like Schwitters, then, constitute a genuine avant-garde, for they have set a lead into new ways of seeing and being that has been followed.

It would be fatuous to claim that Schwitters, as my case in point, prefigures all the aesthetic innovations of postmodernism and Lach, too, would surely not claim such universality. I have, additionally, pointed out that Schwitters owes his innovations to numerous developments by other creative artists and poets. Nevertheless, Schwitters' embracing of the negentropic principle, as I see it, acts as a force in contemporary concrete poetry and L=A=N=G=U=A=G=E poetry; his particular use of juxtaposition and assemblage seems to have been followed by Robert Rauschenberg; found objects appear in the work of Anselm Keifer, an artist trying to come to terms with Germany's Nazi past; and chance is an important part of John Cage's aesthetic. (These are just a small selection of the many postmodernist examples that are discernible.)

I hope my provisional speculations about aesthetics, politics and the negentropic principle provide stimulation for further analysis and discussion of Merz. We live in an age when the general debilitation of millions of men and women, and a concomitant destruction of fauna and flora, are global. Never before has there been greater need for artefacts that sensuously embody a critique of waste and, simultaneously, question the definitions, and the teleology, of man under increasingly dominant capitalism. The transformation of power for human liberation, emancipation and love, rather than the squandering of lives and resources has a broad horizon to aim toward. Aesthetic commitment can, even now, project man into a negentropic future, before all human, and especially the Western, cultural enterprises exhaust their credibility.

NOTES

1 F. Lach, 'Schwitters: Performance Notes', in S. Foster (ed.), *Dada/Dimensions*, Ann Arbor, UMI Research, 1985, p. 45.

2 K. Marx, quoted in T. Eagleton, *The Ideology of the Aesthetic*, Oxford, Basil Blackwell, 1990, p. 204.

3 I have recently seen the particular 'Python' video again and, much to my further surprise, as soon as the commentator claims Schwitters as British, a bystander says 'he's German', which I missed before, adding a further chiff of contradiction.

4 R. Sheppard, 'What is Dada?', *Orbis Litterarum*, vol. 34, no. 3, 1979, includes Schwitters in his discussion of 'What is Dada?', while Hans Richter sees Merz as 'Hanover Dada', in H. Richter, *Dada: Art and Anti-Art*, London, Thames & Hudson, 1965, pp. 137–52.

5 H. Lewis, *Dada Turns Red: The Politics of Surrealism*, Edinburgh, Edinburgh University Press, 1990.

6 P. Bürger, *Theory of the Avant-Garde*, Manchester, Manchester University Press, 1984.

7 Richter, op. cit., p. 138.

8 'Read' includes viewed, observed and general notions of sensuous engagement; all reading takes place within some theory, however implicit, so I shall take it to be the case that it is, perforce, critical reading. Generally speaking, though, the greater the reflection by the reader, the more critical his or her reading. I use the term 'realize' in the sense that it is used in music, to expand or complete, or to reconstruct from an incomplete set of parts.

9 J. Elderfield, *Kurt Schwitters*, London, Thames & Hudson, 1985, p. 198. Schwitters's art was amongst that proscribed by Adolf Hitler and was part of the 1937 'Degenerate Art' exhibition in Munich. The show also included Dada, Expressionist, Cubist and Bauhaus works.

10 K. Schwitters, quoted in Elderfield, op. cit., p. 35.

11 Further details of Schwitters at this time can be found in S. Themerson, *Kurt Schwitters in England*, London, Gaberbocchus, 1958.

12 Eagleton, op. cit., p. 230.
13 Lach is primarily concerned with Schwitters as performer and with later Merz artefacts that I briefly touch on. These, though, seamlessly extend the ones I discuss and further demonstrate Schwitters's ever-evolving interest in formal properties of art and language. I come to a similar conclusion to Lach about Schwitters's position as regards art and the twentieth century, though I do not rehearse his argument.
14 M. Berman, *All that is Solid Melts into Air*, London, Verso, 1983.
15 Ibid. p. 15.
16 To put a precise date on the commencement and subsequent developments of modernity raises a host of questions that I have too limited a space to answer here, though, in addition to Berman, Siegfried Giedion, *Mechanization Takes Command*, New York, Oxford University Press, 1948; Stephen Kern, *The Culture of Space and Time: 1880–1918*, London, Verso, 1983; and David Harvey, *The Condition of Postmodernity: An Inquiry into the Origins of Cultural Change*, Oxford, Basil Blackwell, 1989, provide stimulation for sorties into this much discussed area.
17 K. Marx, quoted in Eagleton, op cit., p. 79. I shall be basing my reading of Marx upon Eagleton's characterizations, hence my procedure of citing Marx through Eagleton's eyes.
18 Marx, ibid., p. 218.
19 Berman, op. cit., p. 95.
20 Walter Benjamin's notion of the 'aura', as explored in his seminal essay 'The Work of Art in the Age of Mechanical Reproduction', W. Benjamin, *Illuminations: Essays and Reflections*, edited with an introduction by H. Arendt, London, Verso, 1970, is the genesis of the general point I make here.
21 In considering Merz artefacts as information mechanisms, I am partially extending the poetics of Ezra Pound and William Carlos Williams, who wanted poems to be as efficient as modern technology. However, any notion that Merz artefacts provide the kind of ekphrastic completeness of image or moment of totality that early Pound and Williams aimed for, is inappropriate. The information mechanisms of Merz are decidedly open and indeterminate.
22 K. Schwitters, quoted in Elderfield, op. cit., p. 44.
23 Ibid., p. 49.
24 Schwitters was extremely conventional in some ways, including this example of working as a graphic artist. This conventional side, as I have shown, alienated him from Huelsenbeck. Nevertheless, even here he was responsible for innovations in typography. See M. Lavin 'Advertising Utopia: Schwitters as Commercial Designer', *Art in America*, October 1985.
25 Schwitters, quoted in Elderfield, op. cit., p. 26.
26 Ibid., illustration 95.
27 Elderfield, op. cit., p. 80.
28 Rhythm, an awareness of abstract regularity in a series of perceptions, is etymologically derived from a Greek word which originally meant form, shape or the pattern of dance-step positions in space and time.
29 Self-preservation would naturally require that certain experiences, such as physically or psychically dangerous ones, were best avoided.
30 Schwitters, quoted in Elderfield, op. cit., p. 42.
31 Ibid., p. 93.

32 Jean-François Lyotard raises some interesting questions about the sublime that obliquely extend my probings here. J.-F. Lyotard, 'The Sublime and the Avant-Garde' in A. Benjamin, *The Lyotard Reader*, Oxford, Basil Blackwell, 1989.

33 Eagleton, op. cit., p. 212.

34 Ibid., p. 217.

35 Ibid., p. 207.

36 J. Campbell, *Grammatical Man: Information, Entropy, Language and Life*, Harmondsworth, Penguin, 1984.

37 W. Köhler, quoted in R. Arnheim, *Entropy and Art: an Essay on Disorder and Order*, London, University of California Press, 1971, p. 13.

38 Campbell, op. cit., p. 26.

39 Roman Jakobson's communication model, with its elements of addresser, addressee, code, context, message and contact, is similar to the information model I am proposing, though Campbell's theories, with their wider application, have greater efficacy for my purposes. R. Jakobson is quoted in W. Steiner, *The Colors of Rhetoric: Problems in the Relation between Modern Literature and Painting*, London, University of Chicago Press, 1982, p. 125.

40 Campbell, op. cit., p. 68.

41 Ibid., p. 29. I am reminded, too, of Noam Chomsky's 'Powerless green ideas sleep furiously', a perfectly correct syntactic sentence, although its semantic value is highly problematic.

42 Arnheim, op. cit., p. 4.

43 Lach, op. cit., p. 42.

44 L. Roudiez in J. Kristeva, *Desire in Language: a Semiotic Approach to Literature and Art*, Oxford, Basil Blackwell, 1980, p. 15.

45 Ibid., p. 15.

46 Kristeva, op. cit., p. 18. Kristeva's theories are extensions of her studies of Mikhail Bakhtin whose morpheme (smallest unit of meaning) is always dialogical, or in my context here, intertextual.

47 Elderfield, op. cit., p. 37. Schwitters, influenced by Constructivism and suprematism (and Dada's phonetic poetry), was moving towards what he considered to be ever more abstract poetry, and the formal properties of words he later delighted in may be embryonically perceivable in earlier poems, such as 'Eve Blossom has Wheels'. 'Abstract poetry', he wrote in 1924, 'has released words from their associations – this is its great merit – by paying special attention to sound it plays off word against word, more particularly, idea against idea.' Schwitters, quoted in Elderfield, op. cit., p. 130. Ultimately, Schwitters was led to claim that 'the basic material of poetry is not the word but the letter. The word is:
1. A combination of letters
2. Sound
3. Denotation (significance)
4. The bearer of associations of ideas.' Schwitters, quoted in Richter, op. cit., p. 147. An extreme working-out of this theory is Schwitters's sound-poem 'Ursonate', its genesis being an elaboration upon a phonetic poem by the Dadaist Raoul Hausmann. These brief excerpts from (a) the beginning and (b) a later section of 'Ursonate' (1922–32), show how far Schwitters had stripped language down:

(a)

Fümms bö wö tää zää Uu,

            pögiff,

                    kwii Ee,

Oooooooooooooooooooooooooooooooooooooo,

```
      dll  rrrrrr  beeeee  bö,
      dll  rrrrrr  beeeee  bö  fümms bö,
           rrrrrr  beeeee  bö  fümms bö  wö,
                   beeeee  bö  fümms bö  wö  tää,
                           bö  fümms bö  wö  tää  zää,
                               fümms bö  wö  tää  zää  Uu ...
```

(b)

```
                        Iiiii
                          Eeeeee
                             m
                             mpe
                             mpff
                             mpiffte
                             mpiff  tilll
                             mpiff  tillff
                             mpiff  tillff tooooo,
  Dedesnn     nn  rrrrr, Ii  Ee,   mpiff  tillff tooooo, ...
```

Schwitters, quoted in Elderfield, op. cit., illustration 193. This is as extreme as all but the most courageous contemporary concrete poets, such as Bob Cobbing, have attempted. In conversation with me, Cobbing has generously acknowledged the influence of Schwitters.

48 Schwitters, quoted in Elderfield, op. cit., p. 38.

49 Elderfield, op. cit., p. 39.

50 The hostility between Schwitters and Huelsenbeck is detailed in Elderfield, op. cit., pp. 36–7 and 39–40.

51 J. Derrida, *Writing and Difference*, London, Routledge & Kegan Paul, 1978, p. 261.

52 I. Hassan's list is quoted in Harvey, op. cit., p. 43.

AFTERWORD

Avant-garde, Modernism, Modernity: A Theoretical Overview

Steve Giles

The reissue in 1991 of the Pelican European Literature guide to modernism some fifteen years after its initial publication[1] lends a certain poignancy to Walter Benjamin's characterization of the modern as the recurrence of the ever-same in the guise of the ever-new.[2] At the same time, Benjamin's dictum ought to make us think twice before dismissing critical attempts to engage with modernism as anomalous simply because of the 1980s theoretical obsession with the postmodern. The conceptual coherence of the debates on postmodernism and postmodernity turns, after all, on the theoretical viability of their respective specifications of modernist cultural artefacts and modern societal formations. And, given David Harvey's comment at the end of the 1980s that nobody agrees either on what is meant by the term postmodernism or on the relationship between postmodernism and modernism,[3] the reader bombarded by the explosion of academic interventions in these areas (itself, no doubt, a postmodern/ist phenomenon) might be forgiven for experiencing a hermeneutic *anomie* akin to Josef K.'s in *Der Proceß/The Trial*:

> Er war zu müde, um alle Folgerungen der Geschichte übersehn zu können, es waren auch ungewohnte Gedankengänge in die sie ihn führte, unwirkliche Dinge, besser geeignet zur Besprechung für die Gesellschaft der Gerichtsbeamten als für ihn. Die einfache Geschichte war unförmlich geworden, er wollte sie von sich abschütteln.

> He was too tired to be able to grasp all the implications of the story, it led him into unfamiliar trains of thought, unrealities better suited to being discussed by the community of court officials than by him. The simple story had become amorphous, he wanted to put it out of his mind . . .[4]

Rather than assume the position of an obfuscating custodian of the law, however, I wish in this Afterword to attempt, at least, to clarify the issues

171

involved by considering the relationship between modernism and the avant-garde, modernism and postmodernism, and modernism and modernity, before concluding with some more speculative methodological reflections.

MODERNISM AND THE AVANT-GARDE

The problem of establishing valid criteria by which to identify modernism is, as various commentators have pointed out, a function of the ambivalence and plurality of modernism itself.[5] Although no single checklist of 'typical' textual strategies or aesthetic predilections commands universal assent amongst theorists and critics – rendering simple binary models of the modernist–postmodernist divide even more problematic[6] – McFarlane and Bradbury's characterization of modernism in terms of certain key shifts in aesthetic sensibility remains a valuable starting point. In the course of 'The Name and Nature of Modernism',[7] they identify five key modernist tendencies:

1 away from representational realism and towards abstract and autotelic art forms;
2 towards a high degree of aesthetic self-consciousness;
3 towards an aesthetic of radical innovation, fragmentation and shock;
4 towards the breaking of familiar formal and linguistic conventions;
5 towards paradox.[8]

One difficulty with this type of approach is that it brackets together ostensibly disparate textual strategies and incompatible aesthetic ideologies, but, as Richard Sheppard has indicated above, this should not lead us simply to abandon the term modernism as a way of designating an apparently non-cohesive series of cultural phenomena. Instead, we must seek to identify the deep-structural factors which make it possible to establish the social and ideological problematic informing movements as diverse as Symbolism, Constructivism, or Expressionism.[9] At the same time, Andreas Huyssen had argued that despite evident areas of overlap between such movements, all of which can be construed as manifesting the sensibility of modernity, 'it makes little sense to lump Thomas Mann together with Dada, Proust with André Breton, or Rilke with Russian constructivism'.[10]

Huyssen's account, both here and in 'Mapping the Postmodern',[11] is indebted to Peter Bürger's *Theorie der Avant-Garde*,[12] one of the most important theoretical contributions to the modernism debate in the last twenty years. There, Bürger contends that a radical and critical difference separates what he calls the historical avant-garde, as instanced in movements such as Dada and Surrealism, from other modern/ist movements such as Aestheticism and Symbolism which are predicated on the notion of aesthetic autonomy. Readers schooled in more traditional approaches to the avant-garde might be somewhat surprised by Bürger's approach. Georg Lukács, after all, effectively equated the avant-garde with modernism,[13] while Renato Poggioli's classic account showed how the concept of the avant-garde shifts, in nineteenth-century France, from denoting an unequivocally activist view of art before 1848 to invoking a depoliticized Aestheticism after 1870 in the wake of the defeat of the Paris Commune.[14] This assimilation of modernism and the avant-garde has been something of an academic cliché ever since.[15]

Bürger's central thesis is that the basic aim of the historical avant-garde movements was to destroy the institution of art in bourgeois society. The bourgeois institution of art, argues Bürger, was founded on the principle of aesthetic autonomy, which involved art's separation from life praxis in bourgeois society and was embodied in the organic work of art. In contrast, the avant-garde rejected aesthetic autonomy and organic art, and produced non-organic artefacts in an attempt to reconnect art and life praxis. In his detailed exposition of these propositions Bürger makes many valid points, particularly in relation to Dada and Surrealism, but in certain crucial respects his argument is questionable. In view of the theoretical significance of Bürger's work, I shall consider its limitations in some detail and focus on three key issues: his specification of the avant-garde, his assertion that bourgeois aesthetics is founded on the notion of autonomy, and his account of the institution of art.

According to Bürger, the institution of art involves two dimensions: the apparatus of artistic production and distribution, and the ruling ideas about art in any given epoch. While the basic principles of Bürger's theoretical framework need not be disputed, his own use of it is problematic. First, unlike Brecht in *Der Dreigroschenprozeß* (*The Threepenny Lawsuit*),[16] he pays insufficient attention to the artistic/cultural apparatus, both in relation to technological and socio-economic factors and in more narrowly institutional terms (e.g. the role of publishing houses and art galleries). Second, he tends to equate 'ruling ideas about art with high points of aesthetic theory', especially German Idealism. He defends this approach by claiming that such theories represent ruling aesthetic ideas in their most developed form (p. 138), but even if one shares his valorization of the philosophy of Kant and Schiller, it does not follow that the most advanced theoretical ideas are societally hegemonic. Indeed, the evidence of Hohendahl's *A History of German Literary Criticism, 1730–*

1980 suggests that, *pace* Bürger, the dominant view of art in Germany from the mid-eighteenth to the late nineteenth century was pragmatic and Enlightened, based on the principle of teaching and pleasing (*prodesse* and *delectare*), whereas the autonomous conception of art associated with Weimar classicism remained culturally marginal until circa 1870.[17]

In this case, Bürger's contention that the dominant conception of art within bourgeois ideology was autonomous must also be reconsidered. The first point to note is that Bürger's characterization of aesthetic autonomy is surprisingly ambiguous given its centrality to his argument. He uses the term in at least five distinct senses, to refer to (1) non-sacral, post-medieval art; (2) art which in general has sundered the link with life praxis; (3) art's functional status in bourgeois society; (4) the artist's socio-economic position under capitalism; (5) works of art which are autotelic, self-contained, and *sui generis*. In other words, Bürger's category of aesthetic autonomy has shifting conceptual boundaries, and this factor may account for difficulties in his historical argument. He asserts, for example, that post-Renaissance bourgeois aesthetic theory was intrinsically autonomous, yet also concedes the significance of pragmatic aesthetics until at least 1780, and he overlooks the emergence of expressive aesthetics in the German *Sturm und Drang* and English Romanticism.[18] Moreover, his comments on the nineteenth-century Realist novel seem to undermine his general thesis, for if, as Bürger claims, the nineteenth-century novel played an essential role in establishing the self-understanding of the bourgeoisie, then mimetic realism should furnish the cornerstone of bourgeois aesthetics.

These latter points necessitate a revision of Bürger's account of the historical avant-garde itself. While radical modernist movements such as Dada clearly do reject notions of aesthetic autonomy, they also distance themselves from expressive aesthetics and mimetic Realism. Furthermore, German Dada in particular not only aggressively attacked the structure of the art market and its institutional presuppositions, but also ridiculed the anthropocentrism and anthropomorphism characteristic of bourgeois ideology in general.[19] And, whereas Bürger's conception of avant-garde critique needs to be expanded, his delineation of the avant-garde in contradistinction to other modern/ist art movements must be refined. He never decides whether the historical avant-garde is different from or coextensive with European modernism, given the clear similarities between the avant-garde and other modern/ist movements such as Cubism, Futurism and Expressionism.

Bürger's account of modernism and the avant-garde has recently been supplemented in a series of essays entitled *Prosa der Moderne* (*Prose of Modernity*). It might have been expected that the verbal shift in emphasis from *Avantgarde* to *Moderne* would signify a fundamental rethink on Bürger's part, but the theoretical sections in this later volume do little more than extend and rearticulate his assertion of the centrality of aesthetic autonomy in bourgeois culture. His starting point now is the philosophical problem of modernity in the alien, secularized world of post-Enlightenment, post-Revolutionary Europe.[20] Modern humanity is confronted by a world torn asunder, by a split between objectified nature and subjective human intervention. Under the impact of the Jacobin Terror in the French Revolution, Enlightened moral agents could no longer recognize themselves in the results of their actions, and so were impelled to construct a realm of action where individual deeds are not alien to their producer, but congruent with the structures of individual subjectivity. This was the realm of aesthetic autonomy, which, because it had no instrumental function in society, constituted a counter-institution to modernity and its ever-encroaching principle of Weberian *Zweckrationalität*.

Bürger's argument is, of course, entirely justified to the extent that the emergence of autonomous aesthetics from German Idealism onwards can be explained in these terms.[21] At the same time, though, Bürger also uses this paradigm to characterize 'modern' aesthetics as such. We have already seen that this approach oversimplifies the theory and practice of bourgeois art from the late eighteenth century onwards, but Bürger's new focus on 'die Moderne' raises further difficulties. The German term 'die Moderne' can be used to refer to both modern*ity* (in, say, political or sociological terms) and modern*ism* (construed as an aesthetic or cultural category). But by deploying this term in an undifferentiated fashion to designate both modernism and modernity, Bürger glosses over that essential conceptual distinction. Although his equivocations on this point enable him to reassert his original thesis that the distinctive feature of the historical avant-garde consists in its rejection of the autonomous aesthetic of modernity, they also render virtually impossible the task of clarifying the complex and contradictory set of relationships between (artistic) modernism and (societal) modernity.[22]

MODERNISM AND POSTMODERNISM

Ever since its inception in the late nineteenth century, theorists of modernism have insisted that it involves a radical aesthetic response to a deeply felt sense of cultural crisis contingent on, for example, the disintegration of the Providential world picture, the depredations of imperialist capitalism, the collapse of traditional notions of self and character in the work of Nietzsche and Freud, and the undermining of long-standing assumptions about language and reality.[23] Typically, though, this perspective on modernism is then compelled to confront the extent and profundity of the rifts just outlined. Should modernism be construed as a decisive break with the entire tradition of Western humanism dating back to the ancient Greeks, or is it simply a late Romantic response to the ravages of industrialization, most drastically embodied in the horrors of the First World War ? Is modernism essentially an aesthetic phenomenon, or a seismic movement in culture as a whole, impinging on social forms of consciousness in their entirety? And, whether modernism is to be construed as a variegated set of broadly cultural or narrowly aesthetic responses to a perceived crisis striking at the heart of modern civilization, how can its anxieties be related to so-called postmodern/ist critiques of the modern?

Much of the controversy involved in confrontations between modern/ism and postmodern/ism derives from terminological and conceptual confusions. David Harvey, for example, first outlines the postmodernist rejection of the modernist view that there is a tight and identifiable relationship between signifier and signified, only to remind us two pages later of the modernist tradition of thinking on language which questions fixed systems of representation.[24] Similarly, Fredric Jameson is unsure whether postmodernism represents a continuation of or a break with modernism, [25] and theoretical commentaries on postmodernism from Jameson onwards tend to present four distinct but incompatible ways of defining the relationship between modernism and postmodernism:

1 postmodernism represents a clear break with and rejection of high modernism in favour of aesthetic populism;
2 postmodernism is the dead end of modernism, which is now exhausted and played out;
3 postmodernism extrapolates from the more radical of the modernist movements (e.g. Dada) but is different in kind from modernism;
4 postmodernism intensifies modernist tendencies but remains within the ambit of modernism.[26]

Not surprisingly, debates on post/modernism seem to involve the participants in talking past one another like the decentred subjects of Expressionist theatre, but in recent years there have been more rigorous attempts to elucidate the apparently intractable relationship between modernism and postmodernism. Huyssen and Sheppard have drawn significant conceptual parallels between European modernism and contemporary post-structuralism,[27] with intriguing implications for the myth of origins, but the work of the leading German postmodern theorist

Wolfgang Welsch has been particularly instructive in this context.[28] In his essay 'Die Geburt der postmodernen Philosophie aus dem Geist der modernen Kunst' ('The Birth of Postmodern Philosophy from the Spirit of Modern Art'),[29] Welsch seeks to identify a highly specific set of connections between postmodern/ist philosophy and modern/ist art, suggesting that postmodern/ist philosophy articulates discursively what modern/ist art demonstrated artistically. Taking Lyotard to be the postmodern/ist philosopher *par excellence*, he demonstrates striking resemblances between Lyotard's ideas and modern/ist aesthetics, identifying affinities between the fragmentation and de-composition of modern/ist art and the end of metaphysical meta-narratives, between a philosophy in search of its own rules and artistic reflexivity, between the aesthetics of the sublime and the philosophy of paradox.[30] Furthermore, like Huyssen and Sheppard, he elaborates on the ways in which modern/ist art pre-empted conceptions of meaning and logic associated with the deconstructive critique of logocentrism, as well as rejecting humanism and anthropocentrism. At the same time, Welsch insists that there are no significant connections between modern/ist philosophy and modern/ist art, so that it is precisely this lack or absence which constitutes *post*modern/ist philosophy as a distinctive enterprise. It is here, however, that Welsch's argument breaks down. Because he too employs the term 'die Moderne' to designate both modern and modernist, he cannot distinguish modern philosophy (e.g. Kant and Hegel) from its modernist counterpart (e.g. Nietzsche and Heidegger) and so, like Lyotard, labels the latter postmodern. But, as Sheppard and Pippin have shown, there are evident and important overlaps between modernist art and modernist philosophizing,[31] suggesting once again that only a theoretically more robust account of the complex imbrications of modernism and modernity can sustain a view of postmodern/ism capable of transcending the vibrant superficiality of the colour supplement.

MODERNISM AND MODERNITY

We saw earlier that a perennial feature in discussions of modernism has been the assertion that it stands in a specific yet contradictory relationship to cultural modernity and societal modernization. Thus, Bradbury and McFarlane define modernism as 'our art', 'the one art that responds to the scenario of our chaos', 'the art of modernization' (p. 27), while Harvey wishes to connect 'the definition of a modernist aesthetic' to 'the material basis of modern life' (p. 20). The classic statement of the view that modernism is the art of modernity remains, though, Habermas's speech

on receiving the Adorno prize, in which he takes the progressive auton-
omization of modern art at the societal level to be an integral part of the
project of modernity.[32] Habermas characterizes this project in Weberian
terms as the post-Enlightenment disaggregation of science, morality and
art, while modernism is said to articulate the consciousness of modernity
following the emergence of aestheticism and market-determined artistic
production (p. 45). Although Habermas stresses the importance of
distinguishing between cultural modernity and societal modernization,
the focus of his essay is philosophical. The notion that modernism
involves a critique of the self-understanding of modernity construed in
terms of the Enlightenment project is, of course, essential to any
theoretical understanding of modernism, as Pippin and Sheppard have
indicated.[33] Nevertheless, we must also bear in mind the fact that the
Enlightenment tradition assailed by modernism is both societal and cultural, and a particularly suggestive way of linking these two dimensions
has been to foreground the modern/ist experience of temporality.

For Habermas, the entire tradition of aesthetic modernity from
Baudelaire to Surrealism is generated by a new consciousness of time,
imbued with a sense of acceleration and discontinuity.[34] While it is true
that the latter is a core modernist experience, Giddens's response to
Habermas's Adorno lecture offers a necessary expansion and refinement
of Habermas's thesis by referring us to the 'transformation of time–space
relations introduced by the spread of industrial capitalism in the late 18th
and 19th centuries' thanks to what he defines as the *commodification of
time–space*.[35] Giddens continues by viewing modernism in art as 'in
some degree an accurate expression of the "emptying" of time–space',
and so implies a way of interrelating structural features of industrial
capitalism with aesthetic form.

To take the argument a stage further, an essential factor mediating
between the commodification of time–space and the practices of modernist art has been proposed by Harvey, who suggests that the radical
readjustment in time–space experience in the latter half of the nineteenth
century provoked a crisis of representation, best exemplified in the
disintegration of post-Renaissance conventions of depiction in modernist
painting from Manet onwards. This crisis is not, however, simply a bizarre
quirk of post-Impressionism or Cubism. Rather, as Sheppard and Wragg
also observe,[36] it constitutes a fundamental rift in conceptions of reality,
indeed in all the various modes of representing the world to ourselves, so
that radically new cognitive and experiential maps are required.[37] It might
be objected, of course, that the notion that modernist texts and paintings
embody a radical shift in conventions of spatio-temporal representation

is hardly novel. Nevertheless, the originality of Harvey's argument consists in his proposal of a mechanism which integrates processes of societal modernization and cultural or aesthetic revolutions such as modernism. Harvey's central thesis is that 'the history of capitalism has been characterized by speed-up in the pace of life, while so overcoming spatial barriers that the world sometimes seems to collapse inwards upon us'. (p. 240). Furthermore, periods of crisis and maximal change are marked by what Harvey calls 'time–space compression'. Time–space compression involves 'processes that so revolutionize the objective qualities of space and time that we are forced to alter, sometimes in quite radical ways, how we represent the world to ourselves' (p. 240). The rhythm of modernity is punctuated by epistemic crises in, say, the Renaissance and the Enlightenment, but the occurrence of such crises cannot be accounted for in purely philosophical terms, because ultimately they are generated by the dynamics of capitalism. The monetization of relations in social life transforms time-space experience by, for example, imposing ever stricter temporal regimes on the working day, while capitalist commodity exchange requires increasingly efficient spatial organization as well as more rapid turnover time of capital: it is processes such as these which are the driving force behind time–space compression.[38]

Modernism and postmodernism can thus be understood as aesthetic/cultural responses to drastic intensifications in the dynamics of capitalism in the late nineteenth/early twentieth century and the late twentieth century respectively. The seemingly incongruous linkages between the depredations of imperialism and cosmic dislocation in Joseph Conrad's *Heart of Darkness* now become self-evident,[39] while Nietzsche's madman, expostulating on the disintegration of the post-Copernican universe, is transmuted into a model of sanity.[40] The postmodern/ist obsession with surface and signification can be understood as the reflex of a situation where we are caught up in a universe of events impenetrable to our understanding and beyond our control, and deconstructive philosophy of language, far from being the abstruse creation of perverse Gallic intellectuals, can be explained in similar fashion. Deconstruction is the inevitable consequence of the increasing abstraction of capitalist socio-economic relations in the condition of postmodernity, where language – like money – 'does not relate to time (or, more accurately, time–space) as a flow, but precisely as a means of bracketing time–space by coupling instantaneity and deferral, presence and absence'.[41]

Nevertheless, the argument that contemporary capitalism is postmodern, that modernity is essentially capitalistic, has not gone unchallenged. While sharing many of Harvey's concerns and diagnoses, Giddens has argued in *The Consequences of Modernity* for a more

179

differentiated model of modernity, particularly as regards its institutional as opposed to its cultural or philosophical dimensions. He therefore characterizes modernity in strictly societal terms as designating 'modes of social life or organisation which emerged in Europe from about the seventeenth century onwards and which subsequently became more or less worldwide in their influence' (p. 4). Giddens's initial account of modernity is very close to Harvey's as, in the spirit of his earlier piece on modernism, he stresses the importance of spatio-temporal transformation. At the same time, he connects the spatio-temporal aspect of modernity with what he terms processes of disembedding and reflexivity. Disembedding involves 'the "lifting out" of social relations from local contexts of interaction and their restructuring across indefinite spans of time–space' (p. 21). Giddens argues that the key features of time–space relations in modernity are the separation of time from space (e.g. standardization of dating) and of space from place. As a result, human interactions in or across space no longer require participants to be physically present in the mode of face-to-face interaction. The classic disembedding mechanism is money, whose increasing abstraction, as we saw earlier, 'brackets' time–space in a manner ostensibly similar to language, particularly writing. Somewhat surprisingly though, Giddens does not count language as a disembedding mechanism, on the grounds that it is an intrinsic feature of social action. This may be true of basic speech situations, but modern media of information transfer from the Gutenberg press to the fax clearly do satisfy Giddens's disembedding criteria as stated above. At the same time, Giddens concedes that writing plays an indispensable role in the development of modern reflexivity. By creating a perspective of past, present and future, writing makes it possible to distinguish traditional and new knowledge, a procedure intrinsic to modernity: 'The reflexivity of modern social life consists in the fact that social practices are constantly examined and reformed in the light of incoming information about those very practices, thus constitutively altering their character' (p. 38). In addition to having important methodological implications for sociology, as we shall see later, reflexivity is at the heart of modern scepticism and uncertainty. As Giddens observes, even in science '*nothing* is certain, and nothing can be proved . . . in the heart of the world of hard science, modernity floats free' (p. 39).

So far, Giddens's account of modernity might appear to be far more abstract than Harvey's, but he insists that it states essential preconditions for modernity's dynamic and globalizing tendencies at the institutional level. The general tendencies towards time–space distantiation, disembedding and reflexivity are, according to Giddens, embodied in four specifically

modern sets of institutions: (1) the capitalist system of commodity production; (2) industrialism; (3) apparatuses of surveillance and administration;
and (4) control of the means of violence. It is important to note that for
Giddens, no single one of these institutions has casual priority in explanatory
accounts of modernity, so that he would reject the propositions that the world
of modernity is essentially capitalistic or intrinsically 'administered'. At the
same time, because in his view the contemporary world has not so much
broken with the processes underpinning modernity and its institutional
framework, as intensified and extended such processes, he also argues that
we are currently not on the threshold of post-modernity, but moving into a
period 'in which the consequences of modernity are becoming more
radicalised and universalised than before' (p. 3).[42]

REFLECTIONS IN CONCLUSION

This intricate discussion of sociological accounts of modernity may seem
to have taken us worlds away from the paintings of Cézanne or the poetry
of W. B. Yeats, and more traditional literary critics and art historians will
no doubt baulk at the suggestion that understanding and explaining
modernism is unavoidably multi- or interdisciplinary. Nevertheless, if we
follow Giddens and Harvey by retaining the term *modernity* as a general
societal category, then we could perhaps conceive of *modernism* as a
cultural phenomenon which, though located within the ambit of modernity, is post- or even anti-modern in ideological terms. Similarly, because
modernism was pressured into existence by the dynamics of time–space
compression and separation, it can be characterized too as a classic
product of modernity. The radicality of the cultural crisis perceived by
modernists turns on the fact that the late nineteenth century witnessed the
simultaneous collapse of two models of reality associated with the development of modernity, those of the Renaissance and of the Enlightenment,
and the overdetermined nature of this conjuncture helps explain the
perennial controversy about the depth of the modernist crisis. And, just
as modernism stands in an ambiguous and ambivalent relationship to a
multi-layered modernity, so too *postmodernism* may be understood in
analogous terms, as the cultural counterpart of what Giddens calls *radi-
calized* modernity. Although there are important differences between the
ways in which Giddens, Harvey and Jameson characterize the latest phase
of modernity, there is a strong case for attempting to synthesize their
various approaches in order to rethink the question of postmodernism's
relationship to both modernity and modernism.

This is an issue which Jameson sidestepped when, in 'Postmodernism, or the Cultural Logic of Late Capitalism', he argued that even if the constitutive features of postmodernist art are essentially modernist, then this does not really matter, since the meaning and social function of modernism and postmodernism differ fundamentally because of their respective positioning in the economic system of (late) capital. While the latter point is well taken, it is also the case that any attempt to understand and explain the social function of modernism or postmodernism must start from a valid identification of the cultural phenomena in question, and this is not the only area where Jameson's theoretical approach conjures up a host of methodological conundrums.

The very title of Jameson's piece, with its neo-Marxian foregrounding through alliterative chiasmus, invites us to consider the relationship (cultural logic) of societal forms of consciousness (postmodernism) to the economic base (late capitalism). Like Sheppard and Bürger,[43] Jameson wishes to reject oversimplified reflectionist accounts of cultural phenomena, but it is far from clear that construing aesthetic artefacts as responses to societal modernity, whether in its capitalist or late capitalist phase, is sufficient to keep the reductionist demon at bay, for the same patterns of socio-economic determination could still be at work, albeit in a more complex and indirect fashion. What is required, of course, is a solution to the perennial problem of mediation – of establishing a non-reductive link between social experience and the discursive practices of the text. Jameson deals with the problem of mediation by trying to relate the linguistic strategies of modernist texts to their societal subtext, which Jameson describes as 'the experience of *anomie*, standardization, rationalizing desacralization in the *Umwelt* or world of daily life'.[44] While this enterprise is crucial, Jameson's specification of the subtext is altogether problematic. In addition to assuming that the sociological theories of Durkheim and Weber can be combined in a relatively straightforward fashion, Jameson also implies that *anomie* or rationalization can be experienced. But even if it could be shown that individuals or groups of individuals in Western society experienced an acute sense of disorientation or dislocation at the turn of the century, it is only within the parameters of a specific sociological theory that such experiences could be categorized and thereby explained as instances of *anomie*, rationalization, or even alienation. 'Lived experience' is not a theory-neutral category, and must be identified with reference to agents' own understanding of their social situation, however limited that understanding may be. Elaborating the 'subjective problematic' of modernism, to use Sheppard's terminology, presupposes that social – and psychological – reality is always pre-interpreted, in the sense that it has been conceptualized by social actors.

How, though, do we move from this 'subjective' problematic to the 'objective' problematic which underlies it? In the context of his remarks on reflexivity, Giddens makes the important point that sociology is characterized by a 'double hermeneutic' interrelating its conceptual schemes and those of lay agents, each feeding off the other, but this seems to bring him dangerously close to espousing the phenomenological fallacy, according to which the perspectives of social actors must have veridical or explanatory status. A critical sociologist or cultural analyst, on the other hand, is bound to argue that the spontaneous understanding of social agents may be incapable of adequately characterizing or explaining their own social reality. From a Marxist point of view, for example, the perspectives of agents may fail to grasp the essential nature of the real political and economic relations which produce the manifest phenomena of social life as conceptualized by them.[45] It is, though, precisely such relations, together with the social and psychological mechanisms which articulate them, which constitute the 'objective' problematic of modernism, a problematic which modernism in its multifarious guises engages with both as *explanans* and *explanandum*, reflecting it, articulating it, displacing it, responding to it, or even intervening in it in the variety of ways delineated in this volume.[46]

NOTES

1 Malcolm Bradbury and James McFarlane (eds), *Modernism 1890–1930*, Harmondsworth, Penguin, 1976.

2 David Frisby, *Fragments of Modernity: Theories of Modernity in the Work of Simmel, Kracauer and Benjamin*, Cambridge, Polity Press, 1985, p. 36.

3 David Harvey, *The Condition of Postmodernity: An Enquiry into the Origins of Cultural Change*, Oxford, Blackwell, 1989, pp. 7, 42–4.

4 Franz Kafka, *Der Proceß*, edited by Malcolm Pasley, Frankfurt am Main, Fischer, 1990, p. 303; translated as *The Trial*, Harmondsworth, Penguin, 1981, p. 243 (translation amended by Steve Giles).

5 See Bradbury and McFarlane, op. cit., pp. 25, 46, 49; Eugene Lunn, *Marxism and Modernism: An Historical Study of Lukács, Brecht, Benjamin, and Adorno*, London, Verso, 1985, pp. 33–5; Peter Bürger (in collaboration with Christa Bürger), *Prosa der Moderne*, Frankfurt am Main, Suhrkamp, 1988, pp. 439–42; Richard Sheppard, above, pp. 1–13.

6 See Harvey's discussion of Hassan's model, Harvey, op. cit., pp. 42–4.

7 Bradbury and McFarlane, op. cit., pp. 19–55.

8 My schema is based on Bradbury and McFarlane, op. cit., pp. 25–30, 49–50; but see also Lunn, op. cit., pp. 34–7, together with his extensive discussions of Lukács and Adorno. It is unnecessarily restrictive and misleading to equate modernism with autonomous art, a position most recently advanced by Robert Pippin, *Modernism as a Philosophical Problem: On the Dissatisfactions of*

European High Culture, Oxford, Blackwell, 1991, p. 31, but see also Jürgen Habermas, 'Die Moderne – ein unvollendetes Projekt', in *Die Moderne – ein unvollendetes Projekt: Philosophisch-politische Aufsätze 1977–1990*, Leipzig, Reclam, pp. 32–54 (pp. 43–5), translated as 'Modernity versus Postmodernity', *New German Critique*, no. 22, Winter 1981, pp. 3–14 (the abridged English translation omits this crucial part of Habermas's discussion); Andreas Huyssen, 'The Search for Tradition: Avant-garde and Postmodernism in the 1970s', *New German Critique*, no. 22, Winter 1981, pp. 23–40, esp. p. 27.

 9 Sheppard, above, pp. 11–13.
10 Huyssen, op. cit, p. 26.
11 Andreas Huyssen, 'Mapping the Postmodern', *New German Critique*, no. 33, Fall 1984, pp. 5–52, esp. pp. 20–1.
12 Peter Bürger, *Theorie der Avantgarde*, Frankfurt am Main, Suhrkamp, 1974, translated as *Theory of the Avant-Garde*, Manchester, Manchester University Press, 1984. The most stimulating critique of Bürger's work in English remains Jochen Schulte-Sasse's 'Foreword: Theory of Modernism versus Theory of the Avant-Garde', in Bürger, *Theory of the Avant-Garde*, pp. vii–xlvii; but see also Russell Berman, *Modern Culture and Critical Theory: Art, Politics, and the Legacy of the Frankfurt School*, Madison, University of Wisconsin Press, 1989, pp. 42–53.
13 Georg Lukács, 'Die weltanschaulichen Grundlagen des Avantgardismus', in *Essays über Realismus*, Neuwied, Luchterhand, 1971, pp. 467–99, translated as 'The Ideology of Modernism', in *The Meaning of Contemporary Realism*, London, Merlin, 1963, pp. 17–46.
14 Renato Poggioli, *The Theory of the Avant-Garde*, Cambridge, Mass., Harvard University Press, 1968, pp. 9–10. The activist conception of avant-garde art is eloquently affirmed by the Fourieriste Laverdant, cited by Poggioli:

> Art, the expression of society, manifests, in its highest soaring, the most advanced social tendencies: it is the forerunner and the revealer. Therefore, to know whether art worthily fulfils its proper mission as initiator, whether the artist is truly of the avant-garde, one must know where Humanity is going.
>
> (Ibid., p. 9)

In view of the existence of analogous tendencies in modernism (well exemplified in the early work of the Expressionist Ernst Toller) I see no problem in holding onto this early characterization of the avant-garde.
15 Raymond Williams's work is a notable exception; see 'The Politics of the Avant-Garde', in Raymond Williams, *The Politics of Modernism: Against the New Conformists*, London, Verso, 1989, pp. 49–64, esp. pp. 50–1.
16 Bertolt Brecht, *Der Dreigroschenprozeß*, in Siegfried Unseld (ed.), *Bertolt Brechts Dreigroschenbuch*, Frankfurt am Main, Suhrkamp, 1978, pp. 117–76.
17 Peter Uwe Hohendahl (ed.), *A History of German Literary Criticism, 1730–1980*, Lincoln, University of Nebraska Press, 1988, pp. 13–276.
18 See M. H. Abrams, *The Mirror and the Lamp: Romantic Theory and the Critical Tradition*, Oxford, Oxford University Press, 1971, especially Chapter 4.
19 See Richard Sheppard, 'What is Dada?', *Orbis Litterarum*, no. 34, 1979, pp. 175–207.

20 My discussion here is based on Bürger, *Prosa der Moderne*, pp. 13–19, 439–50.
21 See Andrew Bowie, *Aesthetics and Subjectivity from Kant to Nietzsche*, Manchester, Manchester University Press, 1990.
22 See Bürger, *Prosa der Moderne*, pp. 451–2; the clarity of Bürger's position is not enhanced by his reference two pages earlier to 'programmatischer Modernismus' ('programmatic modernism'), ibid., p. 449. Similar equivocations also compromise Habermas's account of modernism in Habermas, op. cit., pp. 52–3.
23 See for example Bradbury and McFarlane, op. cit., Harvey, op. cit., and Sheppard above, pp. 13–33.
24 Harvey, op. cit., pp. 49–51. See also Richard Sheppard, 'The Crisis of Language', Bradbury and McFarlane, op. cit., pp. 323–36.
25 Fredric Jameson, 'Postmodernism, or the Cultural Logic of Late Capitalism', *New Left Review*, no. 146, July/August 1984, pp. 53–92, esp. pp. 53–7.
26 This schema is based on the accounts of postmodernism proffered by Habermas, op. cit., Harvey, op. cit., Huyssen, op. cit., Jameson, op. cit.
27 Huyssen, 'Mapping the Postmodern', pp. 39–40, 42, 44; Richard Sheppard, *New Ways in Germanistik*, Oxford, Berg, 1990, pp. 1–2, 189, 240–41.
28 See, for example, Wolfgang Welsch, *Unsere postmoderne Moderne* (*Our Postmodern Modernity*), Weinheim, Acta Humaniora, 1988.
29 Wolfgang Welsch, 'Die Geburt der postmodernen Philosophie aus dem Geist der modernen Kunst', in Welsch, *Ästhetisches Denken*, Stuttgart, Reclam, 1990, pp. 79–113. Welsch also uses the term *Moderne* in an indiscriminate fashion to refer to modern and modernist: hence my use of 'modern/ist' in discussion of his essay.
30 Ibid., p. 97; Welsch discusses Lyotard in some detail on pp. 86–93.
31 Pippin, op. cit., *passim*, Sheppard, above, pp. 13–33.
32 Habermas, op. cit., pp. 33–45, English translation, pp. 4–9. Good accounts of the projects of modernity and Enlightenment are also contained in Harvey, op. cit., p. 12, and Pippin, op. cit., pp. 8–10.
33 Pippin, op. cit., p. 32, and Sheppard, above, pp. 8–9.
34 Habermas's account is pre-empted somewhat in Lukács, op. cit., pp. 477, 490–2, and echoed in Frisby, op. cit., p. 13, and Harvey, op. cit., pp. 279–80. Habermas, Frisby, and Harvey all give Baudelaire a key role in establishing a specifically modernist sense of time (Habermas, p. 33; Frisby, pp. 1–2, 14; Harvey, pp. 10–12) but the presentation of time in *Les Fleurs du Mal* (*Flowers of Evil*) is not fundamentally different from the time consciousness of Baroque poetry.
35 Anthony Giddens, 'Modernism and Postmodernism', *New German Critique*, no. 22, Winter 1981, pp. 15–18, esp. p. 15.
36 Sheppard, above, *passim*; Wragg, above, *passim*, Harvey, op. cit., pp. 27–8, 263–8.
37 See also Frisby, op. cit., p. 4, Jameson, op. cit., pp. 89–91.
38 Harvey, op. cit., pp. 226–33, pp. 240–52.
39 Joseph Conrad, *Heart of Darkness*, Harmondsworth, Penguin, 1983, pp. 22–4.
40 Friedrich Nietzsche, *Die fröhliche Wissenschaft*, Leipzig, Reclam, 1990, para. 125, translated in R. J. Hollingdale (ed.), *A Nietzsche Reader*, Harmondsworth, Penguin, 1984, pp. 202–3. See also Harvey's discussion of Nietzsche, op. cit., p. 274.

41 Anthony Giddens, *The Consequences of Modernity*, Cambridge, Polity Press, 1990, p. 25. Giddens is actually talking about modern theories of money, but could just as easily have been citing Derrida.

42 Giddens presents a useful tabular opposition of 'radical modernity' and 'postmodernity', ibid., p. 150.

43 Sheppard, above pp. 1–13.

44 Fredric Jameson, *The Political Unconscious. Narrative as a Socially Symbolic Act*, London, Methuen, 1981, p. 42. For further discussion of Jameson's work see Steve Giles, 'Against Interpretation? Recent Trends in Marxist Criticism', *British Journal of Aesthetics*, vol. 28, no. 1, Winter 1988, pp. 68–77, and Sara Danius, 'The Mystery of Totality: On Narrative History in Fredric Jameson's *The Political Unconscious*', in Bernard McGuirk (ed.) *Truth, Self, Action, History*, London, Routledge, 1993.

45 See, for example, Roy Bhaskar, *The Possibility of Naturalism: A Philosophical Critique of the Contemporary Human Sciences*, Brighton, Harvester, 1979, pp. 83–91.

46 I wish to thank David Norris, Bernard McGuirk and Richard Sheppard for their helpful comments on an earlier draft of this Afterword.

INDEX

187